LIMITED
LIVELIHOODS

GENDER AND CLASS IN
NINETEENTH-CENTURY
ENGLAND

Sonya O. Rose

University of California Press
Berkeley · Los Angeles

University of California Press
Berkeley and Los Angeles, California

© 1992 by
The Regents of the University of California

Library of Congress Cataloging-in-Publication Data

Rose, Sonya O.
    Limited livelihoods : gender and class in nineteenth-century
England / Sonya O. Rose.
        p.   cm. — (Studies on the history of society and culture)
    Includes bibliographical references and index.
    ISBN 0-520-07478-5
    1. Sex role—England—History—19th century. 2. Sex
discrimination in employment—England—History—19th
century. 3. Working class women—England—History—19th
century. 4. Women—Employment—England—History—
19th century. 5. Capitalism—England—History—
19th century. I. Title. II. Series.
HQ1075.5G7R67   1992
305.3′0942—dc20   91-17418
                                                              CIP

Printed in the United States of America
9 8 7 6 5 4 3 2 1

Material from Chapter 3 appeared in " 'From Behind the
Women's Petticoats': The English Factory Act of 1874 as a
Cultural Production," *Journal of Historical Sociology* 4
(1991): 32–51. An earlier version of Chapter 5 appeared as
"Gender, Technology, and Industrial Relations: The English
Carpet Industry, 1860–1895," *Material History Bulletin* 31
(1990): 79–90.

For Guenter

Contents

vii

Acknowledgments

This work has been my central preoccupation for many years. At various points I was alternately captivated and frustrated by archival research, struggling with a continually exploding literature on topics germane to the book, and experiencing indescribable elation when I found myself writing down ideas I did not know I had. I was carried through all of this by my utter fascination with nineteenth-century England, a fascination which was nourished by three institutions and nurtured by several individuals.

This book, and the research that is at its base, would not have existed without the support of several institutions. Colby College has been unstinting in its generosity, providing funds for me to do the research, allowing me a sabbatical year to begin it (even though at the time I was primarily an administrator), serving as a surrogate home and extended family, and, like the best of families and homes, allowing me to grow and develop in my own way. The faith its president, Bill Cotter, and two deans, Doug Archibald and Bob McArthur, have shown in my abilities has been central to my personal development. I owe them individually and collectively an enormous debt.

The research for this book began at the University of Essex, England, whose sociology department and center for social history took a risk in 1983–1984 on a total unknown. Essex provided me with office space, secretarial and administrative assistance—including the invaluable help of Mary Girling and Brenda Corti—library facilities, and, most important of all, supportive and intellectually stimulating colleagues. Essex has been and continues to be my second home.

The book was completed during my stay at the Mary Ingraham Bunting Institute. To all of my "sister-fellows" whose own work, intensity of purpose, and artistic and scholarly visions were sources of inspiration, and to Florence Ladd, its director, whose elegance, good humor, and friendship helped to lighten my spirits, I owe much more than I can express.

In addition to the support given to me by these three institutions, the National Endowment for the Humanities gave me a fellowship so that I could take a leave of absence to complete the book, and the American Council of Learned Societies provided me with a grant to do some of the research that forms the basis of my argument.

Several very special people have figured in my development as a scholar. Leonore Davidoff has been variously my mentor and my very dear friend. My affection and respect for her are boundless. Ava Baron's scholarship, intelligence, and sisterhood have sustained me as we have pursued our separate but very similar struggles. Marcy May has given me friendship, support, and important critical readings at numerous different points in the development of my work. Alison Scott has been a colleague and confidant. Her work and the acuity of her insights and analyses have been important in challenging me to think on. Jane Hunter's presence, critical reading, and partnership in beginning an engagement with post-structural theory were in their different ways crucial to this work. Without Gail Hershatter's careful readings, I would still be writing and rewriting the introduction.

A number of other colleagues have offered helpful criticism on various chapters and/or have engaged me in enormously useful discussions about the ideas in this book. They include Kathleen Canning, Mary Ann Clawson, Mary Blewett, Vicki Bonnell, Eileen Boris, Johanna Brenner, Joan Busfield, Cyndi Daniels, Laura Frader, Nona Glazer, Erica Harth, Ludmilla Jordanova, Susan Kellogg, Alice Kessler-Harris, Michael Kimmel, Robert Leibman, David Levine, Jane Lewis, Isabel Marcus, Sonya Michel, David Nugent, Joy Parr, Susan Porter, Kay Sanderson, Mariana Valverde, Lise Vogel, and anonymous readers for the University of California Press. Eleventh-hour stimulating discussion and criticism from the Comparative Studies in Social Transformations Seminar participants at the University of Michigan, Ann Arbor, were hungrily and quickly incorporated. Deficiencies that remain are my own.

Several students have served as my assistants over the years. Lisa Maria did some of the initial coding of census data. Leslie Woron helped me to get the data "up and running," and together we conquered the bugs in BMDP on the Colby mainframe. Rachel Tilney did astonishingly good library research and data analysis for me. Mahua Sarkar coded census data and laboriously entered those data onto my Macintosh, making it possible to free myself from the mainframe. Grace Von Tobel, the manuscript typist at Colby College, made sense out of my end notes and helped me to bring some order to them.

I cannot thank enough the numerous librarians and archivists who provided guidance and access to the sources that form the empirical foundation of this book. I am especially indebted to the librarians and archivists at Brintons Ltd., Kidderminster, the Local Studies libraries in Nottingham and Clitheroe, the Tameside Local Studies Library in Staleybridge, the West Yorkshire Archive Service in Wakefield, the Local History Library in Kidderminster, the John Rylands University Library of Manchester, the University of Sheffield, the Worcestershire and Hereford County Records Office, the Lancashire County Records Office, and the British Library, especially its newspaper archive at Colindale. In particular, I would like to acknowledge the help of Dr. Angela Raspin, archivist at the British Library of Political and Economic Science, whose assistance was invaluable in identifying sources appropriate to my topics.

Courtney Cazden housed me during my Bunting year, provided me with an air conditioner that made it possible to deal with my readers' reports in the sweltering Cambridge summer, and, most crucial, told me that Raymond Williams's *Marxism and Literature* was one of the most important books she had ever read. That book eventually became central to the creation of this one. Mary Smullen provided shelter and food in London, along with innumerable cups of Barry's tea, even though she looked upon my obsession with work as more than a little crazy.

Claire L'Enfant, currently history editor of Routledge in London, read and commented on a very preliminary draft of the introduction; her enthusiasm for my project in those early years was very important to me. Sheila Levine at the University of California Press has been everything one could wish for in an editor. She has been calming, encouraging, and supportive, always sensing the right response for the occasion. Jane-Ellen Long's copy editing was magnificent.

Finally, I want to mention those who have been at the center of my life, the people from whom, in the end, I have learned the most—my children, Laura Orleans, Marc Orleans, and Jenny Rose, who, in their own very individual ways, have enriched my life and made this book possible, and my husband, Guenter Rose. His humor, warmth, love, and friendship have been more important to me than he realizes.

Waterville, Maine
February 1991

I

Introduction

This book concerns the central role of gender in the massive reorganization of lives and livelihoods that accompanied the economic, social, political, and cultural revolutions of industrial capitalism in England. It primarily focuses on the importance of gender in class relations in the second half of the nineteenth century.

England was in the vanguard of the industrial revolution, and it was there, during the nineteenth century, that industrial capitalism came into full flower. In the last half of the century, seeds that had been sown much earlier produced bounteous riches for some, along with bitter fruit for others. Factories replaced homes and workshops, altering landscapes from the level Midlands to the craggy hillsides of Lancashire in the north. Cities and towns swelled to accommodate rural immigrants as novel ways of manufacturing familiar goods replaced older ones and new commodities were produced for sale in markets that often lay an ocean away.

Relations between and among the men and women who created the first industrial nation were transformed by the very development of that society. As working people struggled to secure their livelihoods they found themselves constrained by shifting forms of employment, competition with one another for scarce jobs, and revised legal entitlements, responsibilities, and restrictions. They were forced to improvise new directions for living that altered the familiar routes of the past, and gender distinctions were crucial to these transformed patterns and emerging practices.

The upheavals in people's lives and livelihoods, and the unequal distribution of the costs and benefits of industrial transformation, have been at the center of historical and sociological accounts of this momentous period. Visible disjunctures and fissures in social relationships and their consequences stimulated the development of classical social theory. Following in the pathways defined by Karl Marx, Emile Durkheim, and Max Weber, historians and sociologists have shown

us a social landscape being altered by class conflict and industrialization. Their portraits have focused on issues central to this book: class,
family relations, and labor politics. However, they have failed to recognize gender as a core feature of the social fabric and its transformation.

The historical and theoretical insights of E. P. Thompson have enriched our understanding of working-class formation during the early
part of the nineteenth century.[1] His analysis of working-class culture
and political activism stimulated new ways of thinking about class.[2]
He narrated the story of how working people used their cultural resources to create class-based political responses to the economic changes
that had unsettled and often destroyed their livelihoods. Using an entirely different orientation, an earlier sociological study by Neil Smelser had provoked a generation or more of scholarship dealing with the
relationship between family structure and industrial transformation.[3]
Although Smelser's argument has been criticized for reducing complex
historical developments to abstract structural causes, the evidence he
unearthed has enriched what we know about the industrial revolution.
He observed, for example, that disruption in family lives may be linked
to political activism, a theme that has been explored by feminist scholars.[4] The inquiries of Eric Hobsbawm and, more recently, Patrick Joyce
have contributed to our understanding of the latter part of the nineteenth century. Their work has been an important stimulus to studies
of factionalism within the working class, capitalist strategies, and the
dampening of political protest in the second half of the nineteenth
century.[5] Using diverse approaches, these investigations have contributed to our understanding of the development of industrial capitalism in very different ways. They have suggested the importance of
culture in class formation, the relevance of disruptions in family life
for political activism, and the influence of intra-class divisions and
capitalist strategies on working-class solidarity. However, they were
limited because they omitted consideration of the involvement of women
and failed to recognize the importance of gender in men's actions and
experiences.

My work builds on more than two decades of intensive scholarship
on the subject of women and work that challenges the gender-blind
assumptions embedded in traditional sociological and historical scholarship on this crucial period of history.[6] The first stage of this tradition
of feminist scholarship was to demonstrate women's participation in

economic life. This project began with the careful excavation, by such scholars as Sally Alexander for Britain and Alice Kessler-Harris for the United States, of evidence about women in the labor force.[7] In addition to their own work, feminists discovered a tradition of earlier scholarship about women.[8] Using this earlier material, scholars have shown the complex ways that women's economic contributions changed with the development of capitalism, the variations in the location of women's waged work, and the modes and timing of their contributions to working-class household subsistence.[9]

A second stream of scholarship has been instrumental in refashioning our ideas about industrial transformation. Going beyond the observation that women and men have had different family responsibilities, historians and sociologists have revealed the extent and the persistence over time of gender segregation in waged work.[10] The natures of women's work and men's work have varied historically, but two related factors have generally remained constant: both their jobs and their workplaces have been gender-segregated, and only rarely have women supervised men. Although gender segregation of occupations has been documented time and time again, the reasons for its persistence remain elusive.

Recent scholarship has turned to the place of family, work, and community in the construction of masculinity.[11] As long as scholarship focused on women or remained centered on the differences between women's and men's work, our understandings about economic and social transformation could be broadened but not undermined. Recent attention to men as gendered beings and to men's work as having something to do with men as men has been a vital step in undermining gender-neutral accounts of industrial transformation and class formation.

These developments in feminist scholarship have together challenged the comprehensiveness as well as the bias of previous accounts of working-class history. Yet many sociologists and historians remain unconvinced that gender is central to economic relations. It was not only an absence of evidence about women and work that kept scholars from seeing that "gender matters."[12] The subject of gender could be dismissed, not because there were no observable patterns to women's and men's work, but because no theory of gender existed.[13] In fact, there has been no consensus on the meaning of gender as an analytical concept. Without theory, the differences between women's and men's experiences of working-class history and in the unfolding of their histories could be explained by "biology" or by "economics." Lacking an argument articulating what gender is and how it works, scholars looked to something that seemed logically prior to gender or prior to the different social positions of women and men in society, something outside gender itself. Without a theory of gender to back up the assertion that "gender matters," working-class history could flourish untransformed by feminist scholarship.

Although there has been a wealth of scholarship showing that gender has influenced class relations and class relations have shaped gender, how and why this has occurred has remained obscure. Later in this chapter I elaborate on a cultural or symbolic approach to gender that suggests why gender is basic to all social processes. I use this cultural approach to demonstrate how gender was constitutive of economic practices and class relations, by examining how work was structured in industries ranging from metalworking and chocolate manufacture to the production of lace, as well as focusing on the relations between capital and labor and between men and women in other textile industries that differed dramatically from one another.

In the lace industry, women and men worked at totally distinct jobs, usually in radically different locations. While adult men made high wages making lace in factories, adult women earned a pittance finishing it at home. In contrast, cotton powerloom weaving was a sexually integrated occupation. Women and men often worked together at the same jobs and were paid roughly the same wages. Even then, however, women and men had different experiences at work and in labor organizations. In the carpet and hosiery industries, women and men often competed with one another for jobs. In those industries, employers often attempted to employ women rather than men, because they could pay them lower wages. Despite the differences among these industries, gender affected class relations in each of them in distinctive ways.

THE PUZZLE OF THE HOSIERY INDUSTRY

Knitted goods were made in the cities, towns, and rural villages of the East Midlands, and especially in Nottinghamshire and Leicestershire.[14] The production of knitted garments (generally referred to as the stocking or hosiery industry) at first was organized as a capitalist putting-out industry. It had been located in the East Midlands since the middle of the eighteenth century. Garments such as stockings and gloves were knitted on hand-powered stocking frames by stockingers or frame-work knitters, who were artisans working for merchant capitalists in their own homes or in small workshops. The trade was slow to industrialize. The first factories using steam-powered machinery opened in the early 1850s, but the putting-out system proved to be resilient, and a significant number of stockingers continued to work hand-powered knitting frames into the 1880s, when the putting-out system went into sharp decline.

Throughout the nineteenth century, women and their daughters in knitting households contributed to household income by seaming stockings or by stitching gloves. They did work that was known as "women's work." Many of the women who worked in the stocking trade finished the knitwear using needle and thread. However, in the hosiery trade a fair number of women and their daughters worked alongside their male relatives to weave the knitted garments. From about 1812 on the industry fell on a long, virtually unrelieved depression. In order to eke out a living from ever-declining piece rates, husband, wife, and older children worked frames. Whereas men were responsible to the capitalist for their knitting, women (and children) who knit worked under the direction of their husbands, who were paid for the family's labor.

The labor force in the early factory hosiery industry was divided much as it was under the putting-out system. Although the majority of women in hosiery worked at finishing the goods or preparing them for manufacture, some women were hired to make stockings on power-driven frames. However, the transfer of hosiery making from its domestic location to the factory involved an important change in the relations of production for women who made stockings by machinery: they earned wages for their work on power frames independently of their husband's or father's employment.

The consequences of this change were profound. When women and men were knitters using the same tools or machines and were equally subject to the authority of the employer in the factory, labor disputes occurred as male and female workers competed for jobs. From the beginning, women were paid less than men for the same work in the factory.

With the development of industrial capitalism and the creation of enterprises in which workers were hired as individuals, when employers found it necessary to lower their labor costs they often tried to hire women in place of men. Not surprisingly, from the 1860s through the remainder of the century, the all-male stocking-makers' unions were preoccupied with the actual or potential substitution of women for men. As early as 1861, employers in the hosiery industry attempted to hire women workers in place of men and the men fought to retain jobs for themselves. In one incident, police were called in to quell a disturbance created by men assembled outside Mr. James's factory in Nottingham. The men had been discharged and replaced by women. A news reporter commented that the women could "perform the duties connected with the rotary frame as efficiently as men. The pay of the females is, of course, very much less than that given to male operatives." [15]

The hosiery industry was not unique. In many industries, from textiles to metalworking, women and men were thrown into competition with one another. Employers used women to bring down the wage rates of the men. Sometimes women simply were substituted for men, doing the same job but paid from one-third to one-half less than the men had been. At other times, employers altered machinery to make the work less skilled or purchased new machines marketed as "women's machines" and hired women to run them at lower rates than the men had been paid.

In the industrial period when employers hired women for a trade in which men had been working, men's jobs and wages were threatened. The struggle between women and men for jobs resulted in open expressions of antagonism between them in addition to demonstrations of hostility between workers and employers. Frequently the men went on strike or initiated other kinds of actions to preserve their jobs for men only. Whenever the men could figure out a way of maintaining or creating sex-typed jobs, they succeeded in staving off the threat posed by women. However, that success usually failed to prevent an erosion of their wages over the long term, for capitalists were persistent in finding ways to lower their production costs and to secure a wider margin of profit.

It was much less common for employers to hire men to work at jobs in which women had predominated. The major instance of this happening in the nineteenth century was in cotton powerloom weaving. When men worked at a trade in which women predominated, the low women's wages served to depress the men's wages. Under these conditions, however, the only way men could keep their jobs was to insist on being paid the same wages as women, to eliminate the competition between them.

Important questions are raised by this discussion of gender relations and industrial transformation in the hosiery industry. First, we must understand why women and men generally were found doing different work. Why was occupational segregation—the tendency for women and men to work at different jobs, in different places, and on different machines—so persistent? How did employers' assumptions about gender difference influence their hiring practices and the ways that they structured work and working environments? How were women's and men's patterns of paid employment linked to the conditions under which they lived as husbands, wives, daughters, and sons? When employers attempted to substitute women for men at jobs, why did the men often respond with hostility to the women, and why did they resort to exclusionary tactics? What got in the way of women and men uniting to invent strategies to fight against the ever-present threat to their livelihoods posed by employers who were attempting to lower their production costs? If wages had been equalized to eliminate competition between men and women, would they have managed to build organizations based on equal partnership?

GENDER AND CULTURAL ANALYSIS

Using the techniques of symbolic or cultural analysis, I demonstrate that economic relations were (and are) in part constituted by gender. I examine a variety of forms of data including written texts, spoken words, and rituals, as well as such other practices as the structuring of career paths and the sexual division of labor in factories, in order to uncover how they depicted men and women and to determine how people interpreted the events in which they were embroiled.

This approach to gender is useful for several reasons. First, it illuminates aspects of social existence that people never explicitly commented on, because they were taken for granted. In contrast to sociologists and anthropologists who study living people, those of us who do historical studies have a difficult time discovering what people have taken for granted or have considered to be common sense. They would only remark on such matters when shared understandings were being transformed and could no longer be taken for granted. Gender distinctions and their influence on people's behavior are phenomena of this order. They were part of the stock of "what everyone knew to be true." They have seemed to be "in nature."[16] One way to see how gender distinctions were constituted in the past and how they affected people's actions is to examine how gender difference was represented in language, ritual, and other social practices.

Second, numerous social theorists have argued that people's actions are shaped by the meanings or interpretations they have given to the situations in which they were participants.[17] If the theorists are correct, an important task for the historical analyst is to uncover these meanings. Cultural analysis is a powerful way to recover the ways that people construed the events that affected them.

A third reason why this approach is useful is that people make sense of their experiences through interpretations of them that are created by prominent people in public performances or widely available texts. I will refer to these interpretations as *cultural productions*. They are composed of shared cultural symbols which are used to mediate between what is already widely known or understood and the articulation of ideas about something new.[18] They are rhetorical devices meant to persuade.[19] Cultural productions include rituals such as street demonstrations and parades as well as speeches, newspaper articles and letters to the editor, pamphlets, scientific reports, photographs, drawings, and cartoons.[20] City streets, town centers, large meetinghouses, the halls of government, and the media serve as arenas of political contest about meaning. What is said and how it is said are important constituents of the political process.

Cultural productions, then, are crucial to the story to be told in the chapters that follow. They offer their intended audience interpretations of events and experiences that may become a stimulus for political action. These interpretations are particular constructions which cast the events within a limited and limiting perspective. The constructions repress, negate, or remain silent about alternative views. When these interpretations are built into public policies they directly constrain people's lives. When they are articulated by particularly visible and powerful people in their capacities as members of Parliament or heads of state, owners of significant business enterprises, leaders of unions and organizers of strikes and protest movements, or clergymen, they assume greater significance and wider currency than alternative interpretations offered by those who lack public prominence. In addition, they motivate or suppress action by defining or constructing the subjects to which the discourse applies. They call upon previously formed subjectivities and work on commonsense understandings to generate solidarity and consent. They appeal to particular aspects of people's experiences and connect these experiences to facets of their identities.[21]

Fourth, as I will argue later in this chapter, gender is a pervasive symbolic system which inheres in all social relations, including economic relations. It is primary to the constitution of people as social beings, and it forms a major component of personal identity. Because of these aspects of gender, gender divisions and distinctions are, as many feminist scholars have argued, central to all social processes.

My approach sheds new light on questions the answers to which have eluded scholars who have focused their inquiries specifically on the sex-typing of jobs and occupational segregation. For example, by seeing economic practices as shaped by cultural influences, this study suggests why employers' actions often veered away from the path of "strict economic rationality." By examining the meaning of work and its connections to family life it discloses why competition between women and men for jobs often produced vitriolic antagonism. By illuminating how union leaders generated union solidarity through their rhetoric, this study reveals why women often remained on the sidelines of union activity.

The use of cultural or symbolic analysis, especially the analysis of language, is associated with post-structuralism and post-modernism, and in history it is connected with the recent work of Joan Scott. Her stress on the importance of studying language and meaning, especially as a tool for understanding the importance of gender, has sparked considerable controversy.[22] Many of the critics have feared that symbolic analysis generally, and the analysis of texts in particular, wallows in relativism and ignores the material realities that profoundly affect people's lives.

I share some of these concerns. In particular, I believe it is important to include in one's scholarship a way of acknowledging that "the totality of social practices . . . always outruns the constraints of a given discourse," to quote historian Christine Stansell.[23] In this book I attempt to meet this goal by showing that people construed their experiences in particular ways and that these constructions fit uneasily with the multiple, diffuse, and varied influences on their lives, some of which affected them deeply. I also examine how gendered class relations created specific obstacles for people as they struggled to make ends meet. Moreover, I suggest that not only the practices in which gender distinctions were embodied, but the representations of gender promulgated by people in positions of power and authority, had important consequences for working people's lives. This book, then, unites social and cultural approaches in the study of gender and economic relations.

Central to this project is my assumption (elaborated more fully later in this chapter) that industrial capitalism was made up of a complex set of interdependent practices that cannot be reduced to, or explained by, purely economic factors. This is not to deny the importance of such economic factors as people's wages, the competition among employers, or the process of capital accumulation. How much people were paid, for example, determined whether and how much they could eat, or whether they could afford clothing and medical care. However, these economic factors did not operate independently from political, social, and ideological factors. For example, employers gained relative freedom to fix men's wages so that they responded to market forces as a consequence of changes both in laws and in what was thought to be the "right way of doing things."

The complex processes producing changes in economic relations are better pictured as a Gordian knot than a linear chain of discrete variables. In any case, what we might think of as purely economic facts such as people's wages did not have the same meaning for everyone, nor was their meaning a narrowly economic one. Wages were adjusted to the age and gender of the worker, sometimes regardless of the task the worker was performing. In addition, wages connected people's lives at work with their lives at home and in the community. This is why I have used the word *livelihood* in the title—to signify that people worked in order to live. They lived primarily in family households, and they lived with their families in neighborhoods and communities.

In short, I am arguing against reducing historical development to simple narratives that see people's actions as determined by some abstract force called the economy. In addition, I am saying that economic relations were (and are) formed in complex ways. Like all social relations, economic relations were shaped by culture, and concepts of gender were crucial in their formation.

PROBLEMS IN DEFINING GENDER

Gender is a multi-faceted concept that refers simultaneously to the relations between women and men; to their relative positions in society; to ideas about what it means to be woman or man and the qualities of person that make one more or less womanly or more or less manly; to identity and subjectivity. The attributes associated with gender distinctions are constantly changing and are never totally consistent with one another. Even more confusing, the received ideas about what it means to be woman or man do not reflect what real people actually do or are as women and men, although ideas about gender, articulated in social practices, influence their thoughts and actions in many ways. Finally, images of gender organize and transform ideas about the world and become implicated in complex systems of meaning. They are not confined to an explication of the various relations between women and men, but are also used in the construction of political, religious, and scientific understandings. The term *gender* refers simultaneously to social positions, social relations, and ideas about people and to their ideas about themselves.

I argue that it is through cultural processes—the elaboration of ideas, ideologies, and symbolic representations—that gender affects all social structures and social relations. Many past efforts to define the concept of gender and understand how it works have foundered on the distinctions between materialism and idealism or between thought and action that are implicit in most theories. That dualism makes it difficult to discuss the relevance of cultural forms for social life.[24] These dualisms appear in most historical and sociological analyses, but they are particularly pervasive in studies of economic relations and social class. In such studies culture is too often seen as epiphenomenal, as generated by material conditions rather than being in material conditions.[25] Representations of meaning are viewed as reflections of social reality rather than as being constitutive of social reality. That is to say, they are conceptualized as abstractions rather than as depictions.[26]

This dualism also underlies the view that imagines an analytic abstraction, the economy, to be the prime mover of social reality, which can explain all social processes. Although this kind of thinking is often associated with Marxian analysis, in fact it is implicit in neoclassical economics and in sociological approaches to the study of gender and work that have been influenced by economic theories.[27] Raymond Williams has made this point well: "It is . . . noticeable that in the twentieth century, the exponents of capitalism have been the most insistent theorists of the causal primacy of economic production. If you want to be told that our existence is governed by the economy, go to the city pages of the bourgeois press—that is really how they see life."[28] Economic determinism and dualism persist in those strands of Marxism that emphasize the distinction between base and superstructure and the idea that the economy is "determining in the last instance."[29] The role of culture and the issue of the interrelatedness of the multitude of social relations that comprise social life continue to be disputed by Marxist scholars.[30]

The debates about gender and class among different strands of feminist thought have mirrored those within Marxism. The argument that capitalism and patriarchy are separate systems is based on a narrow view of materialism which bifurcates meaning or ideas and action.[31] In order to place gender relations and economic relations on an equal footing, dual systems theories, as they are called, attempt to make gender as "material" as economic relations.[32] If the study of capitalism is concerned with the way the forces of production and the relations of production drive the motor of capital accumulation, yielding profits to capitalists through their exploitation of workers, then patriarchy is thought to be a system by which men benefit sexually and economically by subordinating or exploiting women.[33] Those who argue for a single system of patriarchal capitalism or capitalist patriarchy either relegate gender to the realm of ideology while leaving economic relations grounded in the material world, or claim that patriarchy is ultimately subsumed by capitalism and see the cause of women's subordination to be their biological role in reproduction (that is, their material bodies), which becomes either part of the dynamic of capitalist exploitation or a focus of class conflict.[34]

The connections made by Raymond Williams among language, ideas, imagination, feeling, lived experience, and practices dissolve the materialism/idealism duality. Williams's ideas provide a starting place for thinking about gender and how it is "in" the practices of capitalism and class relations.[35] He insists on the importance of grasping "the whole social process," not mistaking such abstractions from it as "the economy" as historically autonomous.[36] Williams understands language to be a socially structured system of multivalent symbols, and thought or consciousness to be an inner language made up of the multivalent symbols by means of which people communicate with one another. He argues that thought and action, consciousness and material production are not separable. Finally, he suggests that ideologies or particular systems of meaning never fully capture the lived experience of people, even if they become so accepted as to be seen as common sense.[37] These systems of meaning constitute experience for people by interpreting it, but they do not exhaust it. Experience not interpreted remains in imagination, and, as structures of feeling, act as a resource to be mobilized through political movements.

These ideas suggest a way of understanding how gender works. The social meanings of masculinity and femininity are expressed in a variety of practices that constrain people's lives. Just as humans cannot meaningfully be abstracted from society because through language they are constituted as social beings, so too we cannot view people as outside gender, as neuter.[38] The relations between gendered people are part of the social whole, and, as such, cannot be treated as though they constrained people's lives in isolation. Furthermore, the meanings of gender are legitimated through being naturalized.[39] These meanings are reproduced without question, through everyday practices, and they become embedded in the structures constituted by those everyday practices.[40] Social actors often are unaware that these assumptions are guiding their activities. This conception of meaning, one not restricted to conscious thought and intention, helps us to understand why gender divisions are continually being reproduced by employers who do not question the idea that ordinarily men rather than women should have skilled jobs.[41] However, because images of gender difference always fail to capture the complexities and the multiplicity of lived experience, representations of gender are continually being contested and are inherently unstable.

A WORKING DEFINITION OF GENDER

Gender is a classificatory system that depicts the differing positions of women and men in society. It is a system of meanings articulated in practices that position women and men differently and that structure their lived experience in different ways. Societies differ not only in the content of the meanings of gender but also in the extent to which gender segregates the life experiences of women and men and the extent to which there is overlap in their experiences. Historically, gender distinctions have represented and constituted differences in power.[42]

In Western society, people are assigned to the mutually exclusive social categories of *woman* and *man* solely on the basis of anatomical sexual differences. All other similarities and differences between people are irrelevant to the categories. Regardless of what else may characterize their lived experience, all persons with female genitalia are women, and all persons with male genitalia are men.[43]

In our society, as in most others, people have believed that anatomical differences signaled other crucial differences. One that was especially stressed in nineteenth-century thought was the physiological capability of women, but not men, to bear and nurse children. Note, however, that nineteenth-century categorizations placed a woman in that category whether or not she could or did bear a child (whether or not she was fecund; whether or not she was too young or too old to be fecund). Her sex defined either her potential, her current status, or her former situation. A stress on the differences in reproductive function between women and men made other similarities between them irrelevant, and the differences among women and among men were erased. As Mary Poovey writes, "the similarity of women's childbearing capacity became more important than whatever other features distinguished them."[44]

If a society were to stress reproduction in its depiction of men as well as women, then all men would be thought of as inseminators regardless of whether they could or cared to inseminate. However, in nineteenth-century Britain, although gender distinction was predicated on "essential" biological difference, men were not perceived to be "sexed"; their biological roles were not a focus of attention. Rather, representations of gender in Victorian England stressed the equation of women with biology or nature, and men with culture. Women were "the sex."[45]

Gender categories have also been associated with other attributes that have nothing to do with anatomy or physiology. In the nineteenth century these attributes were counterposed as oppositions: men were active, independent, strong, rational; women were passive, dependent, weak, emotional. Furthermore, the cultural meanings associated with being woman and being man were assumed to be "in nature," to be "in" the original anatomical and physiological difference between women and men. Gender categories were believed to indicate the essence of the person; if the person did not match the attributes of the category, he or she was thought to be deviant.[46] Sorting people into the categories *woman* and *man, female* and *male,* was a moral process mistaken for something "real," something "natural."

The attributes of gender were used to differentiate among people of the same biological sex. For example, in the nineteenth century *manliness* was a term that differentiated men from one another. Manliness often meant being honorable. A male person could gain manliness from the work that he did, from his ability to support his family, from his behavior as a trade unionist or as an employer in labor negotiations. To be a man in British society was associated with the value of "independence." In that way manhood was contrasted not only with womanhood but with boyhood.[47] In addition, manliness was linked in a complex system of representations to the revered Victorian value of respectability. To be manly was to be honorable and respectable, which meant being brave, strong, and independent. For a woman, by contrast, to be honorable and respectable meant to have the virtues of sexual purity, domesticity, and motherhood. Women were not legally independent persons, and images of dependency as a character trait as well as in law coexisted uneasily with the realities of working-class women's lives as they struggled to provide a livelihood for themselves and their families. Ironically, working-class men were considered legally independent individuals, but they were dependent not only on their employers, to secure a livelihood, but often on their wives and children, their legal dependents, who contributed economically as well as in other ways to household survival. The association of different values with being male and female shows how these ideological constructions placed particular interpretations on the lived experiences of working-class women and men.

These constructions and people's experiences often contradicted one another. For example, the complementary ideals of the male breadwinner who earned a family wage and the woman who devoted herself to full-time domesticity could not be realized by the majority of working-class married couples. The tensions between the ideal and the reality, between the constructions of masculinity and femininity and lived experience, were a fertile source of political rhetoric in labor disputes.

In addition to representing distinctions between people, gender appears to be such a central way of representing difference that it can become emblematic, creating distinctions in a host of physical objects and mannerisms such as articles of clothing, types of food, rooms in houses, and styles of eating and drinking. Finally, as Joan Scott has insisted, gender is a fundamental way of constituting power relations.[48] In short, I am arguing that gender is a symbolic system for representing difference. It is more akin to language than it is to any other social process.

Language is a set of social symbols that create distinctions. These symbols can vary in meaning and use, but in order for them to communicate meaning they must be understood. Similarly, gender is a process of making distinctions in ways that are widely recognized and understood. The language of gender is expressed in a variety of social practices that position people differently in relations of power. In nineteenth-century England, these positions were linked to differential access to political and economic resources.

These ideas suggest in an abstract way why gender is deeply embedded in all social relations, including those that have been considered to be primarily or solely economic relations. To put it simply, people enter employer-employee relationships as gendered beings unless something happens that actively suppresses the salience of gender. Nineteenth-century employers were influenced by images of gender when they hired workers, structured the work process, and governed their workplaces. They imagined skilled workers to be by definition men, and their actions produced employment opportunities structured by the assumption that workers lacked domestic ties and responsibilities. The notion of a woman worker, especially a working mother, was a contradiction in terms. Work was constructed on the presumption that workers were nonmothers.

Because gender was deeply embedded in the structuring of employment, working-class women and men had different working situations. Women were paid less than men. Women were often supervised by men, but men were never supervised by women. Women and men had different kinds of responsibilities for their families. Because of the way masculinity was constituted, the struggles between male workers and their employers were over issues concerning gender and class simultaneously. Because of the way femininity was constituted and connected to masculinity, male leaders of working-class organizations and activities defined workers as men and shaped their organizing and solidarity-making strategies accordingly.

In this study I focus on the construction of masculinity and femininity at work in the household and workplace. Ideas about what it meant to be man and what it meant to be woman were certainly also articulated in a host of social institutions, including the chapel, the press, the music hall, clubs, training institutes, and self-improvement associations, and in informal leisure activities. I believe, however, that household and workplace, family and employment were at the center of the lives of both men and women of the working class.

Although this study stresses the ways that gender shaped social, political, and economic relations, the relationship between gender and class is neither simple nor unidirectional. While analytically we may speak of class and gender as distinct processes, people's lives are intersected by class and gender relations simultaneously.[49] In nineteenth-century England gendered class relations fostered the development of working-class associations and institutions which, in turn, affected images of gender. This is most clearly seen in the ways that participation by skilled men and male artisans in political, fraternal, and labor organizations bolstered their shared identity as men.[50] The masculine ideal of the breadwinner, which assumed a wife's primary allegiances to be those of housewife and mother, was articulated by skilled male trade unionists, especially the cotton spinners, and by participants in the Ten Hours campaign and the Chartist movement for universal male suffrage.[51] The very associations created by skilled and artisanal working men to cope with their political and economic disadvantage were crucial in revising images of gender, creating new meanings of manhood and womanhood.

CAPITALISM AND CLASS

To accumulate wealth and expand enterprises, the economic institutions of capitalism depend on the labor of workers who sell their labor in order to subsist. However, capitalism is more than an economic system. The development of capitalism, as I indicated above, involved interconnected political, social, cultural, and economic transformations. Thus, when I use the term *capitalism* I mean social and economic practices, centered on private property and the accumulation of wealth, that contain within them multiple cultural influences. Gender has been among the most important of these cultural influences.

In this book I explore some of the ways that capitalism developed as a gendered set of practices. To do this, I examine how employers structured their work force, organized the labor process, and managed their workplaces. In addition, I show how images of gender influenced state policies and how those state policies were central to the development of industrial capitalism and constrained the conditions under which working-class women and men created livelihoods.[52]

Capitalist practices both depended on and created waged workers (male and female proletarians). However, what it meant to be a worker, how those meanings were created through political practices, and the consequences of that creation for class struggle or relations were not preordained by an abstract logic of capital accumulation. Rather, both the character of class relations and the nature of working-class formation were historically contingent.

Ironically, although the absence of a theoretical construction of gender has inhibited the incorporation of gender analysis into social theory, the lack of a clear consensus about the meaning of *class* has not kept it from being a central point of sociological and historical analysis. Scholars have continued to conflate class position with class experience and class experience with political action, retarding progress in understanding working-class formation.[53] One difficulty faced by contemporary scholars has been the issue of structure and agency in the interpretation of class formation.[54] The problem for class analysts is to recognize both that people's lives are deeply affected by their position in the relations of production and also that their responses depend on how their experiences have been interpreted.[55]

In this study I use the terms *working class* and *working classes* to describe wage-earning people in contrast to employers. By using the term *class* instead of the more neutral *employees* I intend to signify that working people were subordinated to those who employed them. Working-class people shared with one another limitations on their capacity to create their livelihoods which stemmed from their class position. In the following chapters I attempt to show how gender affected those limitations, the conflicts between workers and employers about them, and the extent to which the workers were able to forge inclusive organizations in their struggles. In other words, I examine the consequences of gender distinctions and relations for class relations and for working-class formation.

Scholars following and revising E. P. Thompson's theory of class formation have argued that class is the process by which a set of people collectively act in opposition to capitalists, or the process by means of which they see themselves as a class and use the term to define their experience.[56] Historically, however, these collective actions or definitions have not included all those people whose livelihoods have been constrained by their class position. So as not to lose the sense of limitation and constraint that haunted the lives of working people generally in the nineteenth century, I use the term *class relation* to refer to the structured inequality between workers and capitalists, and *class formation* to signify the collective action taken by some or all workers in response to that inequality. In what follows I attempt to show that gender distinctions and relations were involved in shaping both class relations and working-class formation.

Even scholars who have tried to avoid a mechanical understanding of class formation often assume that deviation from class unity is what must be explained, as though unified class action would happen if nothing intervened to stop it.[57] However, as historian Geoff Eley has written, "The 'unity' of the working class, though postulated through the analysis of production and its social relations, remains a contingency of political agitation."[58]

What needs to be made problematic is how interests are created. We cannot assume that they are inherent in social conditions. Interests are constructed through politics, and these politics create collective identities.[59] They are constructed, however, in relation to the social conditions under which people live. They are not abstract social constructions fabricated without reference to people's lives.[60] Rather, interests are produced through a discursive process that interprets the conditions of people's existence and the constraints on them. These articulated interpretations are prerequisite to collective action.

People operate under many different kinds of constraints, stemming from their various but simultaneous social positions.[61] Political practices involve suppressing the salience of some of these positions and aspects of people's identities and emphasizing others. Unity or solidarity is a fragile accomplishment, and it must be explained by showing how it was accomplished.

ORGANIZATION OF THE STUDY

No precise time-frame for this study is possible, because different industries underwent significant alterations at different time periods. Separate processes within the same industry were marked by different time schedules.[62] The cotton industry, at the vanguard of the industrial revolution, is a good example, with power spinning preceding powerlooming by three decades. Cotton spinning ceased to be a domestic, putting-out industry by the 1780s, when the process was moved out of cottages into workshops or sheds. By the beginning of the nineteenth century, spinning was done by steam-powered machines in factories. However, it was not until the 1830s that the power loom was perfected and factory weaving became widespread. The knitting industry was transformed by steam power only after midcentury. The first steam-powered hosiery factories opened in the 1850s, but hand- and foot-powered frames were operated in domestic workshops until the end of the century. Steam power had been introduced to the lace industry by the 1850s, and it rapidly came to be the general method by which lace was made. Lace finishing remained a hand industry and has continued to be done primarily on an outwork basis, largely as a homeworking industry, to the present day.

Industrial capitalism did not affect the organization of production in all industries in a uniform fashion. Some industries were transformed by labor-intensive methods rather than by steam power and remained a source of home or workshop employment for both women and men throughout the nineteenth century. Mechanization in one division of an industry often resulted in an intensification of hand labor in other processes within the same industry. For example, as I have said earlier, lace was made by men using steam-powered machines in factories, but was hand-finished by women and children, the majority of whom worked in their homes or in the homes of nearby middle-women. As hosiery making was transformed, first by the invention of hand- and foot-powered machines and then by steam, the work of finishing the goods by hand increased. The existence of regional variations within some industries further complicates the possibility of generalizing about the specific ways that work was reorganized by industrial capitalism.[63]

Although I rely on secondary material from the entire century, I use a range of primary source material about events in the latter half of the century to create scenarios about how gender affected the development of capitalism, for it was during those years that industrial capitalism was becoming preeminent.

Chapters 2 and 3 show how industrial capitalism was gendered. I show in Chapter 2 that employers built gender distinctions into the ways they organized work and into the ways they managed their work force. Economic institutions were (and are) connected to other institutions such as the state, discussed in Chapter 3, which generated policies affecting working people's lives at home and at work. In Chapter 4 I show how those constraints affected women's waged and unwaged work as they attempted to provide for their families. Chapters 5 and 6 discuss conflicts that developed over time in the carpet industry as employers attempted to deal with competition and male and female workers fought to preserve their livelihoods. In Chapter 5 I examine the range of views of class relations held by the participants in the disputes. In Chapter 6 I demonstrate how these same conflicts were interpreted as gender antagonism and connect this antagonism to emerging notions of masculinity, domesticity, and respectability. In Chapter 7 I examine the one industry, cotton powerloom weaving, in which women and men did not compete for jobs (because they earned equal pay), to determine whether or not their relative equality led them to form strong and unified trade union organizations. In the final chapter I assess what I have learned about gender and economic relations as they relate to public policy and the relationship between class and gender. In particular I focus on the importance of recognizing the complex, interacting practices that turned the past into the present.

2

"Maintaining the
Industrial Supremacy of the Country"
Industrialists and Gendered Work

Employers patterned their work forces and hiring practices, structured work opportunities, and managed their enterprises in ways that expressed pervasive meanings of gender difference, class relations, and a developing ideology of family life.[1] These cultural constructions influenced how employers divided up tasks and allocated jobs among different workers, which machines they purchased, and how they introduced machinery into the production process. In addition, the intertwined constructions of gender, family, and class affected how industrialists regulated employer-employee relationships to insure that production would proceed with maximum efficiency and a minimum of resistance from workers.[2]

Industrialists responded to a variety of market and personal pressures as well as to actual or potential resistance by workers. Industrial capitalism was gendered as it developed through these complex interactions and constraints. In this chapter I consider how gender distinctions influenced the ways manufacturers organized work and managed their enterprises, two aspects of a very dynamic process that affected and were affected by class relations and working-class formation.[3]

GENDER IN THE LABOR PROCESS

Manufacturers organize production by dividing up the jobs to be done and assigning some workers to jobs that require technical facility and other workers to those that are more routine. Numerous scholars have argued that skill is a social construction, not an objective factor that differentiates one job from another.[4] In the nineteenth century nearly all employers hired men for skilled work and for work that involved what they construed to be "complicated" machinery. They rarely questioned the appropriateness of hiring male workers for such jobs. Skill and the ability to run large, complex machinery were widely believed to be "natural" masculine traits. Generally, industrialists hired women for work that had already been defined as "women's work": jobs that were, relative to men's jobs, low-paid and were believed to require little technical competence or training. Employers reevaluated the gender assumptions behind their hiring practices only when they were forced by competitive market pressures to seek ways of reducing their labor costs.[5]

GENDER AND WAGES

The ideology of separate spheres was a central, organizing motif in the worldviews of bourgeois men and women.[6] Industrialists' assumptions about workers were informed by this doctrine, which portrayed home and work as separate and different spheres suited to the natural proclivities and responsibilities of women and men, respectively. They therefore believed it was "natural" for men to have jobs that were better-paying than those of women, since it was men who were supposedly responsible for the economic welfare of families.[7] However, employers did not take into account the family situations of male workers when they decided on their rates of pay. Whether or not they considered a job to be one requiring technical expertise and training, they fixed men's wages by estimating their other costs, and especially by comparison with what other manufacturers were paying for the same work.[8]

Although employers undoubtedly took into account what their competitors were paying women workers, industrialists based their wage scales for women, unlike those for men, on a *customary* rate.[9] A social investigator of women's work and wages in Birmingham reported in 1906 that "employers can usually give no other reasons for the actual wage than the fact that such and such a figure is what women usually get in Birmingham."[10]

Even before industrial transformation, women had already been designated as a low-waged labor force.[11] Estimates of agricultural wages in medieval and early modern England indicate that wages for work normally done by women were significantly below those paid for work normally done by men.[12] Even women who did skilled work were ill paid. For example, the rate of pay for female flower-painters in Wedgwood's London workrooms in the early 1770s was 60 percent of the rate for male flower-painters.[13] In the period just prior to the mechanization of cotton spinning, manufacturers based spinners' wages on the assumption that spinners were being supported by their husbands.[14]

Occupational specialization by gender, which in part may account for the traditional wage differential between women and men, also appears to have been a feature of economic life for centuries.[15] In fourteenth-century Shrewsbury, women were found working in a more limited range of occupations than men, mainly in the preliminary stages of textile industry, brewing, and petty retail and domestic service; they were not found in the more prestigious and profitable occupations.[16] Although women in early modern urban areas could participate in a range of crafts prior to the spread of capitalism, generally they engaged in skilled work only as an aspect of their family responsibilities as wife or daughter.[17] This complexly woven legacy of low wages and occupational segregation was important in the capitalist transformation and development of many industries.[18]

GENDER AND SKILL

Employers and their managers rarely doubted the commonly made association between skilled work and male labor. They structured training and advancement opportunities in their factories that reflected and reproduced this association. With the major exception of cotton weaving (which I will discuss in Chapter 7), industrialists hired boys for jobs that trained them to do the work of skilled adult men. Girls were not given these jobs. Their work did not lead to more advanced or higher paying positions, but were "dead ends" in the factory.

The lace industry provides a good example of how employers structured work so that women were excluded as a potential source of skilled labor.[19] Until the end of the nineteenth century, when manufacturers adopted special lace machines that made embroidered and braided laces, introducing them to the trade as "women's machines," only males worked lace machinery. The early hand-powered machines varied in size; the larger ones probably were too heavy for most women to operate them productively. Hand-run lace machinery became wider, and by 1841 few narrow lace machines were in use. But the size and heaviness of the machinery alone do not explain the exclusively male appropriation of these tools. When hand machines were turned with a wheel instead of hands and feet, boys were employed to turn the wheel under the supervision of men. Factory inspector R. D. Grainger's report to the 1843 Children's Employment Commission noted that turning the wheel was very hard work for young children who worked at all hours of the night.[20]

When lace was made on steam-powered machinery, a number of boys under the age of eighteen were employed as machine-minders. Inspector Grainger commented that the work consisted "simply in minding or watching the progress of the work and in rectifying errors when they arise; the machine is so perfect that no part of the actual work need be done by the mechanic."[21] Henry Scattergood, for example, started working as a threader when he was eleven and began tending a machine when he was thirteen. Together he and the man he assisted worked two machines.[22] If thirteen-year-old boys were physically capable of operating such lace machines, it should have been possible for a grown woman to do at least that same amount and kind of work.

One reason that women were not considered for such jobs is that a number of the early manufacturers of lace, the men who owned machines and employed operatives to work them, had worked as skilled mechanics before becoming entrepreneurs.[23] In the early years of the factory lace industry it was not uncommon for the twist hand to own his machinery.[24] Independent machine-holders moved from their domestic workshops into factories because they were able to rent steam power. In boom times, twist hands became entrepreneurs, and in bad times manufacturers became twist hands again. Even the men who came from families of moderate wealth and headed giant lace-manufacturing firms had earlier acquired mechanical skills.[25]

Given the development of the lace industry and the background of many manufacturers, it is not surprising that the job of twist hand was perceived as one for males. Yet labor costs were a concern. The trade was subject to wild fluctuations caused by changes in fashion, and it was a fiercely competitive industry, with masters attempting to edge out their neighbors and battling challenges from Continental competitors. In lace making, employers looked to boys rather than women as sources of inexpensive labor to assist lace makers and that employment of boys as assistants guaranteed that twist hands would be men.

The Factory Act of 1861 limited the hours that women and children could work in lace factories. Eighteen was the stipulated age at which males ceased to be subject to regulation in other textile industries, but for the lace industry the age was sixteen. Lace manufacturers had insisted that boys from the age of sixteen be allowed to work the same hours as adult men. Mr. Heymann, a major Nottingham lace manufacturer, told parliamentary commissioners who had investigated the industry that it was essential for boys from the age of sixteen to work the same hours as adult men in order to supply skilled labor to the trade. He said, "If legislation prevented our transferring lads at sixteen to the machines, they would go away into other trades, and the best of them would get on those trades, and we should never see them again."[26] Working men opposed the exemption, arguing that boys under eighteen could learn the trade during legally restricted hours by operating the numerous "small, simple machines" that were available.[27] One workman said that the boys should work at the less remunerative work until they were eighteen because it would be better for them from "a moral point of view"; otherwise "they become men too soon."[28] Neither the employers nor the workmen even mentioned the possibility that girls or women could work these machines.

Both employers and working men believed that there was a natural progression in a male's career in the lace industry. A boy worked first as a threader, and then either on the small lace machines or as an assistant to an adult male twist hand on larger machines. Next he moved on to become a twist hand in his own right. Girls had no such career progression. They began their work in lace factories as bobbin winders and they remained bobbin winders, or perhaps they did the job of removing the lace from the machine after it was loomed (called "jacking off"). In any case, they remained in ancillary processes at low wages.[29] To employers and workmen alike, the trade of twist hand was the work of men, which excluded both boys and women. The controversy over whether or not boys sixteen to eighteen should be subject to the factory acts was one concerning a supply of low-waged workers for the lace trade, framed as a debate about when it was appropriate for boys to become men.[30]

In nineteenth-century Britain, employers in a host of industries in addition to lace hired boys for jobs that trained them to be skilled workers. In cotton, manufacturers hired male spinners. They, in turn, hired boy piecers who helped them to mend broken threads and tend the machines. By doing this work during what could be a very long apprenticeship, piecers learned the technical difficulties of working the machines they hoped in the future to run as spinners.[31] Piecers remained in their subordinate position until they could become spinners.[32] Spinners supervised piecers and in turn were supervised by overlookers.[33] Overlookers were recruited from the ranks of the spinners. As in lace making, technical facility with machinery, the method of training, and the stepping-stones in an operative's career were interwoven and were gendered male.

Although there were places that women were hired as compositors, most printers, too, were men. In a move reminiscent of what happened in parliamentary hearings on the lace industry in 1861, Charles Wyman urged a parliamentary commission in 1876 to make sixteen the age when boys could work men's hours, because he believed learning to set type was educational.[34] In the paper industry, employers preferred boys to girls because although girls were believed to have an advantage from their smaller fingers and lighter touch, boys had "more aptitude to manage machines and are better worth teaching, as they may grow up into competent mechanics."[35]

In numerous manufacturing industries, employers and working men alike assumed a connection between "career ladders," technical competence, and masculinity. The term *career ladder* refers to the structured progression that made it possible for male workers to move from low-paid and less skilled to higher-paid and skilled jobs. The gender structuring of career ladders guaranteed that if a job required or was thought to require skill, it was a job for a man. Women had very little opportunity for job mobility.[36] In most trades, industrialists or their male managers guaranteed that the positions of skilled workers would be filled by men by hiring boys at entry-level positions that trained them for their future occupations. With the exception of cotton powerloom weaving, women were excluded from these jobs and restricted to jobs without a career progression.

Employers considered mechanical aptitude to be a purely masculine trait.[37] They talked about men's "natural" technical ability and women's mechanical ineptitude as though this was a gender difference everyone recognized; it was common sense. The belief that women naturally lacked facility with machinery was in fact widely held, and employers used it to justify paying women less than men for the same jobs.

On those occasions when male trade unionists who were threatened with replacement by women tried to insist on equal pay for women and men (often as a ploy to prevent the employment of women), employers in a wide range of industries—hosiery, carpets, woolen weaving, and paper making, to name but a few—insisted that women would not be able to tune or repair their machines. The employers maintained that they paid women less then men because if they hired women they also needed to hire costly male supervisors who could tune machines and do minor repairs.[38] A government report on women in the hosiery industry stated that only men were employed as mechanics in the trade, and therefore men supervised the women who worked the circular hosiery machines. Showing insight into why women lacked mechanical facility, the writer of the report commented, "Women sometimes by practice become very clever at adjusting their machines, but they have not been trained as mechanics and do not undertake repairs."[39] Employers, however, appeared to believe that the reason women did not know how to fix most machinery was because they were born female. By structuring career paths as they did, employers created a self-fulfilling prophecy. Women lacked competence with machinery because they were not given formal, recognized training. And they were not given training for skilled jobs because they were believed to lack technical aptitude.

Not only were women considered inappropriate for jobs already defined as skilled and requiring mechanical competence, but their own skills and abilities with the machinery identified with them were undervalued, underpaid, and denigrated in comparison with men's skills and mechanical competencies.[40] As contemporary social investigator B. L. Hutchins wrote, "There is no reason, save custom and lack of organisation, why a nursery-maid should be paid less than a coal miner. He is not one whit more capable of taking her place than she is of taking his."[41] In structuring work employers exploited traditional definitions of what was skilled work and what kinds of machines required mechanical aptitude. They also accepted without question that formal apprenticeship or specific entry-level jobs were the only source of training. By conflating masculinity and skill, industrialists obscured and naturalized the training that women received for what were assumed to be their "natural" talents.[42] Thus, women's sewing, whether done by hand or by machine, was assumed to be a "natural" talent because young girls presumably learned it as a part of growing up.

Because it was a "natural" talent, it was not a skill. In contrast, the predominantly men's trade of tailoring was considered to be a skilled trade, and employers attempted to deskill it by contracting to have the work done by women.[43]

GENDER AND TECHNOLOGY

In addition to structuring career ladders in a way that prevented women from acquiring particular technical skills, employers also adopted "gendered" technology. Machines designed to be worked by skilled workers were built to be operated by people with the hands, height, and weight of an average male, unless a manufacturer had in mind reducing labor costs by replacing men with women and therefore contracted with a machine maker to build a machine that would be suitable for female bodies.[44] Studies of gender and technology in the twentieth century show that men gain a sense of masculinity from their association with machines.[45] In the nineteenth century the technology itself was gendered.

Not all machinery was thought to be solely appropriate for male operatives. Throughout the nineteenth century, in a variety of industries manufacturers introduced machines that were designed to be marketed as "women's machines." These machines were designed to require little training or stamina of the operatives who would run them. In the hosiery industry the invention of circular frames, attributed to the engineer Marc Isambert Brunel, was aimed at use by women, and employers bought them as "ladies' machines" from the earliest years of the factory industry—although male operatives contested women's employment on them from the start.[46] In the lace industry manufacturers introduced the Schiffle, a machine, widely used by women on the Continent, that made embroidered and braided laces. In the carpet industry, the machine that produced Royal Axminster carpets was thought by employers to be one especially suitable for women's work. As one of the employers remarked when the men's union disputed the continued hiring of women to work on the Axminster looms, "there could be no denying that the Axminster was a girl's loom and not fit for a man at all."[47]

When labor costs were an issue, employers were more likely to be successful in battles with the unions over the substitution of women for men if they could find a new machine designed specifically for women. A new machine was appropriate for women's labor if the running of it required little training. If the machines were large and heavy or required technical know-how, industrialists assumed that men should run them.

Manufacturers, however, did not always reserve machines requiring strength for men. For example, in Kidderminster, the center of the carpet trade, when manufacturers tried to employ women on any machine that made carpets or could possibly be used for making carpets, male carpet weavers protested vigorously (as I will describe more fully in Chapter 5). However, they made no objection to women making rugs on the Chenille handloom. Weaving on this loom was physically taxing. As a female weaver said, "it needed bone and muscle" to do the work.[48] Lottie Mary Cooper, born in 1890, remembered visiting her mother in the factory where she wove cashmere rugs on a Chenille handloom:

> I can see our mother now, working at her loom, there wasn't a stool to sit on, only a bar held by ropes. You couldn't sit on it properly, only lean back against it while your feet worked the treadles. It was very hard work operating the treadles which worked the heddles. . . . You could always tell someone who'd been working on the weaving all their lives for they walked in a special way, all that treadling.[49]

Even though the work required strength, both employers and the members of the all-male union thought of it as women's work.[50] Men in Kidderminster had other sources of employment that were better paid; they were not interested in rug making.

Employers, then, hired men for work defined as skilled; they structured the labor process in such a way that only men could learn the skills; and ordinarily they purchased machinery built with male bodies in mind. Usually women worked at jobs that required little or no formal training. However, when faced with sufficient pressure to lower production costs, industrialists hired women for jobs for which they had previously employed men, sometimes purchasing special "women's machines."

INDUSTRIALISTS' JUSTIFICATIONS FOR EMPLOYING WOMEN

Substitutions or attempted substitutions were common in numerous industries in the last half of the nineteenth century, including the hosiery industry in Nottingham and Leicester, the carpet industry, and the silk industry.[51] Industrialists in a variety of businesses in addition to textiles hired women to do work that had been done by men. As was noted above, women were employed as compositors, especially on weekly papers in country districts and in small printing establishments, presumably because they were cheap labor.[52] At the turn of the century, women filled the former jobs of men in making tin canisters, and the introduction of new technology in some areas of engineering encouraged capitalists to replace men with women.[53] By the last decade of the century, women were soldering fine pieces of wire together to make loops in "self-opening" pins, for wages that averaged seven to ten shillings weekly, having replaced men who had earned from fifteen to twenty shillings weekly doing exactly the same work.[54]

Numerous parliamentary commissions and social investigations focusing on women's work questioned employers or their managers about their motives for hiring women. Employers invented various justifications. The implicit assumption framing both the questions and the responses was that the particular jobs women were doing conflicted with widely accepted ideas about women. The assumption became explicit when the industrialist expressed a justification that overtly undermined accepted gender ideology.

Unlike the majority of employers in the nineteenth century, Arthur Chamberlain, a Birmingham brass works owner, proposed that there should be no restrictions on what work women could do. During Parliamentary Commission hearings in 1876, Chamberlain was badgered about his statements. For example, when he expressed the view that because they were excluded from so many occupations women were forced to take jobs that were "ill-suited" to their sex, the commission chair said, "I want you to consider whether, really, the very startling general statement which you made could be quite supported upon consideration."[55] Chamberlain continued to press his point, claiming that "if women were free from restrictions, in twenty-five years they would be earning equal rates with men."[56] He wanted to employ women to work in his brass works and told the commissioners he would employ them "largely in what has hitherto been considered men's work, and work which is consequently much better paid."[57] A shocked commissioner asked, "Are there not parts of the work where a woman could not wear a woman's dress?"[58] At the turn of the century Chamberlain told a social investigator that he employed women wherever possible, including in some of the particularly dangerous processes in his works—processes which required "greater care and recollectedness and are better paid."[59]

It is clear that Chamberlain reaped the benefits of implementing his beliefs. The average wage for women and girls in his works was little more than eleven shillings; the average wage for boys and men was just over twenty-eight shillings.[60] W. Atkinson, who also ran a brass foundry in Birmingham, refused to follow Chamberlain's lead in hiring women for "men's jobs." He remarked that Chamberlain attempted to put women to work on the automatic lathe, which up to then had been regarded as men's work, for the sake of "their cheapness."[61]

Some employers responded to parliamentary commissions in ways that displayed either a conflict in their values or contradictions that were produced by the line of questioning taken by their interviewers. For example, Frederick Carver, president of the Lace Merchants Association of Nottingham and owner of a warehouse employing more than six hundred women and young persons, testified before the 1876 Commission on the Factory and Workshops Acts. Asked about the employment of married women, he responded:

> As to married women, in one particular department of our establishment we have forty-nine married women and we wish that the present state of things as regards married women should not be disturbed because we find that the married women we employ are . . . the best workers, that is, they are more diligent and attentive to their work . . . but we have as a rule an objection to employing married women, because we think that every man ought to maintain his wife without the necessity of her going to work.[62]

A brass ornaments manufacturer of Birmingham seemed more clearly to portray himself as using business practices that went against his principles as he described them to a social investigator. Employer Morris said that he had been hiring girls to work power presses for about two years, although he thought it was "hard work and in some respects undesirable." However, he found it very difficult to obtain boys cheaply enough: "they won't come under nine or ten shillings, and girls do it as well for five shillings."[63] Similarly, Herbert Green, paper manufacturer at Maidstone, told B. L. Hutchins, "It is undesirable and objectionable to employ women at night and [I have] never done it, but at the same time, if an industrialist really requires night work and needs a supply of cheap labour, women should be allowed to work at night for the sake of maintaining the industrial supremacy of the country."[64] Green justified employing women workers as cheap labor by elevating such a practice to an action in the national interest.

Some employers justified hiring women to do jobs that might be characterized as "unfeminine" because they were heavy, dangerous, or dirty jobs, especially those that had formerly been done by men and had not been made lighter or easier with the help of machinery, by seeing the women who worked at them as contemptible and undeserving of improved conditions. A jewelry manufacturer from Birmingham reported that women were employed at the turn of the twentieth century power-polishing metals, work that men had been doing twenty-five years earlier. He noted that it was light work the women did, but it was "dirty and only the coarsest women do it."[65] A bookbinder from the Isle of Dogs said that he hired girls because it was hard to get boys and only the "roughest girls will take the work. . . . Also no nice girl could put up with the insults she would receive from the men of the factory." He went on to describe the various kinds of work at which women were employed in his trade and said that while some branches were suitable for women, there was "the deadly bronze work, which ruins the health of the girls employed in it—the heavy ledger work, only suitable for men and mere mechanical processes which degrade the work." He asked, "What can be expected of a girl who spends her days standing on a ladder feeding or unloading a machine?"[66]

PATERNALISM AS A
MANAGERIAL STRATEGY

Paternalism was a set of practices that relied on a familial metaphor in which the employer was the head and father and working men and working women were his dependent children. From the 1850s until after the turn of the twentieth century, paternalistic factory regimes proliferated in family-owned and -operated factories in Lancashire and elsewhere.[67] Industrialists who implemented such workplace regimes hoped to instill in their workpeople feelings of obligation and gratitude that would produce harmonious industrial relations.[68] Worker resentment of harsh working conditions and strict supervision, economic insecurity and persistent poverty, were evident to the employer classes in the cities and the factory communities of the industrial north.[69] The Chartist uprisings and the bitter Preston strike and lockout of 1853–1854 undoubtedly led some industrialists to realize that their economic success depended on the cooperation of workers, and that this could not be exacted by coercion. Paternalism evolved as a management strategy to dampen the conflict between labor and capital in the workplace by putting a positive face on capitalist authority.[70]

Most scholars have viewed paternalism as a mechanism of class control by employers.[71] Judy Lown has enriched the study of paternalism by demonstrating how management strategies at the Courtauld silk mills, which primarily employed women workers, were constituted as a set of patriarchal practices.[72] Paternalist employers of both women and men did structure their workplaces in order to diminish worker resistance and enhance worker loyalty, but they used gender distinctions between women and men as workers and as members of families as a template for structuring their enterprises. Paternalist practices, then, both represented gender distinctions and structured gender divisions and relations.

Bourgeois Masculinity

In order to understand paternalist management fully, it is necessary to look at industrialists not just as employers but as men who, with their wives, shaped bourgeois culture. They were businessmen whose own livelihoods depended on the profits of their firms. They headed families in addition to enterprises, and they believed it was their duty to provide for their families. Mid-Victorian capitalists wanted to build a successful business for their heirs to inherit. Instead of land serving as a father's legacy to his son, property in productive capital could be bequeathed by a flourishing businessman.

John Bright, a major Victorian political figure who owned a large textile and carpet concern in Rochdale, "quite frankly admitted that as a manufacturer in a considerable way he did not profess to keep on his factory for the benefit of his workpeople or even for the sake of clothing his customers, but in order to procure for himself and his family a decent income."[73] Leonore Davidoff and Catherine Hall's important study of the centrality of gender and family in the making of middle-class society suggests that Bright's ingenuous comment expressed his vision of his mission and place in society.[74] He spoke from a worldview that linked his manliness and his status as a breadwinner to his business practices. Laissez-faire political economy was a secular creed that sanctioned his business practices and bolstered his self-respect as a husband and father. However, taken to its extreme, this doctrine envisioned workers as mere instruments of production; relations between employer and employee "were to be merely those of the cash nexus."[75]

Church doctrines from evangelical Anglicanism to a range of non-conformist denominations gave men like Bright, a Quaker, sacred justification for engaging in the world of commerce.[76] Religious teaching spoke simultaneously of the employer's responsibilities to his own family and his ethical obligations to his workpeople. On the one hand, religious values underscored the manliness of commerce linked to a man's obligations to his family. On the other, they stressed his "service" to his "family in work."[77] Many middle-class employers deployed these teachings to put a human face on the harsh dictates of political economy to which these same employers subscribed. By espousing and implementing their moral vision, they attempted to distance themselves from those whose stations were above and below them in the blueprint of social space that they were drawing.[78] Living these ideals marked their moral legitimacy as a ruling class by differentiating them from their decadent "social betters." At the same time they proclaimed their domination of the "great unwashed." A man could fulfill his mission by making his factory into a moral community where he presided as father and master.[79]

Numerous middle-class entrepreneurs fashioned paternalistic factory regimes that incorporated this intricately fashioned middle-class ideology. Such regimes, especially the more elaborate ones, were metaphoric dynasties, dominions presided over by the middle-class family provider who, at the same time that he secured his own livelihood, exercised his assumed responsibility for insuring that his workpeople conduct themselves properly both at work and in their family lives.[80]

DISCOURSES ON CLASS RELATIONS

Employers' interests in the moral propriety of their workpeople stemmed not just from their assumed Christian mission to help those less fortunate than themselves. Like their counterparts who were colonizing whole continents to build the British Empire, they feared the people

whom they governed. The very economic structures that bound employer and employed in relations of domination and subordination
nurtured middle-class anxieties about the working classes as a threat
to those relations. These fears were not groundless. Labor unrest in
the Luddite years and in the turbulent 1830s and 1840s, and culmi-
nating in the Chartist demonstrations and the Preston strike and lockout of 1853–1854, fueled ideas of the disruptive potential of the masses.
As Catherine Gallagher has argued, both paternalism and the ideology
of domesticity were promulgated as cures for the social upheavals and
human misery of industrial capitalism.[81] These themes were prominent in social tracts and fiction as well as in the rhetoric of social
reformers.

Middle-class cultural productions formulated "the working-class
woman" and "the working-class man" and proceeded to treat those
constructions as though they were reality.[82] These fabrications were
created through various media, including newspaper accounts of
working women and men who were in trouble with the police; reports
of coroners' inquiries; surveys by social investigators and journalists;
essays in scholarly journals and the publications of professional societies and the reports of Domestic Missions. The working classes were
represented in parliamentary investigations of social problems, especially the work of Children's Employment Commissions, and, as I discuss in the next chapter, in parliamentary debates. They were catego-
rized with statistics in medical officers' health reports and studies by a
nascent social-science establishment. When an event deserving of national coverage involved working people, they were sketched in the
London Illustrated News. They were represented in the fiction of Elizabeth Gaskell, short stories by Charlotte Tonna, and in Dickens's
Household Words and his novels, as well as other industrial novels of
the period.[83]

These portraits were composed of a multitude of themes, but the
one with most relevance to the present discussion was the character-
ization of the masses' potential for disorder and violence.[84] For example, novelist Elizabeth Gaskell's generally sympathetic descriptions
of working people are tempered by her accounts of their threatening
ferocity. In *North and South* she describes an attack by strikers on
employer Thornton's home. The heroine, Margaret, pleads with Mr.
Thornton to

go down this instant, if you are not a coward. Go down and face them like a man. Save these poor strangers, whom you have decoyed here. Speak to your workmen as if they were human beings. Speak to them kindly. Don't let the soldiers come in and cut down poor creatures who are driven mad. . . . If you have any courage or noble quality in you, go out and speak to them, man to man![85]

Margaret's sympathy for the masses of people who advanced on the factory is evident. She entreats the employer to be kind and manly. Margaret, however, tells Mr. Thornton to speak to his workers "as if they were human beings," suggesting that even one as sympathetic toward the working classes as was Margaret may have seen workers as a species apart. In her description of the crowd Mrs. Gaskell uses phrases that elaborate a view of the working-class "other" as having the potential for barbarous action: "angry eyes"; "savage satisfaction of the rolling angry murmur"; "gaunt as wolves, and mad for prey"; "there was a momentary hush of their noise, inarticulate as that of a troop of animals"; "the people were raging worse than ever"; "savage lads, with their love of cruel excitement"; "the thread of dark-red blood which wakened them up from their trance of passion."[86] The words convey images of chaos and violence. By the novel's end, however, Thornton is transformed by Margaret's feminine and humanizing influence into a "new model employer," a paternalist who constructs a canteen for his workpeople and experiments with new forms of industrial relations that bring "the individuals of the different classes into actual personal contact."

Such representations of the working classes simultaneously envisioned them as needing to be controlled and authorized the bourgeoisie to preach, prescribe, legislate, and rule. Paternalism was central to this legitimation, for it both reflected and enforced a deeply hierarchical and gendered worldview held together by the glue of familial obligation. Paternalists, like Christian missionaries, were on civilizing crusades.[87] Providing moral uplift for their workers and securing their consent to participate as subordinate partners in production were two sides of the same coin.[88]

PATERNALISM AND INDUSTRIAL RELATIONS

Paternalistic rule quieted the capitalist's unease about dormant resentments on the part of his workers that might unleash havoc on his firm and family. At the same time, such factory organizations were ways for the employer to secure the loyalty of workers. Loyal workers meant higher profits.[89] Paternalistic practices created conditions that promoted compromise and cooperation between capital and labor.[90] Edward Cadbury, a social investigator who was associated with the Cadbury Chocolate firm, suggested as much when he wrote:

> The supreme principle has been the belief that business efficiency and the welfare of the employees are but different sides of the same problem. Efficiency depends not only on the physical condition of the employees, but on their general attitude and feeling towards the employer. The test of any scheme of factory organization is the extent to which it creates and fosters the atmosphere and spirit of cooperation and good-will, without in any sense lessening the loyalty of the worker to his own class and its organization.[91]

Cadbury's mention of "the loyalty of the worker to his own class and its organization" is telling. Increasingly, in the last quarter of the nineteenth century, unions and their major weapon of negotiation, the strike, were accepted by many employers. Cooperation and controlled dissent were compatible. Although employers generally abhorred strikes because they disrupted trade, what they found truly frightening was mob violence and the threat to social order that they believed was lying just below the surface of working-class life.[92] By the last quarter of the nineteenth century only a thin line separated respectable dissent from fearsome disorder. Orderly strikes were tolerated, but even name-calling—for example, taunting workers hired by employers to break strikes by calling them "knob sticks"—was not only disrespectable, it was illegal.

However, paternalism did not produce workers who deferentially agreed with all of their employers' practices. For example, it did not prevent strikes. Both during and after altercations between workers and employers, however, workers continued to express the harmony of their interests with their employers'. For example, just five months after a major dispute in the Kidderminster carpet trade which was arbitrated in the employer's favor, employer John Brinton commemorated the installation of a new engine in his factory by providing a dinner for his fifteen hundred workpeople and their families. The workers presented Mrs. Brinton with a bracelet and Mr. Brinton with an illuminated address that read:

As those who have to gain their daily bread by manly toil, we are not unmindful of the value and dignity of labour; and we hope to be found faithful both in discharging its duties and in maintaining its just rights. But we do not forget how much Labour stands in need of Capital and how largely dependent it is upon the energy and capacity of those who direct the operations of Industry and who open up the markets of the world to its products.[93]

Similarly, many employers did not cease their paternalistic gestures when their employees were on strike, or even when they had locked them out. In the great Lancashire strike and lock-out of 1878, employers who demanded total surrender by the workers opened soup kitchens for the unemployed.[94]

Rituals of Paternalism

Underpinning paternalist practices was a vision of family relationships as hierarchical, gendered, harmonious, and cooperative. By creating such familial bonds between capital and labor, paternalist employers hoped to mute the labor unrest they feared would bring down the social order. Recalling Max Weber's discussion of the sources of legitimacy in traditional authority, Patrick Joyce has suggested that it was the factory owner's personal "embodiment, in the family or the family head, that gave paternalism its cutting edge."[95] The incorporation of highly selective aspects of employers' family lives into the factory communities symbolized their benevolent mandate. These symbols and attendant rituals helped to constitute the culture of the factory and surrounding community.[96] This symbolic order worked simultaneously to solidify the paternalists' class position and to preserve gender distinctions.

Events in the employing family's life cycle were made the occasion for formal ceremonies involving the factory community. Communities celebrated births, especially the birth of a son and a son's coming of age, as well as marriages and deaths.[97] Such festivities and community rituals were frequent at Oxford Mills, a cotton textile firm in Ashton-under-Lyne which was owned by Hugh Mason. Mason was a leading example of a paternalist employer of the last half of the nineteenth century. He created his own community in the city of Ashton-under-Lyne, building houses for his workpeople and providing them with recreational and educational facilities. The Masons built an institute that housed a library, a chess room, and swimming baths, as well as a gymnasium and recreation grounds for their male operatives. In honor of their son Arnold's twenty-first birthday, Mr. and Mrs. Mason entertained their five hundred workpeople and tenants at a dinner. Some of the guests made elaborate decorations, including scrolls that proclaimed, "Employer and employed, may their true interests be understood by both," and an illuminated poster with the word *Gratitude* written on it.[98] All the houses in the Oxford Mills community were festooned with banners in honor of the occasion, and the workpeople presented Arnold Mason with his portrait. Dinner featured roast beef and plum pudding, and colorful paper bags containing dessert were set at each place.[99] When son Rupert was married, the workers took up a collection and purchased a costly black marble clock with matching vases as "a token of affection" for the young man. As part of the marriage celebration Mason gave the workers a free trip to Blackpool and paid them the wages they would have earned had they not gone on the trip.[100] When Mason died in the winter of 1886, the "Mothers of Oxford" sent the family a wreath and their expression of sympathy. Mason's daughter wrote in acknowledgment:

> For the "Mothers of Oxford", my father had always a special and kindly regard and it was to them he looked for the assistance necessary to enable him to carry out successfully all his plans for the benefit of his workpeople and their children in the cottages. We therefore deeply feel the quick and ready sympathy which the "Mothers" have shown toward us in our great and sorrowful bereavement.[101]

Such ceremonies and rituals both reinforced paternalism and celebrated male authority and the traditional family structure.[102] In addition, working-class motherhood and domesticity were proclaimed to be vital to family (factory) harmony.

Through their participation in the daily practices and ritual occasions of paternalism, working people came to accept capitalist relations of production as legitimate. By going on company-sponsored outings and picnics or taking an all-day excursion to the seashore on trains provided by the firm, and certainly by elaborating on the theme of the harmony between capital and labor in speeches and illuminated memorials at ceremonial teas and dinners, working people and their families paid tribute both to their employers and to the legitimacy of the emerging capitalist order. However, they did not necessarily welcome the intrusion of the industrialist into their private lives. Not infrequently they rejected his benevolence and disregarded his exhortations to refrain from drink and to substitute the library of the Mechanics' Institute for the pub. Often they regarded the feasts and employer-provided amenities with disdain. In addition, their participation in the ceremonial events and rituals did not mean that they gave up resisting employers' encroachments on their wages, hours, and working conditions. Rather, male trade-union leaders contested these encroachments—within certain rules of the game.[103] Paternalism helped to legitimate these rules.[104] As a gendered cultural construction modeled on a vision of "natural" family relationships, paternalism was a managerial style that helped to turn industrial capitalism into a way of life.[105]

Paternalism and the Reproduction of Gender Relations

Paternalist industrialists shaped their factories using as a model the inequalities of status and authority that existed in the family. These inequalities were presented as "natural differentiation" in the workplace, just as they were at home. The construction of a paternalistic factory regime with the factory owner and employer as head of the reconstituted "family in work" had specific consequences for the structure of gender relations. Paternalistic employers created a model for appropriate gender relations in the community at large.

The Cadburys of Birmingham are a prime example of employers who structured the factory milieu to symbolize the differences between women and men as workers and as members of families. Cadbury Chocolate at Bourneville was a complete community of semi-detached cottages with gardens.[106] Separate recreational grounds were provided "for men and for girls," and also one for children under the age of twelve. One of the aims of William Cadbury in planning the community was that no child should be further than a five-minute walk from a playground. Every house had at least three bedrooms, a kitchen, a parlor, and a scullery. The Cadburys also provided a boarding house for girls who came from some distance away. At the turn of the century about thirty-four young women lived in the house, sharing six or seven bedrooms, bath and washing rooms, and sitting and dining rooms. Their rent was low, and in addition they were offered a low-priced dinner at the works.

In 1902, Cadbury's employed twenty-three hundred young women and a thousand men and boys, working at strictly gender-segregated employment. The girls were supervised by forewomen; the men and boys, by foremen. Men and boys were responsible for the earlier processes of cocoa making and the making of tins. Girls finished the "confectioning" and chocolate, packed it and stored it, and made boxes. The firm preferred to hire young people "to train its future adult workers." [107] Between six and seven hundred boys and girls who responded to announcements through the local labor exchange were hired each year. The segregation of the sexes began with the method of selecting them. Girls assembled for testing on one day, boys on another. They were tested on their educational attainment, their "general tone and character," and their physical efficiency.

All of Cadbury's young employees were required to attend evening continuation schools. At first these schools were required for all those under the age of fifteen, but early in the twentieth century evening school was made compulsory until age eighteen. Boys and girls were given separate educations. Boys could choose between a commercial course or an industrial course. In the commercial course they learned English grammar and spelling, literature, mathematics, history, geography, and French. Then they studied modern bookkeeping or shorthand. In the industrial course they learned industrial art, elementary science, mechanics, and physics. At the end of two years the boys' progress was tested, and those not making a certain standard had to take a further year in one of these courses. Those who were successful went on to technical school; the most capable of them were eligible for Cadbury's apprenticeship program.

The girls' education included English grammar, spelling, and literature, arithmetic, art, needlework, home dressmaking, physiology, cookery and laundry work, and the laws of health. In the fourth year they took a course on housewifery which included cookery, mending of household linen, sick nursing, and the care of infants. According to Edward Cadbury, the girls' course was designed to assume an increasingly domestic character as the girl approached the age of eighteen.

Those boys who were eligible (by virtue of a report from their foremen and a report from the evening school) for apprenticeship undertook a formalized syllabus of training for each of the apprenticeship classes. After they had finished the evening-school curriculum, girls could go on to take classes in cardboard box-making and confectionery making. It is clear that the Cadburys saw their mission as being to educate boys and girls for their different adult statuses as well as to protect and nurture young female employees.

One way they protected the girls was by strictly segregating them, both at work and in the recreational and educational facilities that they provided. Edward Cadbury wrote that when youth of both sexes were "indiscriminately mixed" in factories under unsatisfactory conditions, grave moral danger would result. He believed moral danger would also be the consequence if married men and women mixed with "single girls and young persons." He advocated careful planning and organization if married women and men were both employed (no married women were employed at the Bourneville works). Cadbury suggested separate entrances for women and men and recommended the construction of separated passageways so both sexes would not use the same hallways in going to and from their separated dining rooms and dressing rooms. At the Bourneville factory, it was forbidden for anyone to be away from their work area without an excuse. Only carefully selected men, wearing badges, were allowed in the girls' work areas. The only times boys and girls and women and men mingled was at the annual gathering of employees, to which the adult men brought their wives; there the assembly heard music written for the occasion, watched plays, and listened to poetry.

The separation and differentiation of the sexes were crucial symbolic and material links in the interlocking chains of paternalistic practices that made up the Bourneville plan. The education scheme was carefully designed to prepare young male and female workers for their different destinies with the firm. Deserving boys earned an apprenticeship to a skilled trade in the factory. Girls were prepared for marriage and motherhood and were rewarded with a gift of money when they left the works to be wed, after which time they ordinarily could not return; the Cadburys only rehired a few married or widowed women in "poor circumstances" to work as cleaners for an hour or two each morning.[108]

Cadbury's scheme for organizing work was, perhaps, the ultimate in paternalistic plans to reinforce gender distinctions and to cast the relationship between employer and employee in a familial mold. Although not all employers could afford such measures, however, many employers adopted some of them. For example, W. Atkinson, formerly a worker himself, was head of a brass foundry in Birmingham that employed both women and men. Atkinson had the women leave the shop five minutes before the men, an arrangement he considered to be orderly and useful. At the Dog and Ship Biscuit Company in London, the employer objected "on principle" to women and men working together, as "there is too much larking."[109] At this factory employing six hundred men and seventy girls and young women, women and men were segregated both by work process and physically. One or two "staid men" were used to lift or carry where the women worked. Women were supervised by forewomen, and their dining, wash rooms, and kitchen were shut off from the rest of the factory and men were forbidden to use the stairs in the women's section.[110] Thomas Adams, a Nottingham lace manufacturer who employed large numbers of women in the preparation of lace for sale, built a warehouse in 1855 which was touted as providing idyllic working conditions. In addition to work rooms, it boasted a library, a classroom, and separated tea rooms, washing facilities, and dining rooms for women and men. Adams, an evangelical, created a chapel within the warehouse premises where a chaplain conducted compulsory services each morning. In Nottingham the story is still told that a Manchester physician visiting his factory "was astonished that his factory girls looked so healthy and fresh—almost as if they had been haymaking rather than lace making."[111] Few employers would have matched the zeal with which Mr. Corbett, a salt manufacturer from Stoke in Worcestershire, reorganized gender relations at his firm.[112] Corbett owned the entire town in which his works were located. There he built for his workpeople cottages and a church and paid the stipend of a clergyman of the Church of England. He restructured his work force, at considerable expense to the business, so that only men would be employed. He wrote to B. L. Hutchins that he did so because he saw

> Men who with their wives earned perhaps 2 pounds a week or 100 pounds a year living in squalor, their children in the streets cursing, lying and stealing and families growing up with the lowest possible tone— not so much immoral or vicious (always free from crime) as depraved and low. It all appeared to me to result from homes without a mother and as soon as a sister was big enough to scrub the house she was drafted off to tap salt which paid better. As this was passing in my mind

one evening I saw three women—in hot weather—leaving work later than usual faint and done up. I went to the man at the pan and found him sitting on his shovel, smoking a pipe and fresh as paint. I at once put an end to women's work at those works and . . . I have never employed them again. I believe it to be wrong as a general practice, that is to say, barbarous.[113]

According to a newspaper description of Corbett, "The people . . . in their appreciation . . . have erected a stained glass window in the adjoining parish church of Stoke Prior to commemorate the circumstance."[114] To refuse employment to all women was a logical extension of paternalism. However, many employers could not afford to reorganize the labor process to eliminate all women in the name of creating working-class gender and family relations on the model of those in the middle-class family. What they could do was to hire only women who were single.

THE MARRIAGE BAR

The marriage bar was a rule, voluntarily adopted by numerous employers, that a woman would have to leave employment when she married. Some employers, upholding women's responsibilities as mothers, even refused to hire widows, or, like the Cadbury chocolate manufacturing firm, would only employ them for a few hours a day.

Employers' concerns about married women's labor had a number of different aspects. To some employers, a married woman working was a sign that her husband was profligate. Industrialists such as Hugh Mason of Oxford Mills in Ashton-under-Lyne seized upon this issue with fervor. On learning of a medical officer's report on infant deaths in Ashton-under-Lyne in 1875, Mason contrasted the findings with the extent of infant mortality in his factory community of Oxford. He believed that the comparatively good showing of Oxford was due to the fact that only a few Oxford mothers worked in the factory, and when they did there were "exceptional justifications for it." Mason inquired rhetorically, "But how often was the mother, from the drunken habits of the husband driven to the factory to feed and clothe herself and her children? If the husband would only be sober as he ought to be, the mother might be kept at home, and the household changed from one of misery to one of comparative happiness."[115] Such employers rarely, if ever, acknowledged that women might continue working for pay after marriage to boost family income to a more comfortable level than could be obtained by one earner alone. Even less likely would have been an admission by industrialists that able-bodied men could not earn sufficient wages to provide a reasonable level of comfort for their families because employers set their wages too low or because industry offered unstable employment. Employers in a host of trades simply refused to hire married women because they were convinced that this practice degraded the home lives of workers. The marriage bar was routinely enforced in the boot and shoe industry of Northampton, in hosiery in Nottingham, and in the Huddersfield woolen textile industry, among others. At Dickinson's paper mills at Croxley Green in the south of England, for example, the employment of married women was banned. The plant manager said he objected to their employment because "it is bad for the home and quite unnecessary here as the men earn good wages."[116]

In the last half, and especially the last quarter, of the nineteenth century, there was a growing public consensus on the evils of married women's labor. Discussions about infant mortality and its connection to maternal employment proliferated after midcentury and provided the context within which public opinion condemned the employment of married women and even of widowed mothers outside their homes. Employers responded by voluntarily banning married women's employment.[117] As the president of the Northampton Boot and Shoe Trade Employers' Association said, married women were kept out of the labor force because "of local feeling against their employment in factories, a strong feeling which the employers shared with the general public."[118] Given employer policies and the intensity of condemnation of married women's labor, it is not surprising that overall official participation of women in the labor force declined in the last quarter of the nineteenth century and that the number of married women working at the end of the century may have been as little as half of what it had been at midcentury.[119]

The marriage bar embodied the domestic ideology and the cult of motherhood. It developed as an employer practice in the same milieu as paternalism. It was not the product of an economic calculus. The bar would have been a convenient cost-cutting mechanism in a civil service system or in industries dominated by union seniority rules in the twentieth century. Most of the industries we have been examining, however, paid workers by the piece or paid them an hourly wage for work that was quickly learned, so wages did not increase with the employee's tenure on the job. Numerous accounts of women's work as light and simple suggest that the jobs were such that women could learn them and make their maximum wages after a relatively short time on the job. Only rarely did an employer in the nineteenth century pay his employees a pension; however, even when men were paid a pension, women were not.[120] Thus, there was little or no direct monetary incentive for late-nineteenth-century employers to remove women from their employment when they married. Furthermore, there are indications that in some areas, such as Northampton, the voluntary ban on the employment of married women made women's labor scarce and drove up wages.[121] Some employers complained that the practice of women leaving work when they married meant that firms lost their best workers.[122] The marriage bar is best understood by situating it among the other gendered employment practices discussed in this chapter. It should unquestionably be viewed in the context of the growing public disapprobation for married women's employment.[123] Edward Cadbury, for example, believed that the Factory Acts were not stringent enough regarding married women's employment. He proclaimed, "we are taking the responsibilities of empire upon us without having a race of human beings fit to deal with them."[124]

CONCLUSION

Industrialists structured work in ways that simultaneously reflected and fostered taken-for-granted ideas about gender difference which were linked to an ideology of family life. They deviated from these practices when they were forced by market pressures to lower their labor costs. The way employers were called upon to account for such deviations and their justifications for them suggest that these were indeed perceived as deviations and not as the norm.

Paternalism was the outgrowth and the expression of complex dynamics that transposed hierarchical and gendered family relations onto class relations. Paternalistic practices emphasized and manipulated gender divisions. They associated capital and labor relations with the "natural" relation between fathers and their dependents. The dynamics that were the source of paternalism also led to the marriage bar, a common practice by the end of the century and one that represented the voluntarily undertaken masculine/paternal responsibility for protecting motherhood.

Gendered employment practices were central to the development of industrial capitalism and to the structuring of gender relations in the working classes, in several interconnected ways. Hiring practices reinforced the commonsense association between skill and masculinity and created the differences presumed to be innate in women's and men's natures. These practices both structured workplaces and produced cultural meanings that nurtured divisions between working women and working men in their contests with employers over work. Paternalistic practices emphasized gender difference and structured gender relations at work. These relations served in part to set the terms under which labor and capital struggled. In addition, paternalism was instrumental in "naturalizing" capitalism, since "the family" and gender distinctions were seen to belong to the laws of nature.

There is no clear-cut evidence that indicates the numbers of firms adopting paternalistic practices and workplace regimes. Employers did not have uniform ideas about managerial practices. Some believed that employee welfare should not concern them, judging workers as they would their machinery, solely on the basis of their relative cost. For these manufacturers, workers were mere tools, "instruments of production."

However, Patrick Joyce has argued that if full-blown paternalism was not characteristic of large numbers of employers in the last half of the nineteenth century, significant numbers of them at least adopted some of these measures in a piecemeal fashion.[125] It is possible that only very grandiose schemes were touted publicly and that employers who implemented more commonplace measures that symbolized and reinforced gender differences among their workers were not visible. Yet, the very visibility of these "model" employers made their managerial practices a powerful cultural force in nineteenth-century labor relations.

This cultural force had two faces. One looked toward harmonious workplace relationships between employers and employees and the legitimation of capitalism. The other provided multiple representations of gender that defined women's and men's spheres. The two faces were simultaneously present in the managerial strategies of Victorian industrialists. Furthermore, many industrialists who were prominent paternalists and advocates of the marriage bar also became significant national political figures. For example, Kidderminster carpet manufacturer John Brinton was elected to Parliament, as was Ashton-under-Lyne cotton industrialist Hugh Mason. John Bright from Rochdale was a major political figure. As members of Parliament they could shape policies and engage in public debates that articulated some of the same principles they represented as industrialists. It is to these public policies and debates, and their importance in circumscribing the conditions under which working people created their livelihoods, that we turn next.

3

"We Never Sought Protection for the Men Nor Do We Now"

The State and Public Policy

Laws and public policies work through a series of representations.[1] They construct and authorize particular ways of thinking about social problems. They create subjects with legal identities and responsibilities. Laws work to order society by claiming to be neutral, by asserting that they rule in the interests of the society as a whole rather than any particular segment of it.[2] Although, collectively, laws are based on conflicting principles and contain contradictions, they have power because they appear to be based on truth, on unified fields of knowledge.[3]

Individual laws have the power to impose a specific interpretation of reality in opposition to alternative views. In addition, they regulate people's lives, making some alternatives possible and closing off others. They gain their force to create order and to regulate aspects of people's lives through their symbolic power and through the coercive might of the state in whose name they govern.

Once a problem has been defined as one requiring state action, the ensuing debates that produce laws or public policies enter the public domain. They contribute special weight to the developing discourse about the problems that the laws or policies are meant to solve. The debates and the public policies that result from them reflect ideas about gender held by dominant groups. In this way the state contributes to the dissemination and legitimation of representations of gender which constrain the ways that those who are the subjects of the laws or policies live their lives.[4] Legal regulation of gender and family relations was integral to English state formation and can be traced back in law at least to 1200.[5] Through the centuries, state policies had presumed the family to be a monogamous and heterosexual unit, and it had specified the relations of dependency between husband and wife as well as between parents and children.[6] Until the Married Women's Property Acts were passed in the 1870s and 1880s, women could not control their own property, and it was not until 1935 that they had the right to hold and dispose of property. Generally, a married woman's legal status in the nineteenth century and earlier was that of her husband's dependent. This was the common-law principle of *couverture*.

The fact that laws linked marital relations and property relations reveals that moral regulation and economic regulation have often been intertwined.[7] By the same token, laws that on their face were concerned directly with community and economic relations also were instrumental in defining gender and familial relations. Policies governing community responsibility for the poor and regulating the hours and conditions of employment were particularly crucial in stipulating the responsibilities of women and men as workers and as members of families. The 1834 Poor Law Amendment Act and, beginning in 1844, the Factory Acts which restricted the hours and conditions under which women (and children) could work in factories were especially significant in structuring gender and economic relations for the working classes in nineteenth-century England.

The Factory Acts and the Poor Laws are particularly interesting ones because they "state" the state's relationship to individual and family economic welfare on the one hand and to the labor contract on the other.[8] In very different ways, both contributed to the fiction that the state was and should be uninvolved with economic and familial relations. This fiction masked the very real involvement of government in the lives of working-class people, an involvement that constrained their livelihoods and was integral to England's gendered capitalist society.[9]

These laws and the debates that led to their enactment created a framework for thinking about and dealing with the relations between working women and men, the relations between labor and capital, and the relations between the state, capitalists, and working-class families.[10] In addition, the legal enactments themselves were public policies that provided particular solutions to the problems they were meant to solve, blinding both the lawmakers and the governed to alternatives. Finally, the laws had direct consequences for the different relationships of women and men to paid employment.

THE NEW POOR LAW

The New Poor Law limited the community's responsibility for the economic welfare of its residents.[11] Although it ostensibly dealt with poverty by stipulating who was and who was not eligible for relief, in fact its purpose was to reduce, if not totally eliminate, the number of paupers, those poor who sought economic assistance from their communities.[12] In other words, the intent of the law was to confine community assistance to those people who were poor by virtue of severe illness, disability, or old age.

The new poor-law policy replaced the "Speenhamland system" of 1795, which had established for agricultural workers a tax-subsidized minimum wage, based on the cost of bread. This system had the effect of keeping wages for agricultural laborers very low. It subsidized farmers' labor expenditures by supplementing whatever wages they chose to pay. As a result of the mechanization of agriculture, as well as the dislocations accompanying early industrialization, the number of paupers began to increase in the early years of the nineteenth century, and so did the costs of maintaining them. In many areas of the country the misery of poverty became palpable as rate payers succeeded in introducing various schemes to reduce their taxes.[13] By the 1820s the elite classes were putting considerable pressure on Parliament for a change in the laws. All that remained to be determined was the extent to which poor relief of any kind would be abolished, and when.[14] The Poor Law reformers who shaped the 1834 act were convinced that poverty would be minimized if the state played no part in regulating economic relations. Influenced by political economists such as Nassau Senior and Thomas Malthus, they focused the attention of Parliament on curing pauperism, which, they argued, was a moral problem. Poor Law reformers persuaded influential parliamentarians that poverty was "natural," and they argued that destitution, unless it was caused by illness or old age, was the fault of the destitute.[15]

The centerpiece of the Poor Law Amendment act was the principle of "least eligibility." The idea was that if economic assistance was to be given, it would be under conditions that were less endurable than those made possible by the most demeaning and ill-paid employment. The 1834 act stipulated that for those men deemed able-bodied, relief would be available only in strictly monitored and punitive workhouses where they would be taught the habits of work-discipline.

Implicit in the Poor Law Act of 1834 was the idea that if able-bodied people who were poor sought assistance from the state, it was because they were indolent. That is, unemployment was not seen to be endemic in capitalism or exacerbated during slumps in the business cycle. It was not the low wages of employed men that made it hard for the poor to feed their families. Rather, the Poor Law reformers believed, the cause of the poverty of the able-bodied was their refusal to work. The solution was to put those whom the local guardians of the poor deemed able-bodied into the workhouse and force them to do backbreaking and demeaning work. The policy makers hoped to do away with assistance given to poor people outside the workhouse, especially assistance in the form of supplementing wages.

The idea that poverty was incurable and that, because their destitution was of their own making, those who were capable of working should be humiliated for receiving community assistance was to have an important and lasting impact on English society in the nineteenth century. The Poor Law Amendment Act marked a significant turn in class relations, and its stipulations were met with hatred by the poor. As Eric Hobsbawm has written, "It created more embittered unhappiness than any other statute of modern British history."[16] One of its most significant symbolic consequences was to strengthen an association that working men made between manliness and independence. Increasingly, working-class people in the nineteenth century associated independence with remaining out of the clutches of the Poor Law authorities.[17] They associated manliness, independence, and employment at least in part because of the dire consequences of the Poor Law Amendment Act and its administration.

The lawmakers "took for granted the universality of the stable two-parent family, dependent upon the father's wage, and the primacy of the family as a source of welfare."[18] The 1834 act extended the principle of *couverture,* that women were the wards of their husbands, to the dispensation of relief to poor women. The law proclaimed that men were solely responsible for the economic welfare of families. This assumption belied the reality of life during the entire century for the vast majority of working-class people, characterized as it was by low pay, underemployment, episodic unemployment, and the dependence of men and children on the wages of working women. By limiting the responsibility for family welfare to male heads of households, the law repressed the possibility that capitalists or the community at large had any part to play either in causing or in remedying poverty.

Although the severity of the application of the law varied from one

Poor Law Union to the next, administrative regulations passed by central commissioners in general served to reinforce the false notion of women as non-wage-earning dependents and men as sole family providers. Those who administered the Poor Law could demand repayment from a man whose wife claimed poor relief, whether or not they lived together. As historian Pat Thane has written, "if the husband entered the workhouse, the wife would have no choice but to follow. A destitute wife could be refused entry to the workhouse if her husband would not enter, or permission to leave if he would not leave. If a male pauper was officially classified 'not able-bodied,' so was his wife, whatever her personal physical condition. If he received outdoor relief, including medical relief (until 1886), for himself alone, she also was listed as a pauper."[19]

The 1834 Poor Law was an instrument of moral regulation for women as well as for men. Whereas the law was silent about widows and deserted wives, it singled out unmarried mothers and their children for disapprobation. The regulations embodied the idea that the mother of an illegitimate child should be its sole support; if she could not manage, then either her parents would have to support mother and child, or the two would be placed in the workhouse.[20]

In accord with the widespread and growing adherence by the English elite classes to the doctrine of laissez-faire political economy which lay behind the philosophy of poverty of the Poor Law reformers, the 1834 act articulated a very limited responsibility of the state for the economic welfare of the people. It perpetuated the myth that individuals (in this case, men) were responsible for their own welfare and that the state, by withdrawing charity from the able-bodied, was and would be uninvolved in economic affairs.[21] The labor market would be "self-regulating." However, the Poor Law Amendment Act of 1834 was an instrument that forced people to work for wages that were inadequate to support a family, and often to labor under conditions that ruined their health and thus their long-term capacity to sustain themselves and their families. The state's refusal to sanction community responsibility for the economic welfare of the poor (unless they were physically or mentally incapacitated) in a perverse way underscored the myth that government stood outside economic life. However, in refusing to sanction "outdoor relief" to those deemed ablebodied, the state in fact played an important part in creating a pool of people available to be hired for low wages because they had no choice other than the dreaded workhouse.

In addition, during strikes and lock-outs Poor Law administrators often sided with capital to force workers to meet their employers' terms, rather than assisting the unemployed and their families who were in need. There is ample evidence of this in the strike and lock-out that idled nearly the entire adult population of North Lancashire in 1878. For example, even though Preston workers had voted not to strike and were unemployed because their employers had locked them out, the Poor Law guardians refused aid to male applicants unless they agreed to spend twelve hours a day at stone-breaking.[22] In Clitheroe the guardians threatened strikers with jail if they sought assistance and refused to do the "test" work.[23] In Blackburn, the center of the cotton operatives' strike activity, the guardians opened the smallpox hospital to accommodate the growing numbers of people who had to be put in the workhouse because they were starving.[24] In Burnley the guardians wanted to open one of the mills to force applicants for relief to continue to work, but because other mill owners objected to that idea, those on relief were set to breaking stones.[25] These actions on the part of guardians which might have starved the workers into submission sharply contrasted with the myth advanced by the Poor Law Amendment Act of 1834 that the state stood outside the economy.

The Poor Law Amendment Act of 1834 was crucial, then, in establishing the idea that economic well-being was the individual's problem; neither was hardship caused by forces beyond the control of an individual, nor would it be solved by the state. Furthermore, it portrayed working-class men's fecklessness as the cause of their families' destitution, and in doing so it contributed to notions of working-class masculinity that centered on men's responsibility for women and children. Finally, by its refusal to sanction community assistance in support of wages, it contributed to the idea that the state would not interfere with economic relations and was a neutral third party in the relations between capital and labor.

THE FACTORY ACTS

Like the Poor Law, the Factory Acts supported the myth that the state would be uninvolved in the economy. They did this by limiting their regulation to those defined as "not free agents," that is to say, women and children working in specified industries and workplaces, and excluding men who were employed in those same industries and workplaces. In addition, as the debates on the measures proposed in the

1870s reveal, lawmakers and those who contributed to the debates about the hours that women worked in factories reinforced the idea that men were responsible for the economic well-being of their families, whereas wives were responsible for motherhood.

Beginning in the 1830s, the debates that preceded the passage of the major Factory Acts and the framing of the bills enacted by Parliament resulted from a struggle, led by male factory operatives, to reduce the length of the working day for all workers. The operatives were opposed by capitalists who feared that their competitive might would be weakened and by members of Parliament who were loath to intervene directly in economic relations. Although the legislation included provisions for safety and sanitation, the primary focus of the debates concerned restriction of the hours of work.

THE TEN HOURS BILL

Pressure from Short-Time Committees involved in the Ten Hours Movement led to the Factory Act of 1833, which purported to protect children, and the initiatives in the 1840s that specified women with children as needing the intervention of the state to protect them. The 1847 Factory Bill was enacted to reduce women's and children's work in textile factories to a ten-hour day and to prohibit them from working at night. At first the cotton-textile operatives active in the Ten Hours Movement had hoped to shorten the hours of labor for everyone and preferred a bill that would have limited the hours machinery could be worked.[26] However, in the 1830s they pushed for a limitation on the hours children could work, hoping that an act limiting children's hours would also limit their own hours. The government responded by setting up a commission to investigate the necessity for factory reform. Because of growing public concern about working children that was fostered by factory reform activists such as Richard Oastler, factory commissioners in 1833 recommended a bill reducing the working day for children between fourteen and eighteen to twelve hours and for younger children to ten hours, and banning children under nine from working in cotton factories. To make the restrictions jibe with laissez-faire principles, commissioners defined children as "not free agents" because they were sent to work by their parents.[27] The Factory Act of 1833, which dealt only with the hours that children of different ages could work, fell far short of legislating the ten-hour day

for which the Short Time Committees of working men had been pressing. Because children could be worked in relays, the hours of adult
workers were not affected by the act at all. As a result, the movement
for a ten-hour day continued.

Although some middle-class reformers had been concerned with the
"problem" of women working in factories in the 1830s, it was not
until the 1840s that male unionists, encouraged by aristocratic and
middle-class reformers who were inspired by evangelical religious
rhetoric, began to argue that women's hours and jobs ought to be
restricted.[28] In his report of 1843, factory inspector Leonard Horner
proposed that women's hours of work in textile factories be limited as
children's hours were, because, in contrast to men, women were "much
less free agents." He argued that "Twelve hours' daily work is more
than enough for anyone; but however desirable it might be that excessive working should be prevented, there are great difficulties in the
way of legislative interference with the labor of adult men."[29] Horner
seems both to have acknowledged the necessity of reducing the hours
that all people worked and to have seen the need to promote a bill
restricting the hours of women and children as a political expedient.
In 1844, women, like children, were officially labeled by Parliament
as "unfree agents" who were in need of state protection and were
made subject to the Factory Acts. Adult men, however, were considered by legislators to be "free agents," so they could continue to set
their own terms in an employment contract without "interference"
from the state.[30]

The 1847 Factory Act, along with modifications legislated in 1850,
had the consequence of reducing the hours of work in textile factories
for all workers, since textile factories could not be run profitably without the participation of both women and children. Interpretations of
legislative initiatives to regulate the hours of work in England have
focused on the questions of how and why the state became involved
in regulating the hours of work in factories, and who benefited from
the laws. These questions have received a variety of answers. Some
have argued that the proposals were pushed through by humanitarian
reformers,[31] and others have suggested that the bills passed because
they aided large mill owners to establish market domination over their
smaller competitors.[32] Still others have interpreted them as the outcome of political conflict between land-owning and manufacturing
classes.[33] Marx's view of the Factory Acts is complex. He argued that

state regulation was necessary to preserve the long-term interests of capital by assuring the reproduction of the labor supply. In his view, the competition among capitalists would restrain enlightened industrialists from shortening the working day, and, without a shortened working day, unfettered capital would use up the labor supply.[34] Furthermore, he saw the passage of the Factory Acts as a victory for the working classes.[35]

Marx's view that the state had to do for capital what individual capitalists were unable to do for themselves has been the focus of continuing debates among Marxist scholars about the relationship of the state and the economy under capitalism.[36] These analyses do not deal with the fact that the acts purportedly regulated only the labor of women and children and were not intended by their framers to regulate the hours of adult male labor. It is possible that these scholars assumed that the gender issue was unimportant because the passage of the Ten Hours Bill of 1847 restricted the working day for all workers (while allowing men to work overtime and at meal times for extra pay). In contrast, scholars focusing on women's participation in the labor force have concentrated their inquiries on the fact that, beginning with the 1842 Mines Regulation Act, it was adult women and not adult men who were subject to regulation.[37] However, their interpretations, like those of scholars who do not take up the issue of gender, are not in agreement.[38] The restriction of women's labor has been viewed by some as the result of a cross-class gender alliance that enhanced both men's position in the labor market and their position at home.[39] Others have argued that capital as a class in the long run benefited from restricting women's hours, because that insured that women would be able to reproduce the next generation of laborers.[40] Finally, it has been proposed that these regulations were sought by working-class women and men who hoped thereby to strengthen the family by enhancing men's earnings and preventing competition between women and men for jobs.[41]

In a recent study centered on the rhetoric of the male spinners active in the Ten Hours Movement, Mariana Valverde suggests that regardless of the motives of its initiators, "the campaign for shorter hours was crucial in helping designate women workers as a threat to male unionized jobs."[42] In addition, Valverde argues that "the patriarchal making of the working class" was aided by the political reality facing the short-time committees: the legislators would not agree to restricting the hours of men, but once they had defined women to be, like children, "unfree agents," the "state was receptive to philanthropic moves" to restrict the hours women could work.[43] Her analysis takes into account both the political circumstances constraining male workers as they attempted to reduce the hours of work for everyone, and the consequences for working-class formation of their rhetoric about domesticity. Similar dynamics were at play in the 1870s. In both periods, such political practices "naturalized" particular assumptions about the relations of women and men to families and employment.

THE FACTORY ACT OF 1874

In 1874 Parliament passed a law entitled "The Factories (Health of Women, etc.) Bill" that limited women's and children's work in textile factories to fifty-six and a half hours a week. The debates about this legislation and about the law itself were cultural productions which contributed to the formulation of the social problem of "the working mother," promulgated an interpretation of who caused the problem, and reinforced a particular view of who was responsible for social reproduction. The rhetoric in the debates about the measure made crucial contributions to the future agenda for public policies concerning married women workers and working mothers and reinforced a worldview that defined state and economy as independent entities.

Political scientist Murray Edelman has noted that social problems often are created to justify solutions powerful people want implemented.[44] The Factory Acts constitute an example of exactly that. Parliamentary action was sought by male trade unionists after the failure of their vigorous attempts to negotiate directly with their employers for a reduced working day for themselves as well as for women and children who worked in textile factories. They were joined in their appeal to Parliament by industrialists who either had humanitarian motives or wanted to restrict production. However, as was the case in the 1840s, legislators refused to consider a general hours bill, for such a measure would have undermined the fundamental principle that workers and employers should be "free" to negotiate the terms of a labor contract without the "interference" of government.

Like the Factory Act of 1847, which instituted the ten-hour day for women and children in factories, the 1874 measure had the effect of reducing the hours of work in textile factories for all workers.[45] Contemporary analysts of the trade union movement, as well as some union leaders, acknowledged that unionists had fought for measures to reduce the length of the working day "from behind the women's petticoats."[46] Interest in a workday shorter than ten hours had existed among workers even in the days of the Ten Hours Movement, and in the late 1850s coalitions of various skilled trade unionists struck, unsuccessfully, for a nine-hour day. However, it was not until the early 1870s that workers engaged in sustained and successful efforts to achieve a nine-hour day. This movement began among both unionized and nonunionized skilled male workers in the engineering trades. It was not a movement for factory legislation; rather, the men hoped to negotiate a shortened working day with their employers. A five-month-long strike of engineers in Newcastle, led by John Burnett, ended in the fall of 1871 with victory for the men. At celebrations commemorating the bitter strike, other workers were encouraged to continue industrial action to secure a nine-hour day in every trade. By January of 1872, engineers and skilled artisans from a host of trades and from all areas of the country were celebrating the inauguration of the nine-hour day they had negotiated with their employers.[47] In the same week that these celebrations took place, Lord Shaftesbury, the champion of the Ten Hours Movement, chaired the inaugural meeting of the Factory Acts Reform Association, which was attended by male trade unionists and sympathetic manufacturers in the cotton textile industry.[48] Trade union leaders had appealed to A. J. Mundella, a Nottingham hosiery manufacturer who was the member of Parliament from Sheffield, a man with known sympathies to the trade union movement, to introduce a Nine Hours Bill in Parliament.[49]

The trade unionists appealed to Parliament because efforts by the Oldham operative spinners—supported, in the cotton textile districts, by all textile workers, male and female, spinners and weavers—to negotiate a shortened work week had failed following a bitter strike and stalled attempts at arbitration.[50] The unionists were joined by several cloth manufacturers who were sympathetic to their cause and were also anxious for a uniform reduction in the hours of work in the textile factories, in order to slow down the production of cotton cloth and thus to raise the prices for manufactured goods on the market.[51] Although women had been active in the strike and work stoppages in Oldham, the Factory Acts Reform Association and its branches were composed of men only. According to Beatrice and Sidney Webb, it is scarcely necessary to say that it was not entirely, or even exclusively, for the sake of women and children that the skilled leaders of the Lancashire cotton operatives had diverted their "Short Time Movement" from aggressive strikes to Parliamentary agitation. The private minutes of the Factory Acts Reform Association contain no mention of the woes of the women and children, but reflect the demand of the adult male spinners for a shorter day.[52]

It is clear from the statements of all of the principal legislative supporters that a general nine-hour bill was out of the question. To have any chance of success in Parliament, the bill had to be made specific to women and children. As the Webbs note, "The experience of a generation had taught the Lancashire operatives that any effective limitation of the factory day for women and children could not fail to bring with it an equivalent shortening of the hours of the men who worked with them."[53] A. J. Mundella agreed to introduce a private members' bill in the House of Commons in the spring. It was given a first reading in April 1872, but Mundella was unable to generate sufficient enthusiasm for the measure. He reintroduced it, to vigorous debate, in June 1873, and withdrew it in August, because there was insufficient time for a full hearing.[54] The following January, the Gladstone government called a general election which resulted in a Tory victory, and Benjamin Disraeli became prime minister.[55] A short time after the government was seated, a deputation, headed by Lord Shaftesbury and composed of Mundella and other members of Parliament who favored the Nine Hours Bill, supportive mill owners, and male operatives, visited the home secretary, Assheton Cross, to seek aid from the Disraeli government for the bill. When Mundella reintroduced his bill in the new Parliament, the home secretary announced that the government would propose its own measure. The government's "Factories (Health of Women, etc.) Bill," restricting the working hours of women, children and young persons employed in textile factories to fifty-six and a half per week, was a compromise between what the operatives wanted and what most manufacturers were willing to tolerate.

Gendered Discourses: The "Working Mother Problem" and "Lazy Men"

A major hurdle faced by supporters of a legislated reduction in the hours of work was that of convincing manufacturers and others who had political influence that it was being proposed for the benefit of women and children. Meetings supporting Factory Act reform increasingly focused on women. However, unlike their counterparts in the 1840s, they did not focus on women in general, but instead emphasized married women, and especially mothers. For example, in late February at a meeting of factory operatives in support of the Nine Hours Bill, Reverend Stephens of Stalybridge addressed the well-attended gathering. On hearing in a speech made by a unionist that there were approximately 92,000 married women in cotton factories, the minister, who had been an active Chartist, said, "Now, anybody can tell at once what the consequences of that must be in the factory population, 92,000 that cannot be homes; 92,000 families without mothers; 92,000 grates without fires in them; 92,000 cradles that mothers do not rock; 92,000 children whom their mothers do not suckle. What can it end in?"[56] The operatives appealed to both Liberal and Tory members of Parliament and sent a deputation to Benjamin Disraeli composed of workmen from a large number of manufacturing towns in Lancashire. The deputation told Disraeli, "The great object of our legislation was that we might protect females and children. We never sought protection for men nor do we now."[57] Disraeli responded, "All I can promise at present is that I will give the matter my earnest consideration." He added, "Lady Beaconsfield says 'it's a woman's question—and therefore [she] thinks it is entitled to [her] good wishes,' " a comment that was greeted with laughter and cheers.[58]

Like the members of the Factory Acts Reform Association, legislators and other middle-class commentators who debated the measures to reduce the hours of work in textile factories focused their arguments on the ill effects of married women's work. However, many of them accused working-class husbands of causing their wives to work in factories. Although male textile operatives supported the measures, once the debates were underway in the House of Commons the workers lost control over the discourse about the working-mother problem.

The marital status of workers was not recorded in the censuses in Britain until the twentieth century. It is not possible, therefore, to determine with any certainty whether the actual proportion of employed married women was increasing in the 1860s and 1870s to an extent that would have produced public concern. Although the absolute numbers of working women were increasing, the percentage of women who were employed remained relatively constant from 1861 to 1871,

at about 36 percent.[59] It was only in 1881 that the percentage declined, from 36 percent to 34 percent. The percentage of women workers
who worked in the textile industries, however, declined gradually
throughout the period, from 21 percent of female workers in 1861 to
19 percent of female workers in 1881. At the same time, the percentage of women working as domestic servants increased from 43 percent
of female workers in 1861 to 46 percent of female workers in 1871.
Forty-five percent of women worked as domestics in 1881. Although,
because the proportions of married women workers are unknown,
these data are not conclusive, they certainly suggest that the "problem" of married women working in textile factories was not caused
by proportionally more women employed in factories during this period. What seems instead to have been increasing was concern on the
part of industrialists and legislators about what married women's labor meant for the working-class family in general and the health of
children in particular.

The controversy about married women's employment and its causes
articulated in these debates was part of a larger public discussion about
the working-class family that intensified in the 1870s.[60] Jane Lewis
has suggested that in the last part of the nineteenth century the state
was increasingly prepared to intervene overtly in aspects of life that
previously had been considered to be private.[61] In 1870 the Married
Women's Property Act, a measure designed to protect the earnings of
working-class women, was passed. In the hearings that led to the framing
of the legislation, proponents argued that the law would enhance the
mother's role as educator of her children and would protect her earnings from feckless men.[62] In 1878 the Matrimonial Causes Acts
Amendment Bill giving working-class wives the right to sue their husbands for separation and maintenance was passed, supported by evidence concerning wife-beating and a propaganda campaign by middle-
class feminists who spoke of "wife torture."[63] It is interesting to note
that Mundella viewed the Married Women's Property Act of 1870 as
coming from the same public concern that justified the regulation of
women's hours under the Factory Acts.[64]

In 1872 the government appointed two physicians, Drs. Bridges
and Holmes, to conduct a formal inquiry into the effects of factory life
on women and children. Both opponents and proponents of Mundella's bill used the findings in their debates, but to different ends. The
aspect of the report that figured heavily in the discussions about the

legislation was their argument that the high rates of infant mortality in the factory districts were caused by the employment of mothers.[65] They recommended the shorter hours of labor for women proposed by Mundella's bill, and, further, that mothers of young children should only be allowed to work half-time. In his report for 1873, factory inspector Alexander Redgrave also advocated that married women, like young children, should be allowed to work only for half a day, arguing that

> At present a married woman can earn sufficient to maintain herself and her husband, who, if he be so degraded, may do nothing but spend her earnings. To some extent such fellows will be forced to work. . . . The only way to remedy this appears to be to ensure to the wife time to do her duty to her children, to be just to herself, and to make a home for her husband, who should be the real breadwinner and mainstay out of doors.[66]

The findings about infant mortality in the Bridges and Holmes report were interpreted by legislators and industrialists as portents of a decline in the quality of the English working population. The public concern with motherhood was linked to eugenicist concerns about the quality of the race.[67] In the last quarter of the nineteenth century, motherhood became a duty women owed not simply to their individual families but to the nation. Whereas men's responsibility was to provide for their families, women's responsibility was motherhood. Moreover, although the health of children was part of a woman's domain, it was men who made it possible for women to carry out their duties. This argument denied state and community responsibility for child health and welfare.

The findings in the Bridges and Holmes report were used by legislators and other bourgeois commentators to legitimate claims that working mothers constituted a pressing social problem.[68] A committee representing associations of employers in the factory districts published a statement about the report in the *Times*.[69] They pointed out that infant mortality was caused, not by factory labor, but, as the Bridges and Holmes report suggested, "by [lack of] natural nutrition and motherly care, owing to mothers working in the factories and resigning the charge of their offspring to others."[70] They argued that shortening the hours of labor of women in factories would do nothing for this problem. There was only one solution, "the gradual removal of child-bearing women from the factory and their resumption of the motherly duties they owe to their offspring."[71] At the debate on the Nine Hours Bill in June 1873, Mundella cited many of the same statistics on the mortality of women and infants contained in the Bridges and Holmes report and argued, "For that state of things there was no remedy but the interference of Parliament, and it was for that interference that both master and men waited."[72] In supporting the bill member of Parliament Thomas Hughes used the same statistics. He was quoted as saying that "As far as he was concerned, he hoped and believed that the time was not far distant when working men would be ashamed to allow their wives to work in factories at all. The sooner that time arrived the better it would be for England; but until then he thought we ought to legislate in such a way as to render the evil of the present system as small as possible."[73] Thus, although they disagreed as to the appropriate remedy, both sides agreed that working mothers were a social problem.

Organized opposition to Mundella's bill and to the government's compromise initiative came principally from two sources: manufacturers who feared that a reduction in the hours of labor would put them at a disadvantage in international competition, and women's rights supporters. This vocal and active alliance was bolstered by members of Parliament, industrialists, academics, and others who believed in the "natural laws of political economy." Ultimately, their position, that women, like men, were free agents and should not be seen as children who needed the protection of government, was defeated. What defeated this argument was a growing consensus that included voices on both sides, concerning women workers, married women's labor, and men's responsibilities toward their families.

The voices of opposition to the Factory Acts included Millicent Fawcett, women's rights activist and suffragist. In a letter to the *Times* she maintained that the legislation would restrict and impede women's labor, and she cautioned that it would result in a reduction of the workday for men as well as women. She argued that adult women should not be treated in law as though they were children.[74] Her husband, member of Parliament for Cambridge, brought the argument to the House of Commons. In his speech, Henry Fawcett stressed that it was the regulation of adult labor to which he was opposed. He said, "My chief contention is this—that the working classes can settle such a question as this far better for themselves than the State can settle it for them."[75] He claimed that limiting the hours of labor of women would only be justified if it could be shown that they were not free agents, as children are not free agents. This issue was central to the legal rationale for legislation and was used to equate women with children in the Factory Acts of the 1840s. By defining women as not unfree agents, legislators in the 1840s extended the principle of *couverture* to all women.

Parliamentarians in the 1870s persisted in maintaining that women were not free agents, even though the Married Women's Property Act of 1870, which modified married women's legal identity, had become law. Mundella argued that "the girls were, up to a certain age, the servants of their parents, and that after marriage they were—unless they happened to have courageous and affectionate husbands—the slaves of the masters."[76] When the deputation of supporters of Factory Act reform visited the home secretary in March 1874, Lord Shaftesbury argued, "Women were not free agents; especially those with children as they would submit to anything—any sort of oppression; some had been known to work three days after giving birth to maintain their child."[77] In Shaftesbury's version, women were not free agents, because they were compelled by maternal instinct to work to support their families. At the first reading of the government's bill, home secretary Assheton Cross argued that women were not free agents but were under "the moral compulsion to support their families, and under the natural compulsion which was exercised by their husbands to go to work in the factories."[78] The home secretary invoked the duties of motherhood and blamed husbands, not employers, for overworking women.[79]

During the debates on the measure, one legislator urged the adoption of "more direct provisions for the protection of married women, especially from the coercion sometimes exercised by their husbands to compel them to work beyond their strength, and at critical periods."[80] Another would have included mothers of children under five years old as half-timers in the legislation. When the bill was in committee, a committee member introduced a clause prohibiting the employment of women in factories within four weeks after the birth of a child; another introduced an amendment that no mother should be employed within twelve months after the birth of her child. Yet another legislator wanted to make women responsible for upholding a law that subjected them to a fine if they returned to work within six weeks of childbirth.[81] These measures were voted down, not because other legislators were unsympathetic to the issue, but because the provisions were thought to be unenforceable.

A principal organization that opposed the factory reform measures was "The Vigilance Association for the Defence of Personal Rights and for the Amendment of the Law in Points wherein it is Injurious to Women." The group, which was made up primarily of bourgeois women, was founded in 1871 to "uphold the principle of the perfect equality of all persons before the law, irrespective of sex or class." As its name suggests, the organization concerned itself principally with legislation affecting the interests of women. Although the writings of the Vigilance Association members were generally clear in maintaining that women were free agents, they often appealed to the same gender ideology as those whom they opposed. In its annual report for 1873, the Vigilance Association suggested that a woman be given the power to request that her husband's wages be attached if he consistently neglected to maintain her. The report stated:

> Your committee believe that such a measure would at once, and of itself, secure the greater number of married women with young children would voluntarily and without compulsion of law, withdraw from labor pursued elsewhere than in their own homes, and would devote themselves to maternal and domestic duties. But they are bound to point out that any law or social custom which puts women at the mercy or pleasure of men for the necessaries of existence, is a direct cause of the grossest immorality.[82]

Such statements reveal the complex ideologies held by these feminists and why even their statements added to what had become the commonsense view that marriage and motherhood conferred on women one relationship to paid work while conferring on men the opposite relation. To these middle-class observers, women were responsible for domesticity, but it was men who were to blame if women could not do their motherly duties.[83] The position taken by the women's rights activists was supported by particularly outspoken opponents of legislative intervention between employers and their workers. *Capital and Labour,* a newspaper published by the National Federation of Associated Employers of Labour, wrote frequently on such topics as "The Freedom of Labour—The Sanctity of Contract and of Law."[84] The paper's arguments against the proposed legislative initiatives were primarily focused on the consequences for men's labor. However, when it dealt specifically with the question of legislation for women, the paper assumed the same gender distinctions as did the proponents of the measure. Speaking against the supporters of Factory Act reform, the writer of an article in *Capital and Labour* stated, "If law is to protect married women against the cry of their children, or the selfish urging of their husbands, it must legislate not for the factory, but for the home. . . . No doubt, women and children do need a certain amount of legislative protection; and what we protest against is the tendency of this protection to become oppressive."[85] The arguments of such opponents of state intervention as the Vigilance Association and the National Federation of Employers also tacitly supported the assumptions of promoters of the legislation. Women, they said, were not autonomous individuals who chose to work; they were coerced by their husbands. It was, then, up to working-class husbands to remedy the social problem of working mothers.

The class position of women became an issue in the debates. On the one hand, the Vigilance Association appealed to George Howell, the head of the Trades Union Congress (TUC) Parliamentary Committee, to set up a meeting between his committee and one from the Vigilance Association. Howell, however, told the Vigilance Association that the TUC had never before received such a deputation and did not want to set a precedent. The association also appealed to Home Secretary Cross to receive a deputation of women factory workers who would, according to the Vigilance Association, "state the case not just in general from the woman's point of view, but in particular from the working woman's point of view."[86] The home secretary refused to see them. He had entertained numerous deputations of men, but admitted no women. On the other hand, a major criticism leveled at the feminist opponents of the legislation was that those who wrote letters to the press or published memorials were women of privilege. Supporters of the acts countered the arguments of the Vigilance Association and such women's rights activists as Millicent Fawcett by saying that they took the position they did because "they did not belong to the humble class who were so shamefully overworked."[87]

Working women participated in various ways in the agitation for reduced hours in Oldham and other districts. For example, after the Factory Acts Reform Association had been formed and Mundella announced his Nine Hours Bill, the predominantly female Leeds flax workers went out on strike for a nine-hour day. Groups of "mill girls" walked from one district to another to induce fellow workwomen to turn out.[88] The women of Leeds were determined to win their battle even though both the Bradford Factory Acts Reform Association and Mundella opposed the strike; Mundella was quoted in a Leeds newspaper as saying, "it was more fitting that agitation should be carried on by the men employed in factories than the women and children."[89] Tempers in Leeds flared as some workers returned to work. Mrs. Newsome, a fifty-nine-year-old woman, was arrested for clapping her hands and calling some of the workers who had returned to work "black sheep."[90] Ultimately the union lost the strike, for employers bought off the male overlookers and a small number of striking women by raising their salaries. At the last strike meeting, which was attended principally by women and children, the union leader, Mr. Kendall, declared that "The men had not behaved with good faith to the union." In the crowd the cry was heard, "They were no men."[91] A last rally was held to demonstrate sympathy and appreciation for Mrs. Newsome, who had been imprisoned for two weeks and who had a large family dependent on her earnings. She was brought to the rally in a cab that had been converted to an open carriage, and Kendall and other members of the Flax Operatives Committee led a procession, to the accompaniment of cheers.[92]

There are records of women's active participation in attempts to reduce the hours they worked by trade union action, but we know almost nothing of their participation in meetings and demonstrations concerning the factory bills, nor even how many women signed petitions that were sent to the home secretary or to members of Parliament. We do know that all the members of deputations and all the officials of the various branches of the Factory Acts Reform Association were men. It is difficult to know why there is so little evidence about working women's views on the factory legislation. One explanation is that many were not organized. Cotton weavers' unions were sexually integrated and were headed by men; moreover, weavers' unions did not exist in all localities during this time period, and those that did exist had not been successful in organizing all weavers. Had the women been organized in their own trade unions or had they had representatives within the ranks of officials in the integrated unions, they might have made known in a more official or formal way their views about the legislation.[93]

This situation changed somewhat in 1874, after the government's bill passed. Emma Paterson, who, although she was the daughter of a schoolmaster, had apprenticed as a bookbinder, founded the Women's Protective and Provident League, later known as the Women's Trade Union League. Mrs. Paterson and the league, as well as women workers who were members of unions affiliated with the league, protested the proposed extensions of the restrictions on female labor under the new Factory and Workshops Consolidation Bill, which was made law in 1878. In commission hearings a number of women spoke out against further restrictions, despite the commissioners' expression of considerable resistance to their point of view. For example, Harriet Ford, a widow with seven children who supervised lace mending in a Nottingham factory, told the commissioners that after her husband's death she had worked in a factory until she had a child old enough to go to work, at which point she went home

> to my little ones; but my health was not so good at home as out. Since I have been out I feel a different woman altogether. I believe a married woman that goes out to work has more spirit and energy than one that always stays at home; and when she does return, and she has no lace work to do at home, she can devote her time to her house and family.[94]

An unmarried Birmingham woman, Miss Sloane, at first agreed with a commissioner who insisted that women were forced by their husbands to go out to work, but then she added:

> If a woman is cleverer than a man and she can go out and earn as much as her husband, I do not see why she should be prevented from earning what she can to bring up her children in a better way than she could if she did not work. Why can't a woman make a pattern of chandeliers? There is no reason whatever. It is easier than scrubbing or taking care of children at home, as I can speak from my own experience. I would rather make patterns; I can do it and do it, and would very much rather do it than stay at home and scrub.[95]

Like the Vigilance Association members in 1874, during debates on the Factory and Workshops Consolidation Bill passed in 1878 unionized women were denied the opportunity to send a deputation to the home secretary and were constrained to register their opposition to the proposed legislation in a memorial. The league, under Mrs. Paterson's leadership, opposed legislative restrictions on women's work, because they believed that women could achieve better working conditions for themselves in the same way that men achieved them—through their unions. As one member of the league said regarding the Factory Acts being discussed in 1877, "What was good for the gander was good for the goose."[96]

The government's "Factories (Health of Women, etc.) Bill" of 1874 easily passed both Houses of Parliament. The bill offered modifications regarding the hours of labor and other small concessions that persuaded most of the manufacturers who had opposed Mundella's bill to withdraw their opposition to the government's initiative. The proposals that singled out married women and new mothers did not become law, but they remained on the minds of many who would have had them included, and they were discussed in subsequent sessions of Parliament.

By 1875 a royal commission was at work to inquire into the working of the factories and workshops acts with an eye to consolidating the measures. The Factory and Workshops Consolidation Act of 1878 extended the restrictions on women's labor created by the 1874 act to industries other than textiles, further reduced the hours of labor, and unified the laws regulating the work of women and children in factories and workshops.[97] A measure requiring women to remain away from their jobs, without pay, for four weeks after giving birth was made law by Parliament in 1891.

Momentum for increasing the protection of women by legislation had been generated by the debates on the Nine Hours Bill and the government's "Factories (Health of Women, etc.) Bill."[98] The debates helped to mold and consolidate a growing consensus about the different responsibilities that marriage conferred upon women and upon men. The very existence of an act of Parliament with such a title was a public proclamation that working women needed and would get state protection.

It is important to realize that such legislation made individual women responsible for the welfare of babies and children and that it did not encourage consideration of alternative policies that would have made either the state or employers responsible for infant and child care.[99] At the same time, the debates blamed infant mortality on working mothers and not on overcrowded and unsanitary towns and cities or on the poverty produced by low wages and the high rates of underemployment and casual labor that marked the period in some areas of the country.[100] In addition, the public drama surrounding the passage of this legislation vilified working-class men whose wives were working in factories. It blamed the employment of wives on working men's moral failings, not on the inadequacy of the pay packet handed them by their employers. The assumption that individual women were responsible for children and individual men were responsible for family welfare set the terms in which people debated the pros and cons of legislation. The public policy that resulted reinforced these assumptions and also blinded people to alternative ways to deal with child care and the economic needs of families.

These ideas about women, men, and social reproduction generated by discussions of the Factory Acts fueled the late nineteenth- and early twentieth-century demand by the general labor unions for a family wage.[101] They underlay such employment policies as the marriage bar (discussed in Chapter 2), which existed in many firms by the end of the century. In addition, the idea that women needed to be protected like children persisted as a basis for future legislation.[102]

I have suggested that proposing factory legislation to restrict the hours that men as well as women and children could work would not have been politically expedient at the time. Such legislation would have set a precedent for state intervention in what was supposed to be a labor market in which capitalists and adult workers freely negotiated the terms of employment. The legislation specifically set limits on the hours of women and children only. The symbolic character of the legislation and the debates about it helped to create public perception of a new social problem: working mothers. Also, it blamed, not the employers who paid inadequate wages, but working men themselves for their inability to support a family. The rhetoric was successful because it was part of a larger discourse by the middle and upper classes about working-class family life.

The arguments about working mothers and their dissolute husbands used to advocate factory reform in the 1870s surely were instrumental in securing political support for the legislation. What I have attempted to show by this analysis is that even though the rhetoric may have been employed expediently in order to secure political goals that served working people in general, the discourses helped to create a new public problem. This suggests that the terms of a debate can have far-reaching consequences.

What happened in the 1870s in the enactment of a factory bill exemplifies a more general phenomenon. Social problems are those issues that emerge as a consequence of collective behavior, often as a consequence of contests over the interpretation of needs and interest.[103] When they are seen to require public solutions, those solutions, especially in the form of laws, symbolically create cultural assumptions that define not only the problem but the appropriate solutions. It is likely that the arguments about the dire consequences their mothers' employment had for infants and children touched a nerve that had already been stimulated in other public arenas. In this way the debate about factory legislation fed a growing public concern about married women's employment and the sanctity of motherhood at the same time that it resulted in success for the movement for factory reform. It built on the earlier rhetorical tradition, embodied in the New Poor Law, that held working-class men to be responsible for their own impoverishment. In addition, it deflected from employers and the state the responsibility for social reproduction. By reinforcing the idea that individual men were responsible for the economic welfare of their families, and that women were fully responsible for the health and well-being of their children, the New Poor Law and the Factory Acts defined the conditions under which women and men devised household strategies. At the same time, the debates were premised on the fiction that economy and state are independent of one another. This analysis of public policies as cultural productions reveals how fabrications about social reality are promulgated through discourse and suggests that one time they become dominant assumptions is when they are embedded in public policies that profoundly affect everyday life.

In addition to influencing approaches to public problems about gender, work, and family, the Factory Acts had a direct impact on women's employment. The Factory Acts did not affect the number of women who were hired, especially since most women were employed, not in factories, but as paid domestic workers. However, the acts did have adverse consequences for women and their work experiences in other ways. At the end of the nineteenth century, the Bowley Commission of the British Association for the Advancement of Science examined the economic effects of legislation on women's labor and concluded that such consequences were minimal. Bowley argued that "the line of demarcation between men's and women's work is, in the great majority of cases, rigidly fixed by physical suitability, by relative cheapness or by custom, and it usually appears that the work which must be done at night is far too heavy and hard for women."[104] Essentially, Bowley was arguing that the sexual segregation of occupations was such that protective labor legislation for women did not discourage employers from hiring them.[105] However, the acts did constrain women's employment to the advantage of men in certain industries, especially those, such as printing, that required night work. Thus, as sociologist Ava Baron has argued, protective labor legislation contributed to women's lack of competitiveness for well-paid employment, at the same time as it failed to protect them from their low-waged position in the labor market.[106]

The regulation of women's employment negatively affected women's position in the labor market in two other ways as well. As I will argue in Chapter 7, although women and men both worked as cotton weavers and earned equal piece rates, legally men, and men only, could clean their machines after working hours, so some men could and did earn higher weekly wages than women. In addition, after large workshops were regulated in 1867, smaller workshops and home manufacturing proliferated, as employers in highly competitive and labor-intensive industries, especially those in which flexibility was vital to survival (for example, in trades that were seasonal or subject to the dictates of fashion), reorganized their production in unregulated environments. For example, parliamentary commissioners investigating women's and children's work heard testimony about how employers in the lace and hosiery industries evaded the Factory Acts by this process.[107]

As the acts increased their purview, the area of unregulated work shrank. The Factory and Workshops Consolidation Act of 1878 created a nine-hour day for women and children in both factories and workshops, but the measure exempted private manufacturing households as long as only family members were involved in the work. That act led numerous employers to subcontract their work to private households, which were hidden from public scrutiny.[108] As Shelley Pennington and Belinda Westover argue, "The limitations on working hours and regulation of standards in the workplace was [sic] a positive incentive to employers to put work out into the one workplace unfettered by restrictive legislation."[109] That one place was the household.

In spite of the public outcry about sweated labor that culminated in the parliamentary commissions on sweating in the 1880s, it was not until 1901 that the government attempted any serious measures to curb and regulate homework. The Factory and Workshops Act of 1901 required employers to keep a list of all homeworkers they employed. In addition, employers were to give each employee a written statement of the work to be done and what they were to be paid. However, as Pennington and Westover have argued, enforcement of the act proved difficult, and it was not until the Trades Boards Act of 1909 that the state seriously addressed a primary issue regarding homework—the pitifully low wages earned by those (mostly women) who did it.

CONCLUSION

The laws discussed in this chapter and the debates that led to their enactment helped to construct gender in such a way that working-class men and working-class women were caught in a trap. Men who could not support their families because of periodic trade depressions or because of the economic instabilities affecting their particular line of work were blamed for their own plight. These public policies reinforced and legitimated beliefs that men were responsible for the economic welfare of families and women's proper job was to nurture their children. Legal representations of gender were important in the construction of working-class manhood and womanhood. In practice, Poor Laws and the Factory Acts constrained the ways the working class could make ends meet. Both forms of legislation stressed individual responsibility for social reproduction, for the maintenance of life on a daily basis and intergenerationally. They limited or denied community responsibility for family welfare.

This chapter has examined how state policies that are instrumental in shaping work and community relations contain intrinsic assumptions about gender. Such policies were important building blocks for industrial capitalism in nineteenth-century England. My interpretation suggests that theories of the state stressing its autonomy or relative autonomy from economic relations are misguided.[110] Economic practices, as well as family relations and the interconnections between these practices and relations, are defined in and are in turn structured by laws. As E. P. Thompson has put it, " 'law' was deeply imbricated within the very basis of productive relations, which would have been inoperable without this law."[111]

4

"To Do the Best You Can"
Women's Work and Homework

The members of Parliament and social reformers who were concerned with infant mortality and the "working mother problem" did not acknowledge that most working-class women had to bring cash into their households at some time during their married lives.[1] With birthrates remaining high and earnings either low, erratic, or both, the income of more than a single wage earner often was necessary for family survival. Some married women remained wage earners throughout the family life cycle. Others sought employment during the times when there were more dependents than could be supported by a single wage earner. Many others were desperate for work when their husbands were laid off or put on short time. And widows often took whatever jobs they found in order to put food on the table.

Employers, however, structured factory jobs as though they were to be held by people without household responsibilities, and certainly by nonmothers—that is, by men.[2] As I argued in the last chapter, public policies reflected the idea that social welfare and social reproduction were private matters. The belief that individual women were responsible for social reproduction, by which I mean childbearing and caring for family members on a daily basis, was enshrined in law as well as in local custom. Individual women were to meet these family responsibilities with no other assistance than the financial help available from spouses or kin.

As a consequence, mothering and breadwinning were oppositional constructs both in their ideological representation and in the ways they were organized socially.[3] Ironically, the social construction of motherhood singled out women to be industrial homeworkers. However, homework did not solve the contradiction between wage earning and social reproduction.

WAGE-EARNING WOMEN

Married working-class women who earned money worked, not because they wanted jobs, but because their families needed them to do so if they were to make ends meet. It is likely that as children were withdrawn from the labor force in the nineteenth century, married and widowed women's wage-earning became increasingly important. Poor Law guardians, responsible for giving community assistance to the destitute, expected widows either to work to support themselves and their children or to get help from their kin. If they could do neither, they faced the workhouse.[4] Many of the widowed homeworkers surveyed in London at the end of the nineteenth century had their earnings supplemented by parish relief.[5] But the amount of that aid was meager. Those without dependents received a weekly sum of 2s. 6d., scarcely enough to pay for a single room. A widow with five children received 5 shillings. One widow who sewed boys' knickers and trousers to support herself and three children under the age of six had been transferred to the Bethnal Green Union, which denied her any poor relief and left her struggling to stay out of the workhouse.[6] In declining framework-knitting communities such as Arnold in Nottinghamshire, approximately 77 percent of widows were working in 1881. All the unemployed widows were very elderly. Most of the widows worked as seamers of knitted garments; the remainder were domestic servants and agricultural workers.[7]

Throughout the nineteenth century the large majority of working-class families had difficulty making ends meet. Many different forms of evidence suggest that most married working-class women often had to provide income for their families, because their husbands' earnings were too low for family subsistence. Historian Eric Hobsbawm has estimated that throughout the nineteenth century, the most skilled and secure of manual workers probably made up no more than 10 to 20 percent of all workers.[8] These figures suggest that at least 80 percent of working-class men either were not sole family providers, or if they were, they and their families lived under continuing economic stress.

Chronic job insecurity haunted even the better-paid skilled workers such as boilermakers and men in engineering. Robert Knight of the Boilermaker's Society said that workers must "make the best of the sunshine we now enjoy, for as certain as night will return, so surely will the clouds of depression again surround us with gloom, loss of work, and consequent suffering to ourselves and families."[9] The nineteenth-century economy was beset by uncontrolled cycles of expansion and contraction which played havoc with even the most skilled workers' jobs. Knight commented, "These unhealthy, feverish spurts, followed by years of idleness, are not conducive to the best interests of the workman and those dependent upon his earnings."[10] People in such cities as London, with its large casual-labor market, experienced chronic unemployment and underemployment.[11] Although reliable national unemployment statistics for this period are scarce, clear evidence exists that rates were high in 1867–1869, 1878–1879, 1884–1887, and 1893–1894.[12]

Working-class family budgets suggest that only a minority of working-class men were sole family providers. For example, the budgets of English industrial workers in 1889 and 1890, years of relative prosperity, indicate that in the majority of households in which there were children aged ten or over, the children contributed to the household finances.[13] In addition, the proportion of total family income earned by the male head of household varied according to the family's developmental cycle and the opportunities for employment that were available.[14] Even among the skilled workers in Scotland studied by sociologist John Holley, the head's income only provided between 44 and 57 percent of total family income.[15]

Contemporary studies of the poor by Charles Booth and B. Seebohm Rowntree documented the number of families living in poverty due to the irregular earnings of the heads of households (usually men).[16] Booth discovered that only 30 percent of the population were able to rely solely on wages earned by the male head of household.[17] Ten years later, Rowntree established the "primary poverty line" as the barest minimum for physical maintenance: for a man and his wife and three children, this sum was 21s. 8d. a week. He showed that 52 percent of the households in York living at or below this poverty line were poor because of the low wages of household heads.[18] In all, he found that 34 percent of York households were either below or very close to this primary poverty line.[19] In addition, Rowntree discovered that there were important times during the individual male's life cycle when he would be especially hard-pressed: as an infant, when he was married and had young children, and then again in old age.

Other evidence from the early twentieth century bears out these conclusions. In 1908 social investigator Edward Cadbury calculated a subsistence wage for a man and his wife and three children to be 25 shillings a week, and the 1906 Wages Census showed that 41.6 percent of men in the cotton industry and 30.6 percent of men in the metal, engineering, and shipbuilding trades earned less than 25 shillings weekly.[20] A study for the Fabian Society published in 1913 documented the extent to which women's earnings were necessary for their own support or as a contribution to the support of others.[21] Maud Pember Reeves, writing a defense of working-class women's abilities as household managers, showed the appalling conditions under which women saved and maneuvered in order to feed their families, and their dire need for additional sources of money so that they would not be forced to pawn their own boots.[22]

In a richly textured portrait based on oral histories, Elizabeth Roberts has described the home- and family-centered worlds of working-class women at the turn of the century.[23] Roberts suggests that these women were preoccupied with "being respectable" and that they preferred not to be wage earners after they married. Yet the majority of her respondents brought money into their households at some point in their married lives. Women used various tactics to help their families survive. They got money by hawking, child minding, taking in washing and ironing, housing lodgers and boarders, pawning their clothes and household furnishings, earning wages at jobs outside their homes, or doing industrial homework.[24]

STATISTICAL REPRESENTATIONS OF
WORKING WOMEN

Although most working-class women earned wages at various points in their lives, including after they had married and had children, official statistics underrepresented the number of women, especially married women, who earned wages during the last half of the nineteenth century. Census data, a primary source that documented employment patterns, underestimated the number of married working women.

It was not until 1901 that the census first reported data on married and widowed women workers as distinct from single women, and not until 1911 that married workers were distinguished from both widowed and single women. Therefore, it is impossible to determine from aggregate census reports the rates of married women's labor-force participation during the period of our study.[25] It has been estimated that married women's employment rate dropped to around 13 percent by 1901, and 10 percent by 1911.[26]

Aggregate statistics also concealed local and regional variations in the rate at which women worked in any given year. Cross-sectional data inadequately reflected the extent to which women found ways to contribute money to the household budget when it was necessary for them to do so, and how they moved in and out of employment or alternated among various subsistence strategies. Such data do not accurately portray the extent to which earning money was an integral and frequent aspect of most working-class women's lives after they married.[27]

Interpreting the data on married women's employment, even when they are derived from the census enumerators' records rather than from aggregate statistics, is hazardous because the subject was distorted by the value judgments of householders and census enumerators alike.[28] Although household census data included information about the occupations of all household members, census categories and statistics were not objective, neutral indicators of social facts. Changing ideas about work and gender shaped occupational categorization, how the information was recorded and analyzed, and how it was obtained.[29] Both householders and enumerators varied in the extent to which they acknowledged women's economic contributions earned either inside or outside their homes as "occupations."[30] Both would have been influenced by prevailing conceptions of womanhood in their community as they took account of married women's work.

From midcentury on, the census office saw motherhood as women's primary responsibility. The 1851 census report put it this way: "The child receives nurture, warmth, affection, admonition, education from a good mother; who, with the child in her arms, is in the eyes of all European nations surrounded by a sanctity which is only expressed in the highest works of art."[31] Census figures were also influenced by the changing meaning of domestic work for married women. Prior to 1881, wives and other female relatives who were listed as doing housework in their own homes were counted among the "occupied" in census reports.[32] Beginning in 1881, women working at home, whether in home production, in domestic work, or helping in a family business, were removed from the tables listing those who were occupied and were placed in a residual category of the "unoccupied."[33] Once house-wifery and other forms of home employment were excluded as occupations for women, their official rate of labor-force participation was cut in half.[34]

Beginning in 1841, the head of the household, usually a man, filled in the census form. In communities where it was generally a mark of shame for a married woman to have to earn wages, because it signified that her husband was unable to provide for her, the husband may have left blank the line reserved for his wife's occupation. In other communities, where it was commonplace for wives to work full-time for much of their married lives, heads of households may have reported their wives' work differently.[35] In such areas as North Lancashire, where women's employment in the cotton mills was central to the organization of textile manufacture, censuses reported relatively high percentages of married women working. For example, 45.7 percent of married women in the Lancashire textile factory community of Clitheroe, Low Moor, in 1881 were working at the local mill.[36] In the framework knitting community of Arnold, Nottinghamshire, where the domestic hosiery industry persisted until the last decades of the nineteenth century, in 1851 41 percent of wives were listed with an occupation, and in 1881 54.4 percent of married women living with their husbands were recorded as having an occupation.[37]

Heads of households were asked to provide details about people in their households on one night of the year, usually one in March or April. It is possible that only those married women who were year-round workers and who were earning at the time the census was taken were reported as having an occupation. The fluctuations in employment level resulting from the ups and downs of business cycles, as well as the seasonal nature of many businesses, would have resulted in numerous men being out of work—especially in a census year like 1881, which was during the great depression—yet only very old men were listed without an occupation. However, even though a married woman moved in and out of employment, she was rarely considered to have an occupation if she was not currently employed. In other words, in many districts a married woman's "trade" would be listed as house-wifery unless she happened to be employed at the time the census return was filled out. Censuses thus masked women's wage earning and men's unemployment.

Women who earned wages as industrial homeworkers were especially likely to be invisible in statistical records of the nineteenth century.[38] The proliferation of industries that relied on homeworkers suggests that toward the end of the nineteenth century ever larger numbers of women, assisted by their children, did industrial homework as a way of making ends meet. But no matter how necessary this work was to the household economy, it tended to be unrecognized as employment both in official tallies of labor-force participation rates, and even by the homeworkers themselves. For example, in an oral history interview a Colchester woman responded to the question, "Did your mother work after she was married?" by saying, "No, I don't know—they seemed to think if a woman worked after marriage . . . it was something to be ashamed of. You were looked down on. You could do it at home and they didn't take too much notice of it. . . . Like my mother, although she did it at home she never went out to work."[39] Because these women have been hidden from history, we are just beginning to learn about those who did industrial homework, the conditions that led them to this form of work, and its consequences for their lives.[40]

INDUSTRIAL HOMEWORK

Homework proliferated with industrial development, especially from the 1850s through the early decades of the twentieth century.[41] From the vantage point of the industrialist, homework was a way of minimizing risks and lowering costs.[42] Above all, it gave him flexibility.[43] From the viewpoint of the majority of homeworkers, it was one form of what Olwen Hufton has called "the economy of makeshift."[44] Countless numbers of women working at home manufactured cardboard boxes and paper bags, artificial flowers, and brushes. They covered tennis balls and racquetballs, mended and finished lace, plaited straw, seamed and embroidered hosiery, and pulled fur. In 1907 four-fifths of all recorded outworkers in the country worked in the clothing industry, stitching collars and buttonholes, and making shirts, trousers, and waistcoats.[45]

Firms and industries that relied on homeworkers sprang up in localities where there were large numbers of underemployed men, and where women had few alternative ways of earning money. They developed in areas where people were desperate for work, and they relied on workers who had so few opportunities that they would work for any price. At a structural level, once homeworking industries became integral to the economy of a city, town, or region, these industries helped to perpetuate the labor surplus and family work patterns that fed them.

As the evidence on the number of families living in poverty has suggested, women did homework because they were self-supporting or were a major support of others in their households. Very few worked for personal independence or for the proverbial "pin money," or to pass the time when they were not preoccupied with domestic duties. A Colchester woman, when asked if the homeworkers in the tailoring trade did the work for "pocket money," replied, "Pocket money! That was pocket money! To fill the kids' tummies. No-one worked on the tailoring at home unless it was to fulfil a need . . . they had to. If the husband lost his job—no dole—no money coming in."[46] If they were in households that were not facing destitution, they lived close to the margin of absolute poverty and worked in order to save against the likely event of an illness, or to provide the minimum income essential for purchasing the clothing, shoes, and household furnishings considered respectable. As a homeworker in London explained, " 'E don't care what the children wears, but I ain't going to let 'em go about looking like a puppet show for all that."[47] The majority worked either to provide the barest essentials for their families or to improve their well-being at least minimally.

Women "chose" to do homework because it was one answer to the problem of surviving with inadequate household financial resources and providing care and nourishment for their charges. This hypothesis is borne out by the domestic situations of Nottingham lace clippers (homeworkers) enumerated in the 1881 census of households in two districts adjacent to the Nottingham lace market.[48] A majority of lace clippers (65.9 percent) were married, many of them to men who were irregularly employed.[49] Construction work was the most commonly listed occupation of the lace clippers' husbands. Of the 105 married clippers in the Nottingham sample, 37.1 percent had husbands who were in the building trades. Their employment and wages depended on the season and the weather.[50] Robert Roberts described the struggle for work among construction workers in a town near Manchester:

> Building laborers I have seen as a child follow a wagon laden with bricks from the kilns, hoping to find a job where the load was tipped. For the

same reason, too, they would send a wife or child trailing behind a lime cart. On some building sites a foreman might find fifty laborers pleading for a mere half-dozen jobs. It was not unknown for him to place six spades against a wall at one hundred yards' distance. A wild, humiliating race followed; work went to those who succeeded in grabbing a spade.[51]

Homework would have been a welcome way for builders' wives to alleviate their household's financial difficulties, especially if alternatives to this work were limited or nonexistent.

Homeworkers in other areas of the country, too, tended to have husbands who were unskilled or casual laborers.[52] The majority of married homeworkers in the Women's Industrial Council study in London at the end of the nineteenth century had husbands who worked in construction or were described as laborers, or who were sickly or unemployed. A study of families in West Ham (London) in 1907 found that over half of the women who earned wages by sewing clothing at home were wives of builders, general laborers, or dock workers, all of whom experienced intermittent employment.[53]

Although homework was especially geared to married women, many working women in poor districts of cities such as the census districts of Nottingham I sampled, were married. According to the Nottingham census data for 1881, even though the proportion of married workers was higher for lace clippers than for any other occupational group, still, 48.9 percent of lace menders (who usually worked in factories or warehouses) were married, 32.2 percent of factory hosiery workers were married, and 34.6 percent of lace-factory hands were married. These data support the idea that married women in many poor households needed to contribute wages to make ends meet. In some localities—and Nottingham is an example—homework was a major means by which they earned wages, but it was not the only income-earning strategy employed by working-class wives.

Lace clipping at home was an economic strategy primarily adopted by married women at a particular stage of their life cycle. These homeworkers were primarily between the ages of twenty-five and thirty-five.[54] Whereas the percentage of married lace clippers who were under the age of twenty-five was almost identical to the percentage of all married women who were in that age group, the percentage of married clippers aged thirty-five and over was lower than the percentage of all married women in that age group. Lace clippers, then, were in their prime childbearing years, the time in their families' life cycle when there would be young children who both needed care and were too young to contribute to the family economy.

When compared with married women thirty-five and over who worked outside the home, the percentage of lace clippers thirty-five and over was substantially lower.[55] This suggests that when their children grew older, married women in very poor families found employment in factories, warehouses, and elsewhere more remunerative than finishing lace at home. Rather than retiring from wage earning when a child was old enough to earn wages, at least some women who had taken in homework when their children were very young probably then went out to work.

Homeworking wives were distinguished from their neighbors who were not homeworkers by the numbers and ages of their young children. Homeworkers were more likely than other wives to have in their households a number of children under the age of fourteen (the age at which children were then permitted to work full-time).[56] Married women who were not working outside their homes were more likely to have at least three children under the age of fourteen than were wives who went out to work, but homeworkers were the *most* likely group of married women to have a large number of young children under their care.[57]

These data suggest that having many young children had two consequences: mothers could not easily leave their houses to seek work in warehouses and factories, and their earnings were especially essential because of the drain on household finances of a large number of dependents. The presence of young children, then, had contradictory effects for mothers: they made their wages essential for survival, but, at the same time, numerous young children limited the access of these mothers to alternatives to sweated labor.

Oral histories of people who were reared in the early years of the twentieth century in Nottingham or its hinterland flesh out this sketch drawn from the census. They describe the impoverished conditions which led their mothers to do lace or hosiery finishing. For example, Mrs. R., who grew up in Arnold, Nottinghamshire, early in the twentieth century, told of the persistent efforts of her widowed mother to care for her family in the face of economic destitution:

> Well, she—she was very poor, very poor because I mean there was no relief in those days same as there is now. She used to take in seaming from somebody at—that lived on Church Drive, and I've heard her say that she's sat up until two o'clock and three—in the morning to get us bread for that following day.[58]

As the census suggested, homeworking mothers were married to fathers with unstable or poorly remunerated employment. One respondent's father "used to do anything, any kind you know of work he was what they used to call a 'labor man' you, know, he'd do any sort of work."[59] Her mother did lace finishing at home, sometimes clipping and scalloping all day; she was helped by the children, who did the drawing. The respondent added, "Course then as we got older me mother used to work at what they used to call 'dressing rooms'; they used to do a lot of these 'ere mosquito nets and that you know, cleaning and starch 'em and stretch 'em on frames . . . in a dressing room."[60] Continuing to earn wages to support her family, this respondent's mother went out to work when she and her siblings were old enough to be left on their own.

In contrast, another respondent whose father was an engineer had to be prompted to recall that his mother worked at home. At first he said that his mother did not work; she only took on voluntary jobs. Then he said:

> Yes, I—I've got to come back a bit, you said did my mother do—did you ask me if my mother did part-time work? She did. Yes, she did chevoning for a hosiery firm, you know, the old—clocking socks by hand. She used to fetch it in a bag from the—I used to have to fetch it as a boy. From the factory and then take it back again.[61]

He reported that his mother's work hours "fit in with the domestic duties naturally you know, an hour at a time." She did more work "depending how she wanted the money to keep the family going when father was—."[62] When asked how much time her mother spent finishing lace, the former respondent reported "Well it depended on how much they gave her to do you see . . . sometimes sit all afternoon and you know, a lot."[63]

These and other oral histories suggest that rather than doing a bit of industrial homework here and there to fit in with their other domestic responsibilities, homeworkers adapted the time spent at housework and their methods of child care to mesh with wage earning.

Industrial homeworkers, in other words, worked much as their preindustrial grandmothers had worked.[64] Under preindustrial conditions of domestic manufacture, wives extended the length of the day that they worked, and when it was necessary for them to spend a large portion of this elongated day at manufacture they modified their domestic duties accordingly. Descriptions of framework-knitting communities mentioned the late hours that women and children would work on Friday nights because Saturday was the day knitters were paid for the stockings produced during the week.[65] Very young children were set to work, both to help their parents and to keep them busy and out of harm's way. Babies were minded by the somewhat older children, by a neighboring girl who was paid a copper or two for her efforts, or by an aged relative who lived close by. Parliamentary commissioners were shocked by the chemists' and medical officers' reports of widespread use of opiates to quiet hungry and fretful infants so that their mothers could do the work necessary for the family's subsistence.

Similarly, children raised in households in which their mothers took in industrial homework helped their mothers to do the work. When there was a rush job, everyone in the family would pitch in. Children, especially daughters, might be kept at home to help out, or they started work immediately on their arrival home after school.[66] As children ceased to be employed in domestic workshops in the last quarter of the nineteenth century, children and young people under the age of eighteen continued to do lace finishing, but most often for their own mothers, who took out work from the middlewomen.

As I suggested in Chapter 3, state regulation of women's work outside the home led to an increase in industrial manufacturing in private dwellings. Homeworkers used family labor to increase their productivity. Many hands were needed to make ends meet when there was much work to be done. The fact that homework tended to be done partly by children and elderly relatives who helped the homeworker obscured the amount of time family members had to spend at the wage-earning activity. It also had the consequence of lowering the piece rates for the products.

The census and oral histories, supplemented by descriptions of working patterns in preindustrial, domestic industry, have suggested that the more needy were their families, the more homeworkers would have to produce to earn a living. This meant that homeworkers had to make housework and child care fit around the incessant demand for production. The more dependent the family was on the wages that would be earned by the household's manufacture, the more those domestic responsibilities, including the care of infants and children, were molded by economic necessity. Although it was possible for wives and mothers to combine the activities of manufacturing and domesticity, since both took place at home, the fit probably was never a very good one. Women then as now, when the majority work outside their homes, had a "double day." Then as now, domestic responsibilities were given short shrift when they competed with activities that could put food on the table.[67]

The connection between economic necessity and the time and effort spent by homeworkers at home manufacture had a perverse consequence: the neediest women earned the lowest piece rates. Nineteenth- and early twentieth-century investigators all found that the lowest rates were paid, not to married women who were "merely supplementing" the wages of their husbands, but to destitute widows. And married women whose husbands were earning regular wages were able to earn more than the women to whom homework was absolutely indispensable.[68]

THE CYCLE OF POVERTY AND REPRODUCTION

The evidence from Nottingham points to the complex ways that social reproduction and forms of production were related. The development of capitalism in this period had particular demographic consequences for some working-class families. Very poor families may have continued to have large families because their subsistence depended on many wage earners. Nonunionized and casual workers might not have had access to burial societies to help provide for them in their old age, or to clubs which insured against accidents and illness, or, certainly, to union funds to help when they were unemployed.[69] The fear of receiving a pauper's funeral was prevalent, and anything the household might manage to save would be likely to be put in a burial club to prevent such a calamity.[70] Old age threatened destitution: old-age insurance pensions were not available until 1911, and then they were denied to those who had "failed to work habitually according to their ability and need, and those who failed to save money regularly."[71]

The family strategies for formation and fertility in such households, particularly when infant mortality rates remained very high, may have paralleled those of households engaged in preindustrial domestic manufacture.[72] They would marry relatively early and would concentrate childbearing in the early years of marriage, producing contributors to the household budget as quickly as possible. However, according to historian David Levine, high levels of infant mortality led families to continue to have children until at least one child was old enough to contribute to the family economy.[73] It would have been at this point, according to Levine, that family limitation would begin.[74]

The data from Nottingham in 1881 suggest that industrial homework for women, like work for whole families in domestic industry, may have encouraged this pattern. The ready availability of homework may have been a stimulus to a relatively high within-marriage fertility rate, concentrated in the early childbearing years. Like protoindustrial employment, homework encouraged what Levine has called "industrial involution," or the "vicious circle of self-exploitation" brought about by low piece rates.

Family survival strategies were not necessarily arrived at by an unchanging, uniform, and uncontested consensus between husbands and wives. The historical evidence suggests that these strategies, including the unequal allocation of food, made living more difficult for women than for men.[75] However, there is little evidence about the intrahousehold negotiations that may have taken place, or how individual women and men construed their different responsibilities.[76] What is known suggests that families of casual workers in urban areas, of unskilled and semi-skilled workers in towns and villages, and of agricultural laborers or cottagers in rural areas faced economic exigencies that placed a double burden on married women. They gave birth to a large number of children who then needed their care, and they also had to contribute to the family economy, especially when they had many young, nonworking children at home. Even though fertility control was possible, however inadequate it may have been, women and men in such families did not limit reproduction by attempting to lower the overall size of their households, possibly because the chances were so high that many of their children would not survive.[77] Poor families were caught in a downward spiral. On the structural level, poverty contributed to the conditions of labor surplus (in particular, large numbers of married women in need of work) that encouraged manufacturers to adopt homework as a form of work organization. Poverty coupled with homework may have encouraged families to adopt fertility strategies producing the "dependency hump" that continued to make women's wage earning necessary.[78]

CHILD-BEARING

We have only sketchy knowledge about how couples during the nineteenth century dealt with sex and reproduction.[79] Working-class women had a large number of children and probably were pregnant or nursing from the time they married until they approached menopause, which may have been when they were in their early forties.[80] In the very poorest families, the number of times a woman gave birth may have been truncated by her generally poor health and poor diet, which may have produced amenorrhea,[81] and possibly by relatively long periods of breast feeding.[82] In any case, what we know about maternity in the period suggests that pregnancy and childbirth were difficult at best, and working-class women could not have looked forward to the succession of births that was their lot.[83]

If the women's earnings were necessary, as they probably were in the majority of households, they would have welcomed opportunities to work at home while they were pregnant, after the birth of a child, and while they were nursing. Combining maternity with wage earning outside the household, even if women could make the choice between waged work out of the home and waged work within it, would have increased the danger of their already precarious pregnancies and recoveries from childbirth. As Johanna Brenner and Maria Ramas have argued, under such conditions the practices associated with biological reproduction acted as constraints on the ways married women contributed to their households.[84]

The social construction of responsibility for health contributed to the consequences of childbearing for women's wage earning. The financial and medical responsibilities for producing the next generation of citizens and workers were considered to be private concerns.[85] In nineteenth-century England, the state or community intervened overtly only when officials and middle-class observers believed that individuals were shirking their responsibilities. The idea behind these early policy initiatives was to supply the individual with whatever missing personal resource was presumed to cause this failure (knowledge about motherhood, nutrition, sanitation).[86] As was suggested in Chapter 3, the assumptions that individual mothers were responsible for children and that employers and the community at large had only limited responsibility for the health and well-being of working families were built into the fabric of everyday practices, commonsense thinking, and public policies.[87]

The state in Britain was not unconcerned with childbirth. Rather, its concern was limited in particular ways. Industrial capitalism in England developed with a set of assumptions about social reproduction, and a pattern of social relations that organized social reproduction.[88] Basically, the welfare of mothers as women was not of concern; their health was a private matter. Their welfare became a subject of state interest only when policy makers became worried about the health of children and about infant death rates. The last years of the nineteenth century in England witnessed a flowering of public concern about the welfare of children. The response of the state was to attempt to regulate the waged work of mothers, making it harder for those who had to work to earn wages. Otherwise, the principal efforts toward maternal and infant welfare were directed at teaching mothers the skills of mothering.[89] State policy in Britain reinforced the opposition between motherhood and waged work by emphasizing the mother's own responsibility for motherhood.

It was in this context that individual mothers and their families coped with the economic hardships accompanying pregnancy, childbirth, and postpartum recovery. The stress of poverty weighed heavily on women.[90] Mrs. Layton recalled her first pregnancy:

> I was beginning to wonder how my confinement was to be paid for when I had to give up work. I was also very anxious about the health of the coming baby. I knew enough about maternity to know I had not had sufficient food to nourish myself and child, and then I felt a great responsibility of bringing a new life into the world.[91]

Exhausted from childbirth, many women nonetheless returned to their work as soon as they could physically manage it, because they needed the money. The law passed in 1891 making it illegal for an employer "knowingly" to allow a woman to work within four weeks of giving birth was difficult to enforce. It was widely evaded by the women themselves, who could not afford to remain unemployed. As Margaret Hewitt put it, "To enforce the Act was to enforce starvation."[92] Since the law made no provision for maternity benefits, when it was obeyed by employers, the women and their families went without.

Knowledgeable people in England knew about maternity benefit schemes in other countries. For example, by the last decades of the century Germany had compulsory maternity insurance that allowed a working mother to receive half her weekly wage for four to six weeks after she gave birth. In Britain, however, such a policy was almost beyond comprehension. As one contemporary British commentator put it, "This expedient could hardly be made applicable to this country."[93]

Data collected by factory inspector Miss Squire about the length of time 124 women remained away from their cotton factory jobs in Preston showed that only two had returned within a month of giving birth.[94] About two-thirds had returned between one and three months after delivery. It is likely that physical exhaustion from the delivery and from caring for a fretful infant who awoke frequently during the night would have made returning to work during those first few months extremely difficult.

Mothers who worked at home probably began their employment even earlier than one month after childbirth. The following is one of several such cases of homeworking women from central London reported in the 1904 annual report of the chief inspector of factories:

> Mrs. H., blouse and children's costume machinist at home, has three children, the youngest 2 1/2, two very delicate. After confinement she has usually begun her blouse work again at the end of a fortnight. But a year ago after a premature confinement (the baby died immediately after birth), as her husband had been out of work, she could not afford to lie up at all. The baby was born between 6 and 7 a.m., and before midday of the same day she was sitting at her sewing-machine blouse-making.[95]

A woman whose mother was a tailoress who worked at home remembered:

> Well my mother had a lot of babies that I knew nothing about much. Every little while I'd come down and see a baby on the sideboard . . . and there would be babies' little coffins and she used to be laying in bed and she'd be putting these buttons on the trousers . . . as she lay there.[96]

In her campaign to have homework regulated, Gertrude Tuckwell, head of the Women's Trade Union League, wrote in 1909, "Work lies on the cradle; often on the bed of a woman whose baby is 24 hours born, and her fingers take it up; work lies on the coffin like a pall."[97] In a society that assigned to individual women the responsibility for child care and that admitted no obligation for the costs of providing for the health of women who both bore babies and were employed, women preferred homework to working outside the home. As long as their babies slept or their cries could be ignored, the women could continue their wage-earning work.

CHILD CARE

In addition to the difficulties of combining maternity with paid work outside the household, arranging for infant feeding and child care would not have been a simple matter for poor working-class mothers. The mother's own milk would have been the safest food for the newborn; other sources of nourishment were expensive and often were contaminated.[98] Unless families enlarged to include relatives who could care for the young while their mothers left the household for employment, child care also would have been difficult.

It was not usual for working-class families to share a residence with relatives who could help them with child care. As a rule, family life in Britain was organized around the nuclear household.[99] For centuries it had been customary for young couples to leave their parents and set up a separate household when they married.[100] Even in old age people preferred independent households.[101] Margaret Hewitt estimated that at most about one-third of the households in her sample from the 1851 census of Lancashire had a grandmother or elderly aunt living in the household.[102] My study of households from the 1881 census of Low Moor, Clitheroe, and Ashton-under-Lyne in the Lancashire cotton manufacturing area showed that only 6 percent of households included either parents, grandparents, or elderly aunts.[103] In 1881 only 8 percent of Nottingham lace clippers and 11 percent of married women working in lace factories who were living with their husbands also had other relatives in the household.[104]

The results of an 1894 survey of the arrangements for day care of 165 children of working mothers in the cotton-manufacturing town of Burnley showed that one in four was left with grandparents, one in four with other relatives, and nearly half with unrelated neighbors; only nine were left with no one to care for them.[105] Numerous working mothers lived in neighborhoods where relatives living close by provided child care. For example, Mary Cooper grew up "surrounded by her father's extensive family and knew that there were always relatives in nearby houses she could go to if there was no one at home when she came back from school."[106] Neighborhood women frequently acted as child minders. Often, too, the woman's older children were responsible for the care of the younger.[107] A letter written at midcentury to the *Morning Chronicle* by a man raised in Birmingham described his child-minding days:

> My mother worked at her trade (button turning) till the last. Often till the day before her confinement she was at the lathe, and often returned to her work within three weeks. It was my business, as the eldest child, to nurse the younger ones. I was a nurse at five years old, and . . . sometimes I had to go to the factory to attend to the infant. My mother was allowed to take it with her, and it used to lie in a tub of sawdust, and sleep or roll about till it wanted the breast. I was obliged to watch over it and amuse it.[108]

However, it was not just mothers who worked outside of their homes who relied on older children to mind younger ones. Mrs. Layton, born in 1855 and raised in Bethnal Green, recalled that she and a sister always stayed away from school on washing day to mind the babies. She reminisced, "In the summer it was real sport, because so many people did their washing on the same day, and everybody had large families and generally kept the elder girls, and sometimes boys, at home to mind the little ones."[109] In spite of attempts by school boards to enforce school attendance, girls were often kept at home to care for younger siblings or help their mothers.[110]

Stricter enforcement of school attendance meant that older children could less often help out with the younger ones. This left mothers even more hard pressed to care for their newborns while they continued to earn wages. Child minding was an expensive service, and many women would not have earned enough to afford it. Elizabeth Roberts's figures for such costs early in the twentieth century suggest that it may have only been weavers in the Lancashire cotton textile districts that could have afforded to pay a neighboring woman to care for their young children.[111] However, when the mother's work was essential for family survival, the children were perforce sent to live with or be watched by others. A man born in 1896 recalled that his mother continued as a silk winder for eight or nine years after she had married and had children, by putting her children out to nurse. He said, "I've got a strict—a strong recollection of that because I lived with these people more than I lived at home." He and his siblings were brought "to some other working-class family, a mining family, a family of colliers, a father and two sons and a daughter, and I was practically brought up with them."[112] A woman was raised by her grandmother until her grandmother's death, when she "went to me mother." She explained, "Mind you when I was young there was a lot of poverty about, you know there was no security pay and no, you couldn't get any money from anywhere or anything like that you know, and so it used to . . . do the best you can."

Public alarm at the impoverished conditions under which the majority of homeworkers lived and worked led social reformers to propose various measures to regulate industrial homework. Given that homework was seen by many women as the least onerous of the available options for making ends meet, it is not surprising that some of them joined the National Home Workers League, formed to protest proposed legislation to limit and regulate homework. A representative of the National Home Workers League argued at a parliamentary commission hearing that opportunities for homework should be protected because of the difficulties married women had in combining wage earning and domestic responsibilities.[113] One homeworker had said to her, "If I go to the factory I must buy milk for my child. If I stay at home I can give it the breast, as I ought."[114] She explained that generally homeworkers preferred to work at home because if they

> go to the factory they must pay for child minding. They must pay for washing to be done and must buy tinned meats. If they stay at home they can do their own housework and their own shopping; and can better care for children. If work is slack there is housework and mending and other domestic chores to be done.[115]

In her interviews with people raised in Lancaster, Barrow, and Preston during the Edwardian period, Elizabeth Roberts found that women preferred wage-earning work in the home to outside work "because it meant less disruption to home routines." Mothers of her respondents had taken in washing, done dressmaking and alterations, and acted as small-scale traders. Some had sold foods and drink from their parlors, and others had been child minders for mothers who worked full-time.[116]

One reason that homeworkers and those who have studied them

perceived homework as a more salutary alternative than working outside the household was that they believed homeworkers had some control over the pace and timing of their employment.[117] Compared with working in a factory or warehouse under the rigid time schedules of centralized manufacturing regimes, being at home made wage-earning compatible with postpartum recuperation, infant feeding, and infant care. However, poverty, combined with the pitifully low piece rates most homeworkers were paid, would in fact have forced the new mother to sacrifice her health and the care of her newborn in order to turn out a sufficient quantity of manufactured products. Homework was more flexible than factory or workshop employment, especially when the need for additional income was not extreme. Then women could reduce the amount of time they spent in manufacturing or refuse to do it altogether. When their economic circumstances became less favorable, they could pick it up again. As Elizabeth Roberts has written about working-class mothers in the Edwardian period:

> It is clear that these women held an idea of an ideal family income, usually one which would adequately clothe, feed and house the family, and leave a small surplus for entertainment, or savings. Once the ideal level was reached, it was more important to have less work than to have more money. Material expectations were very low compared to those of the present day.[118]

Employment in factory, warehouse, and workshop depended on the availability of jobs and was less tolerant of workers who might need wages one month but not the next. Combining wage earning and infant care was marginally more feasible with homework, but, as I have suggested earlier, it was only the lesser of the two evils. With child care defined as solely the responsibility of the mother, combining wage earning and social reproduction was, and continues to be, difficult.

Although the concept of public or civic provision for child care was probably beyond the comprehension of the vast majority in nineteenth-century Britain, it would be misleading to say that there were no such initiatives in the last half of the century. A few paternalist employers who relied on married women as workers provided child-care facilities within the factory gates. The Courtalds in Halstead, Essex, provided such facilities, but they closed for lack of use; apparently, the women who were employed at the mill did not trust them, or perhaps they found them less satisfactory than their own familial or neighborhood arrangements.[119] Less is known about the fate of an employer-initiated nursery begun by Richard Stanway of Enderley Mills at Newcastle under Lyme. In 1883 he equipped his works with a nursery consisting of a playroom and a cot-room, where the cribs were gently rocked by steam machinery.[120] The Enderley Mills nursery charged women the nominal fee of 1s. per child per week.[121] Most manufacturers, however, were not involved in the establishment of the few infant and child care facilities that were established in the factory towns.

A few communities in England experimented with formally organized nurseries. Some nurseries were subsidized by charity, although working women were expected to pay fees. The first day nursery established in England, early in 1850, located in the St. Marylebone district of London, charged 3d. per child.[122] Another day nursery begun in 1850 in Halstead, Essex, to care for infants and children of mothers employed in the silk mill closed in less than three years because of finances.[123] The Anscoats nursery in Manchester, also begun in 1850, charged women 2s. 6d. per week for each infant and 3s. per week for children requiring solid food. Not a charitable institution, it demanded payment in advance.[124] It, too, eventually failed, presumably for lack of paying customers. By the turn of the century, there were approximately seventy-five such nurseries in England, accommodating on average between twenty and thirty children.[125]

These nurseries were means tested and women who wished to place their children in them were screened, not just about their finances, but for their marital status, their husband's employment status, and their personal reputation. For example, the unsuccessful Anscoats nursery in Manchester accepted only legitimate children. A more successful charitable institution in Manchester, the Charles Street nursery, was run primarily for the children of widows and widowers: "Infants of married women were only accepted where it could be proved that it was financially imperative that the mother should be employed at the mill rather than tend her own baby."[126] Twenty-seven of the fifty-five London nurseries in existence in the early years of the twentieth century did not admit illegitimate children.[127]

Turn-of-the-century public health statistician George Newman estimated that many of the nurseries operated at 50 to 90 percent of capacity.[128] Twenty-five years earlier, the Charles Street nursery in Manchester had averaged fifteen children and often cared for as few as ten children, but could have taken twenty children each day. Margaret Hewitt has suggested that these nurseries were underutilized because of the dislike of "charity" in any form among the poor.[129] The women probably also resented the intrusive screening of their personal lives demanded by most of the nurseries.

In spite of philanthropists' efforts to provide safe and sanitary infant and day care for the children of working mothers, responsibility for children remained the mother's obligation.[130] Charitable provisions for day care reached only a small proportion of women who needed them: they were intended to save infant lives in the very poorest families. The emphasis placed on facilities only for the most needy and deserving reinforced the idea that mothers should be the principal caretakers of their young and that only those who were in dire need, and were caring for children conceived in the sanctity of marriage, would be assisted in preserving the health and safety of their offspring.

If the difficulties of combining marriage and motherhood with work outside the home were not sufficient to deter women, as I indicated in Chapter 2, employers in most areas of the country (but not in the cotton districts, which depended heavily on women's labor in factories) tended to relieve women of their jobs when they married, or at least when they had children.[131] This was the policy among many Nottinghamshire employers early in the twentieth century. When Mrs. R. from Arnold was asked whether her mother had worked after marriage, she said, "I don't think so because they weren't allowed to in those days. No. Mother went—I know we were bad off, I'll tell you that—and she went back to get a job, you know, to help out a little bit but they wouldn't have her because we were small—small."[132] Such evidence suggests the possibility that the marriage bar and homework were cut from the same cloth.[133]

Although women do have special needs in pregnancy, childbirth, and nursing, nothing about these biological processes per se would cause women to work at low-paying jobs in general or homework in particular. Instead, the cultural meanings and social practices associated with these biological processes shaped the conditions under which women bore babies and cared for them, and limited the ways they could fulfill their broad responsibilities for their families. In nineteenth-century Britain, nuclear family household formation, the insistence that matters of social reproduction were private concerns, and the ideology that motherhood defined femininity and excluded breadwinning, combined to place working-class women in a contradictory situation that made homework, not a salutary alternative to waged work outside their homes, but their only option.

Homework was not the automatic choice of women who needed to combine paid labor with raising families. In the United States, many more black women than white women who were married and had children worked outside their homes. In addition, they were less likely than white women to do industrial homework.[134] Instead, black women worked in the white women's homes as domestic servants. Simultaneously they struggled to juggle this work with pregnancy, childbirth, nursing, child care, and their own housework.[135] The comparison between poor black and poor white women suggests that something other than biology accounted for women's choice of homework as a strategy for making ends meet. In the United States, racial discrimination often excluded black women from homework, forcing them to work as domestics.[136] In England women became homeworkers because of the construction of motherhood as expressed in public policies and manufacturers' strategies. With the exception of people in some textile manufacturing districts, many women in the working class accepted the idea that being a parent was a mother's responsibility.

As I will argue in Chapter 6, the working-class version of the ideology of domesticity was bound up with the aspiration toward "respectability." If a wife worked in a factory, it reflected badly on her husband's status as provider. As the nineteenth century drew to a close, women were increasingly associated with the home and with domesticity, which could include a variety of strategies to feed a family including earning money, but excluded working away from home.

Middle-class observers and trade-union officials frequently commented that work in factories and workshops reflected badly on women's abilities as housewives and mothers. In the early campaigns against homework and sweated labor, reformers often cited the presumed ill effects such work had on homes.[137] Sir Charles Dilke, prominent in the campaign to regulate and restrict homework in order to curb the abuses of sweating, commented on the special nature of home industries: "The home life of the home worker is often nothing. The home becomes the grinding shop. Factory slavery finds a refuge even in a hard home. 'Home' slavery has none."[138] For Dilke, as for the majority in Victorian Britain, home and factory were oppositional constructs. Brought up by mothers who held their families together by their struggles for a livelihood, and associating those struggles with womanhood, it is not surprising that working-class wives and mothers embraced the promise of ease contained in the ideology of domesticity. In their daily lives, they made ends meet and cared for their families in whatever way they could.

CONCLUSION

This chapter has shown that where women earned wages was less important in their lives than was the necessity for them to combine other aspects of their domestic lives with a variety of makeshift strategies to make ends meet. Manufacturers created industrial homework especially for married women, as a way of cutting labor costs, reducing capital costs, and maintaining flexibility.[139] The women who managed households adopted homework as a response to poverty at particular points in the family life cycle. Living in households that did not bring in sufficient money for the barest necessities, they had to seize what opportunities there were for work. Sources of employment that paid relatively good wages were few and far between, especially outside the cotton-manufacturing towns. Generally women could choose from only a narrow range of occupations, and if there was a large number of women who wanted work, the competition among them depressed their wages; for example, in Nottingham a large surplus of women "crowded" the "female jobs" available in the lace and hosiery industries. Elsewhere, rural isolation and lack of mobility in urban areas limited the jobs women, especially married women, could find.[140] In many areas, as I suggested in Chapter 2, employer policies discriminated against married women, further limiting their opportunities for employment.

The division of labor by gender, and the organization of social reproduction assigning individual women the task of child rearing, were part of a complex web of factors that recruited women to be homeworkers. This complex web included the realities of pregnancy and childbirth in a society that assumed no public responsibility for the health of its populace, a society, moreover, that had long been accustomed to living in nuclear family households. Woven into the fabric of working-class life during the nineteenth and early twentieth centuries was the absolute necessity in the majority of families, at one time or another in the family life cycle, for at least two wage earners.

Gender was central in structuring the poverty-reproduction-homework knot. Homework, as a form of women's work, was generated by a particular conjunction of familial, political, cultural, and economic relations. Employers created opportunities for homework when there were large numbers of married women who needed employment. Its profitability and flexibility for manufacturers depended on the social contradiction between wage earning and mothering. Economic necessity was fed by competition and exploitation. From the perspective of the homeworking women, homework was their only way to put food in the mouths of their families.

5

"Mary Had a Little Loom"

Gender Segregation, Struggles over the Labor Process, and Class Antagonism in the English Carpet Industry

Mary had a little loom and unto it did go.
And every Saturday afternoon you should have seen the show.
With veil, kid gloves and gaiters too, she goes out on the mash.
She fairly knocks the men out now because she gets the cash.

Arthur Smith, *Carpet Weaving and Trade Union
Activity, Kidderminster and District*

This poem by an unemployed male carpet weaver in Kidderminster was written in the 1890s, during a dispute between the all-male carpet weavers' union and the manufacturers of Royal Axminsters. The men were objecting to the long-standing practice of employing women to weave Royal Axminsters. Numerous poems, letters to the editor of the local newspaper, journalistic commentaries and accounts, and a variety of street demonstrations and public speeches produced a discourse about gender and class during the last quarter of the nineteenth century in England's major carpet-manufacturing center. Through such symbolic expressions, workers, employers, and journalists communicated with one another about the meanings of work and gender, and people construed their experiences of industrial strife.[1]

From 1874 until nearly the end of the century, major industrial disputes erupted in Kidderminster when various manufacturers attempted to change the labor process in carpet weaving by introducing new technology, altering machines already in use, or manufacturing a new product, and then hiring women rather than men to do the work. The cultural productions of these controversies reveal that people understood them as deriving from both class and gender antagonism. This chapter provides a detailed view of the changes in the labor process in one industry—changes and struggles, however, that were not unique to the people of Kidderminster. Similar ones occurred in other regions and industries—for example, in the hosiery industry in Nottingham and Leicester, in tailoring in London, in metalworking in Birmingham, and in printing in London and Edinburgh.[2]

WOMEN'S LOW WAGES: A THREAT TO MEN'S EMPLOYMENT

In Chapter 2 I suggested that most employers took for granted that it was men who should be hired to do skilled work. The idea of employing women for such jobs probably would not have occurred to them unless they were faced with significant pressure to lower their costs, or they were unable to hire men or to hire them at the price they were willing and able to pay. Whatever women's supposed "natural" talents, such as "nimble fingers," it was their identity as cheap workers that brought them to mind as an appropriate source of labor.

Because women were identified as a low-waged labor force, employers used them, not only to lower costs, but in battles with skilled male workers over issues of control.[3] Some employers believed women to be more docile and less likely to make trouble than men. Sidney Webb, the contemporary student and champion of the trade union movement, learned in a confidential letter from a foreman in a cigar factory: "The late employer used to say he preferred women to men workers because they were contented with female wages, worked more steadily and struck less."[4] However, employers could not take women's passivity for granted. For example, in Kidderminster, nonunionized women carpet and rug weavers went out on strike against Smith and Sons in 1894.[5] Women workers sometimes proved less willing than men to give in to employer pressure. In a major strike at Leeds in 1872, women flax workers were the backbone of the union and remained on the picket line while the men, primarily overlookers, were bought off by employers and broke the strike.[6]

When employers hired women to do work that men had been doing, either through direct substitution or by adopting new machinery to be worked by women, the trade was feminized if the women were paid less than men. As Clementina Black noted in a letter to Sidney Webb, where women and men do the same work, "there are generally speaking two scales; one lower for the women, another the men's scale.

Gradually the men either diminish in numbers or their scale comes down to meet the women's."[7] As a consequence, economic competition between women and men was a significant feature of industrial transformation throughout the nineteenth century. In the 1820s and 1830s male tailors in London struck in opposition to employers who introduced women into the trade.[8] In the hosiery industry in Nottingham and Leicester, male operatives repeatedly went on strike over attempts by employers to substitute female labor. In 1872, employers in the Derby silk industry, in an attempt to break the newly formed men's union, introduced women into the trade. The ensuing strike lasted twenty weeks and ended with the defeat of the men and the collapse of their union. The majority of the male silk throwsters found themselves seeking work as general laborers.[9] In the carpet-weaving industry in Elderslie, Scotland, new looms, lighter and faster than the old, were introduced in the 1870s. The men struck, objecting to the quicker speed of the looms and the lower rates the employers were paying. Women were hired, and eventually the strike was broken. After that time, women predominated as carpet weavers in Elderslie.[10]

Although a good many of these disputes were in the textile trades, competition between women and men was not limited to those industries. Employers in some quintessentially male trades attempted to hire women. The "woman question" in printing created open and bitter conflict between women and men compositors in both London and Edinburgh.[11] The brass-manufacturing firm of Smith and Chamberlain attempted to introduce women into their brass works to do what was traditionally thought to be men's work.[12] The male workers put up strong opposition, and workers from every brass works in Birmingham struck. In a letter to the *Daily Post,* the union argued that the men "did not ask the firm to discharge women who were employed in legitimate occupations. We oppose and many employers also oppose, the employment of women to turn at the lathe and file at the vice."[13] Although Arthur Chamberlain was strongly opposed to any barriers to women's employment, the men in his firm *succeeded* in barring the employment of women. Also in Birmingham, women were hired to do power polishing of metal at a gas and electric fittings firm, but a strike by the men led to the work remaining masculinized except in nonunion shops.[14] M. J. Davis, secretary of the National Society of Amalgamated Brassworkers, remarked that women were not sought by these manufacturers because they were women, but only because they worked for lower wages than men. He said that if "work was given to women fitted to their special gifts it would remove the present degradation of female labor. But this I fear can never be done because the main object of employing women is to bring down the wages of men."[15]

In order to cope with the threat of being replaced by women, skilled male workers in numerous industries struggled to exclude women and to maintain strict lines of demarcation between men's and women's work. These strategies, whether they succeeded or failed, resulted in occupational segregation. Generally, it was only if women and men were employed to do the same work *at the same rate of pay* that jobs were sexually integrated and could remain sexually integrated. As Clementina Black pointed out to Sidney Webb, instances of women and men doing identical work were rare.[16] The major exception was cotton textile weaving (see Chapter 7, below). Nineteenth-century male trade unionists responded with resistance, exclusion, and consciously constructed gender segregation of work to initiatives by employers to hire women.[17] Sometimes, as in the case of the Derby silk throwsters, the employers won and the trade became feminized. In other instances, as in the brass works in Birmingham in the late 1870s and early 1880s, the workmen carried the victory. Occasionally the men won the battle for the moment, only to lose on another front a few years later. If the men won, their victory often inspired new employer initiatives to cut costs.

The complex of conditions that favored one outcome over another included union strength, alternative sources of income for workers, the extent of competition among employers, and the economic state of the industry at the time. These dynamics were at work in Kidderminster, the main center of carpet making in Britain. In this West Midlands town of approximately 20,000 inhabitants, competition for jobs between women and men was the focus of nearly all of the major labor disputes from the 1870s to the turn of the century.

TECHNOLOGY AND COMPETITION

Competition among firms in the carpet industry formed the backdrop to the continuing struggles between workers and employers over the terms and conditions of employment. Employers battled one another in the search for increasingly productive technology and for methods of lowering their labor costs.

Kidderminster was the center of the trade, but carpets were also manufactured by large concerns in Rochdale, Lancashire, by John Bright's mills and in Halifax, Yorkshire, especially by the Crossleys at the Dean Clough Mills. Competition between and among the Kidderminster manufacturers and carpet firms in the north was pronounced at least from the 1840s and led to a virtual war for technological superiority among firms in the different locales. They competed for patents on steam-powered machinery to produce both the traditional Brussels carpets and tapestry carpets. In the 1850s the Crossleys purchased exclusive British rights to the only successful steam-powered loom, the Brussels power loom invented by Bigelow in America. This purchase gave the Crossleys a monopoly on the patents for weaving both Brussels and tapestry carpets using steam-powered machinery. When John Bright began producing tapestries on a steam-powered loom in 1859, breaking the Crossleys' monopoly, Crossleys initiated a celebrated lawsuit against Bright for infringing their patent rights. The suit was not settled until 1864, but was then decided in John Bright's favor. However, the Crossleys were successful in defending their patent rights in other challenges they made from 1858 to 1863, one of which was appealed to the House of Lords.[18] Both Bright and the Crossleys concentrated their production on tapestry carpets while Kidderminster manufacturers specialized in the manufacture of Brussels carpets.

The two types of carpets were manufactured using different technologies. The Brussels loom wove intricate patterns; the tapestry loom involved a simplified weaving process and used less expensive worsted yarn on which the pattern of the carpet had already been printed. Tapestries came in a wider range of colors, used less wool, and were less expensive to purchase than were Brussels carpets. The power loom output greatly exceeded that of the hand loom; moreover, samples of Bigelow's Brussels carpets shown at the Great Exhibition in 1851 were judged by a panel of experts to be "better and more perfectly woven than any hand-loom goods that have come under the notice of the Jury."[19] Within two years, several Kidderminster firms had leased the rights from the Crossleys and were making power-loomed Brussels. Thereafter, power weaving quickly displaced handloom weaving in Kidderminster.

From the 1860s on, manufacturers and their male powerloom weavers in Kidderminster struggled over the issue of the supply of labor for carpet weaving. In 1864 the employers formed an association with the express intention of controlling the labor supply and protecting their interests in relation to those of their workers.[20] Almost immediately the manufacturers' association announced a new scheme for training boy apprentices that would both increase the number of apprentices and have them begin work at a younger age than they had previously. The purpose of the new plan was to increase the number of trained (male) workers. The manufacturers had offered to increase weavers' wages and expected that the workers would not resist what the employers called their ultimatum on the issue of apprentice labor.[21] In response the weavers waged an unsuccessful strike, but formed a trade union which began with nearly five hundred male members, enrolling 97 percent of the Brussels carpet weavers in Kidderminster and nearby Stourport.

Like the lace manufacturers described in Chapter 2, Kidderminster Brussels manufacturers reduced their labor costs and countered the control the male Brussels weavers had over the labor process by hiring boys and young men to work as weavers' assistants. The carpet weavers' assistants, called creelers, were hired and paid by the manufacturer. Attempts by individual firms to have apprentices work looms, and by the employers' association to increase the number of apprentices and lower the age at which they would be permitted to work looms, was a continuing problem faced by the union for the remainder of the century. Until the 1870s, however, no Kidderminster manufacturers hired women to weave carpets.

In the 1860s Bright's became the first of the firms to hire women to weave carpets. They were successful, in part because in Lancashire, where Bright's mills were located, women and men worked side by side at cotton powerloom weaving, earning equal piece rates for the same work. The Crossleys followed Bright's lead and hired women to run certain carpet looms. Both firms paid women and men the same wages for the same work.[22] However, they paid lower wages than the manufacturers in Kidderminster and provided much of the competitive stimulus for the cost-cutting strategies of the Kidderminster firms.

INDUSTRIAL DISPUTES AND
WOMEN'S WORK

The job of working Brussels looms was gendered male from the start, and it remained "men's work" in Kidderminster because manufacturers could afford to pay relatively high wages to make these high-priced carpets, and they had a supply of low-waged labor in lads who were creelers.[23] Tapestry manufacture presented different problems. Tapestries appealed to customers with lower incomes; they were therefore sold in a highly competitive product market and were more affected by trade recessions than were Brussels carpets. In the 1850s one of the firms making tapestries in Kidderminster went bankrupt. John Brinton's firm, which had produced both tapestries and Brussels, ceased making tapestry carpet by the middle of 1860. Only one Kidderminster manufacturer, William Green, made tapestries throughout the 1860s. In the 1870s, other firms began producing the carpets once again.

One of the first major labor disputes in Kidderminster occurred in 1874, when John Brinton attempted to reintroduce tapestry making into his firm. By hiring women to weave tapestries, Brinton hoped to compete successfully with the northern manufacturers who hired women to weave tapestries. He purchased the "best form of loom for women that could be found."[24] When Brinton put women to work on the new looms, however, all the Brussels weavers in Kidderminster went on strike. The strike lasted only one week and resulted in victory for the union. Although Brinton was not attempting to replace men with women but merely to add women to his weaving work force to make a new type of carpet, his actions produced a concerted and militant response by the union to exclude women from weaving any type of carpet in Kidderminster.

In 1861 Bright's Lancashire firm had introduced new machinery that produced three pieces of carpet in the same time that it had taken to make two and had reduced piece rates paid to male carpet weavers. When the men resisted the reduction and the work speed-up, young women and men were brought in to work the machines, and the strike was broken.[25] During the strike, carpet weavers from Crossleys' in Halifax came to protest with the Rochdale workers, and a number of men were charged in court with intimidating the factory hands.[26] The men were rehired to work these tapestry machines, but at the reduced rate. A few years later Bright's, wishing to compete more successfully than they had been with the giant Crossley firm, hired women to operate a new tapestry loom which they claimed was designed especially for women operatives. The Crossleys then introduced a similar loom and hired women. Now John Brinton in Kidderminster, who also happened to be Francis Crossley's father-in-law, wished to manufacture tapestries and enter the competition (particularly against Bright's firm).

The Kidderminster unionists sent representatives to the north and discovered that Brinton had not introduced the same looms that were being worked by women in Rochdale and Halifax, but had purchased looms that elsewhere were known as "men's machines." There was a difference between the "women's tapestry looms" and the "men's tapestry looms." If the same kind of material was used in both types of looms, the men's looms would turn out a greater number of yards per hour than women's looms. This meant that in the other places in England where women and men both made the tapestry carpets, but on different machines, the cost of women's labor to the manufacturer was lower, but men were more productive. John Brinton, however, wished to pay women "women's wages" to work the more productive "men's machines" in Kidderminster.[27]

In the negotiations the union offered not to object to the employment of women if Brinton would pay them what male tapestry workers in the Kidderminster district were paid.[28] Although this may have been a serious proposal on the part of the union, there is evidence that they knew Brinton would never agree to it. For example, at one of the strike meetings a worker said he did "not think if Mr. Brinton was compelled to pay the females the same price as other tapestry weavers were paid by other manufacturers, that he would long continue to employ females."[29] If Brinton had set wages of female tapestry weavers equal to those of male tapestry weavers, he would have been paying more for women to work this particular loom in Kidderminster than Bright was paying for men to work it in Rochdale. As might have been expected, then, Brinton absolutely refused to employ women at the same rates as men, although he did not advance the argument of competition as his rationale; instead he argued, like other textile manufacturers, that when women were employed, men had to "tune" the looms and perform other tasks that male weavers did for themselves.[30] Therefore, he believed he had to hire more expensive tuners when he employed women than when men were the weavers.

A main contention of the weavers' association was that there were not enough well-paid jobs for the number of men residing in Kidderminster, and there were men without jobs who needed work. In part, this was due to the apprenticeship system insisted upon by the masters, which trained more boys to be weavers than were needed by the manufacturers. As one of the men wrote, "it was a crying evil to see women getting into the trade. The weavers were not situated like some other men, for they had no other occupation to turn to. They were bound to the loom without any alternative."[31] Apparently, when there was insufficient work for Brussels weavers, the men would work on tapestry looms. The weavers' association claimed that out of 160 men weaving tapestries in Kidderminster, 150 of them were Brussels weavers by training.[32] Thus they saw one of their principal alternative sources of employment being taken from them. At a meeting between Brinton and his workmen, one of the workers asked the employer "if it would not be more humane, not to employ women when men were walking the streets."[33] The unionists seemed to fear that they would end by being permanently unemployed: once women were employed in the trade by Brinton, they would be hired by other manufacturers, and the trend would continue until carpet weaving became solely women's work.

The discovery by the unionists that Brinton's attempts to undercut his competition would affect his fellow manufacturers in Kidderminster lost him the support of the employers' association—not that all of the employers had ever supported Brinton's actions. Employer Hughes was interviewed by a deputation of his workpeople about the impending strike. He told the workmen he would not support Brinton; he was not a member of the employers' association and would have nothing to do with it or with the present struggle.[34] Other employers in the town also opposed hiring women.[35] In the end, rather than employ men on his tapestry looms or pay men's wages to the women, Brinton moved the looms to Leeds, where he employed women to produce tapestry carpets.

John Brinton was not a man to be so easily defeated, however. In November 1878 Brinton moved his tapestry looms back to Kidderminster. He had these Moxon looms adjusted so that they would run faster and produce substantially more yardage per hour than the other type of tapestry loom, the Smith loom, that men worked in Kidderminster, and he paid only the lower rates offered men in the north. The union refused to accept Brinton's proposed wage reduction, resolving to strike unless Brinton agreed to pay the same rates for weaving on the "speeded" looms as for work on Smith looms. The unionists had learned that the other tapestry manufacturers in town planned to refuse to pay their men working Smith looms more than Brinton was paying for weaving tapestries on the Moxon loom.[36] They resolved that "men weaving on Moxon Looms be treated in every respect as free Union Men" and that the union would not sanction the principle of adjusting the price of weaving according to the speed of the loom.[37] Rather than sustain a strike, the unionists and Brinton agreed to submit the dispute to arbitration.

The arbitration took place at the end of April 1879 and was decided primarily in favor of Brinton. He was allowed to pay the low wages of the north, but he was required to provide the weavers with extra tuners and other assistants not formerly provided in Kidderminster. Although in the 1874 strike Brinton had claimed he could not pay men's wages to women because the women required more tuners, now he agreed to provide tuners and was also willing to pay Kidderminster men more in 1879 than he had paid the women in 1874, because the looms had been made to run faster.[38]

The disputes over the making of tapestries in Kidderminster illustrate the ongoing struggle between workers and manufacturers. They show the competitive pressures on manufacturers to lower production costs by one means or another and also suggest that many employers could not succeed in these maneuvers without the support of other employers. The very competition that caused employers to cut labor costs could weaken their position in disputes with unions.[39] On the union side, these events show the struggle to retain wage levels and jobs in the face of employer cost-cutting strategies. The disputes at Brinton's illustrate historian Richard Price's claim that labor history is the result of the continual search by both labor and capital for the better bargain in their contests.[40] They demonstrate how gender, and the links among gender, skill, and technology discussed in Chapter 2, figured into transformations of work and workplace struggles. Capitalist John Brinton's search for a "better bargain" in tapestry production led him to hire women rather than men because he could pay them lower rates. In addition, he put them to work on "men's machines," which were more productive than "women's" tapestry looms. When that strategy proved too contentious, to lower his unit costs he altered the technology of the "men's" tapestry looms to make them run even faster. The outcome in Kidderminster, at least for the moment, was the continuation of an all-male carpet work force. However, the men had to sustain a reduction in their piece rates as John Brinton increased his yield from his capital and from his work force and managed to lower his production costs without disturbing the gender division of labor.

Events in tapestry making in 1881 showed that the downward trend in wages would continue in Kidderminster. Crossleys' in Halifax had lowered their rates for working a tapestry loom called the Dandy loom, and Henry Dixon's firm introduced the Dandy at Kidderminster. Dixon paid *male* tapestry weavers the same rates being paid by Crossleys to *women* in Halifax. The Moxon loom weavers were then under pressure to work at the same rate as Dandy loom weavers. The unionists protested, but in the end they agreed to the manufacturers' terms for tapestry weaving.[41]

Only two years later, Henry Dixon, who had tried to mediate the 1874 dispute and who had told the unionists he would never hire women, became embroiled in the most rancorous labor dispute witnessed in nineteenth-century Kidderminster. The year 1883 was not a good one for the carpet industry. Although there was a brisk demand for Brussels toward the end of the year, the tapestry trade was down.[42] In late fall Henry Dixon altered a few of his tapestry looms to make a new fabric, Medici plush, a velvet material to be used for draperies. He then hired women to do the work. When the male weavers protested to Dixon, Dixon replied that he would continue to employ women because "it was not man's work, it was not a carpet that was made on the loom and it was not a Smith loom."[43] Dixon probably thought that he would be able to introduce the women without trouble from the union if he could convince the men that their own looms were not in jeopardy, and that, technically, the women were not weaving carpets. However, the men were not to be so easily convinced that redundancy would not follow if women were allowed to use tapestry looms in Kidderminster. Two deputations from the weavers' association went to see Henry Dixon, in January and in early February, but they failed to convince Dixon to remove the women weaving in his mill. Near the end of February, therefore, Dixon's male weavers went on strike.

The issue of women weaving had been a sore point with the Kidderminster unionists ever since the dispute with Brinton's in 1874. During the strike against Henry Dixon, union meetings on the issue of female labor and on the negotiations with the manufacturers drew huge crowds.[44] One meeting called in early March on only three or four hours' notice was reported by the press to be the largest and most unanimous meeting held for many years; hundreds of people stood for the full three hours.[45] Another meeting in mid-March, held at the Town Hall, was reported to be the largest ever held there; so that everyone could be seated, the adjoining Corn Exchange was opened.[46]

The weavers organized processions and demonstrations to underline their concerns. Weavers who remained at work were harassed; strikers were accused of physical violence; and some strikers were arrested. The unionists became increasingly outraged when Dixon hired men from neighboring communities to replace the striking workers. The local newspaper, the *Kidderminster Shuttle,* reported that the crowds were so unruly that "gentlemen who had prominent positions in the town and were among the largest ratepayers had not been able to pass to and from their works."[47] By the second week of April the demonstrations had reached such a height that the magistrate and members of the Watch Committee agreed to call for assistance from the Birmingham police. The appearance of a number of policemen from Birmingham further infuriated the crowds, who pelted them with stones and attempted to storm Dixon's mill. Henry Dixon walked from his works to the Town Hall heavily guarded by police, and "when he entered a cab and drove away the people indulged in a good deal of groaning."[48] The mayor's son was reportedly hit on the head with a stone, and crowds pelted the mill manager's house with stones, breaking windows and damaging the interior. A second detachment of Birmingham police was sent for, and finally the magistrate telegraphed for the Third Dragoon Guards, who arrived in Kidderminster late on 9 April 1884. The *Shuttle* reported: "The presence of these smart looking men in their highly polished brass helmets and somewhat showy regimentals created a good deal of commotion in the town."[49] The union protested that they had not been consulted about the situation; if they had been, they could have reassured everyone that order would be maintained.[50] A union meeting attended by more than fourteen hundred men passed a "vote of indignation" on the Watch Committee and the magistrate, who had sent for the police and soldiers "to interfere with the rights and liberties of the people."[51]

Not only were the unionists adamant on the issue of female labor, but they were further angered by the report that Dixon was also employing boys to work on his looms during the men's dinner break and that he kept the boys weaving until eight o'clock in the evening. At the meeting at which a strike was called there was a great deal of discussion about boys working "men's looms," and especially about working them at night.[52] Since its beginnings the union had objected to the practice of having creelers work looms at any time. In addition, the union had alleged that Dixon was intimidating the weavers in his employ who had become active in union affairs and at meetings.[53] A weaver who had been fired "for insufficient work" wrote to the *Kidderminster Shuttle* that there had been no serious complaints about his work "until the weavers elected me to serve them on the shop committee."[54]

Dixon had not only become a member of the employers' association, but he also served as its secretary and could count on the support of its members. Indeed, the Kidderminster manufacturers might have welcomed a general shutdown; at the time of the dispute some of the manufacturers had proposed that they operate on short time, since many of them had excess stock.[55] With or without support, Dixon was determined to hold to his position. When he learned that a strike vote had been called, he told his assembled workmen:

> We maintain our right as Englishmen that of perfect freedom in doing what we like with our own. This may be a painful struggle, but you may rest assured we shall do everything in our power to keep our looms fully employed. We shall do everything in our power to increase the prosperity of our firm.[56]

Dixon had decided to introduce this new product because the tapestry trade was doing poorly. He had begun it by altering four of his tapestry looms to make the drapery material, intending to use them either temporarily or in addition to new looms made specifically to weave the new material. The unionists saw it differently. They were angered by the employment of women when men needed work. As one unionist put it, they wanted

> to prevent Messrs. Dixon employing females on the looms when there was plenty of male labor walking about ready and anxious to work. There was not only in Kidderminster, but throughout the country, a surplus of male labor, and they should only be doing their duty in doing all they could in getting men employed on new fabrics.[57]

The carpet weavers said that the dispute was over "whether to sanction females making that fabric on any loom."[58] They were unimpressed by Dixon's insistence that the material being made was for draperies instead of carpets, which in Kidderminster were woven only by men.

Throughout the strike the unionists seemed anxious to find some way to end the dispute. Early on, the union offered to have men work on the altered looms at women's wages. The unionists took Dixon's refusal to show that he intended to displace men. Early in April the union was prepared to offer what the *Kidderminster Shuttle* referred to as "sweeping concessions," but the manufacturers refused to meet with the union representatives.[59] On hearing that the manufacturers would not receive the deputation, the union withdrew its proposals, tempers flared, and some of the unionists took to the streets; it was then that the Birmingham policemen and the Dragoons were called in.[60]

Following the appearance of the troops in Kidderminster, John Brinton, now a member of Parliament for Kidderminster, mediated an end to the dispute because he believed "the honour of the constituency was at stake" in that journalists had portrayed mob scenes at Kidderminster; "people were afraid to go into the city."[61] In the accord Dixon agreed to hire young men to work the four altered tapestry machines. When he purchased new machines designed to make plush, he would employ four women to work them. After that he would hire men and women in equal numbers on future plush machines. The men and women would be paid the same wages.

Although the strike was over, a good deal of bitterness remained. The strike had cost the union more than £2,000, and the union had to pay unemployment benefits to the men who did not find employment immediately after it. Although Dixon rehired some of the striking men, the majority of the strikers did remain unemployed. The union distributed a list of strikebreakers and prohibited members from associating with anyone on the list.[62] According to letters to the *Kidderminster Shuttle* written nearly a dozen years after the dispute, the strike had ruined Dixon, and the plush looms were sent to America.[63] A man was reported to have been refused employment in 1920 for the part he had played in the "Dixon riots" of 1884.[64]

It had been an inopportune time for a strike. Many employers were overstocked and might have benefited if a general strike had been called, which would have stopped the production of carpets. The tapestry trade was in decline, and the workers employed on the tapestry looms were demoralized.[65] Many weavers and young men who had trained as creelers were without employment. The union had therefore been forced to accept the principle of women and men doing the same work. The compromise agreement continued to segregate women's and men's labor on carpet looms, even those that had been altered to produce plush, but it permitted women to work in equal numbers with men on the new looms designed specifically to make plush. For the men, half a loaf was apparently better than no loaf at all, even if it meant that young men would be doing a task thought of as women's work and would be paid a woman's wage for doing it. However, the unionists managed to preserve what they (re)defined as men's work (weaving on "men's looms") for males, and they also staked a partial claim to what the employer had defined as women's work (making plush) because of the employment situation for men in Kidderminster. By doing this, they sexually integrated the making of plush for draperies on the new looms and retained for men the exclusive use of tapestry carpet looms. The employer, for his part, was able to have the work done at women's wages. In addition, the men could not in the future demand higher wages than the women for making plush, because then only women would be hired.

One last skirmish over gender occurred in the nineteenth century between the unionists and manufacturers. At the time of the Dixon dispute, women were working Royal Axminster carpet looms in a nonunion shop in Kidderminster. The Royal Axminster spool loom was introduced by the firm of Tomkinson and Adams in 1878. The carpet woven on these looms was similar to the costly Wilton carpet but used less yarn than Wiltons and was therefore lower-priced. Royal Axminster manufacture was important for capitalists who wished to profit from the expanding trade at the lower end of the market. At the time Tomkinson and Adams introduced them in Kidderminster, the Royal Axminster looms were being worked in America by women. As Tomkinson told the men during their meetings about women's employment in 1895, "It never entered our heads at the time to employ men because women were employed in America upon it—one able to manage two looms."[66] Women had been employed at Tomkinson and Adams from the time the firm began its operations in 1870, on "the old rug setting loom": Tomkinson apparently found it difficult to find men who would weave on rug looms at the price he was willing to pay.[67] The Royal Axminster was a light power loom which was more easily worked and was more productive than the rug loom, and it produced a floor covering with more potential for sales than the rug loom; so the firm put women to work on it instead of on the heavier handloom.

Tomkinson and Adams saw the change as replacing heavy women's labor by light women's labor. But the crucial change for the male unionists, the one that led them to protest fourteen years after the introduction of the looms, was that the Royal Axminster carpet, made by women, had displaced the Wilton carpet, made by men, in the marketplace.[68] For the working-class men of Kidderminster, women were replacing men in the making of carpets. It is likely that the unionists had not protested the introduction of women workers on the Royal Axminster spool looms in 1878 because Tomkinson and Adams was a nonunion shop and because people at that time saw Tomkinson as replacing one woman's loom with another. The men simply did not foresee the rapid expansion in the Axminster trade that would come in the next fifteen years and what it would mean for their own employment.

The issue of women working the Axminster looms first came up at union meetings in the spring of 1891 and then again in early summer of that year.[69] In June, men from one of the firms working the Royal Axminster looms had approached the union committee concerning the employment of women; they indicated their willingness to work for the same wages the women were being paid.[70] Nothing further was done concerning the issue until 1894. During the intervening years, the union was faced with unemployment and falling wage levels due to a rapidly declining tapestry trade and may not have felt the time was right to approach the manufacturers employing women to weave the Royal Axminsters.[71]

By the spring of 1894, unemployment among the union men had increased even more and the question of women's employment on the Axminster looms came up again.[72] A deputation from the union met with Tomkinson, who was not only a major manufacturer of Axminsters but also mayor of Kidderminster. According to a union spokesman, Tomkinson listened to their arguments and said that he would consult with his partner about the matter. However, he said, he believed the looms to be so "fragile that the men would knock them to pieces."[73] In a subsequent letter to the union, Tomkinson wrote that he had nothing more to say about the matter; the loom was a "woman's loom."[74] The once militant and forceful union seemed to be subdued and placating in its posture. There was a general trade depression, and by year's end the only branch of the Kidderminster carpet industry that seemed to be thriving was Royal Axminster manufacturing.[75]

Finally, in early February the unionists again discussed the problem of the employment of women on the Axminster looms and what could be done to convince employers to hire men instead of women. Many unionists believed that it would not be long before the Axminster trade would be the staple trade of Kidderminster.[76] One unionist said he had learned that men worked these looms in Glasgow at night. The men decided to approach Mayor Tomkinson again to ask his help in convening a meeting between all the Axminster manufacturers of Kidderminster and union representatives.

A conference in early March was attended by members of the union and the heads of six Axminster firms. To counter Tomkinson's assertion that women's looms were too fragile for men to work, they reported that men were working them at night in Scotland. Also, they argued that men turned out more and better work than women. As one of the weavers put it, it was only "natural for men were better able to manage machinery, whether it was heavy or light, while men did not require as much assistance."[77]

The mayor argued that women had been working these looms for fifteen years in England, and he had never heard it said that the work was unsuitable for women: "In fact an authority told his firm that theirs was not only a model factory, but that the employment was a model employment for women."[78] The employers argued that if the work was suitable for women, it could not also be appropriate for men. The union, for their part, was trying to get the employers to see that the male unemployment level was so high that the men would be willing to do women's work at women's wages.

The unionists raised the issue of the employment of married women. The mayor replied that he was opposed to the employment of married women and that his firm did not hire them except in unusual circumstances. The other employers present also said they tried to discourage married women from working. The unionists then asked the employers if they would take on men to work looms vacated by married women. The employers were noncommittal. Exasperated and seemingly defeated, the union representatives asked the manufacturers "for some little hope" to give the young men. The union asked that preference should be given to young men who would work for the same wages that were paid to women until "a fair proportion" of men and women worked the Axminster looms.[79] The employers said they would speak with their foremen but made no promises. That ended the matter, except for the usual outpouring of letters to the *Shuttle* arguing over the union's position.

This final dispute about women's employment was conducted when the union's position was weakened, due to unemployment in the industry. In the 1870s the men had unwittingly allowed women to gain entry into carpet weaving, not realizing that only fifteen years later their work would contribute to the high rates of male unemployment in the district. The employers were in a much stronger position than were the men. Some of the firms, like Tomkinson and Adams, primarily manufactured Axminsters, not Brussels, so the union could not threaten them with a strike. Unlike the 1880s conflict involving the weavers' union and Dixon's, the struggle did not restructure gender segregation. Rather, the process under contention remained sex-typed as female.

This analysis of disputes in the Kidderminster carpet industry has shown how the attempts of male unionists and employers to gain a favorable employment bargain affected gender segregation in the industry. In the 1870s, competition among firms and the relative strength of the union led to union victory in excluding women from tapestry carpet weaving in Kidderminster. However, five years later the men had to accept work on a speeded loom at wages made lower by the employment of women in the north of England. In the 1880s, as the tapestry trade declined, the union was able to retain the principle that only men would use carpet looms in Kidderminster, but, to secure employment in a declining job market, agreed that men could work with women at women's wages on a loom designed for women which made plush for curtains. Finally, in the 1890s, the union was hard-pressed by shrinking employment opportunities relative to the supply of male labor. The men were not able to exclude women from carpet weaving on looms touted as "women's looms," nor were they able to convince employers to make the trade sexually integrated.

Some of the Kidderminster disputes were settled in ways that altered the strategies of the capitalists. However, even if the union diverted the employers' tactics, the overwhelming economic threat to the male carpet weavers still remained. In addition, regardless of which side was victorious, the struggles involving strikes resulted in the restructuring of work. With the exception of limited job integration in the making of plush velvet, job segregation by sex in carpet manufacture was reproduced or reconfirmed through these struggles over the labor process.

For women and men to do the same work in the same location over a long period, it would have been necessary for them to earn the same wages. This was the agreement made between the union and Dixon with regard to the new plush looms. It is likely that some of the same conditions that promoted the employment of both women and men to make plush in Kidderminster also led to cotton weaving being sexually integrated. In that industry, male weavers in effect agreed to do what originally had been defined as "women's work" at women's wages rather than be unemployed. As an official of a cotton weavers' union put it: "The weaving is done equally well by men and women and large numbers of women are employed. Of course, therefore, if men demanded more wages than women, women alone would be employed."[80] Since Chapter 7 deals specifically with gender and the politics of labor in cotton weaving, it is important at this point only to stress the idea that gender segregation broke down in nineteenth-century industries when men had no other choice but to work at what were defined as "women's jobs" at "women's pay." Male unionists would rather work under these conditions than not work at all. The fact that Kidderminster was a one-industry town made its residents totally dependent on the prosperity of the carpet trade for their own livelihood. As particular types of carpets declined in popularity and the carpet trade came upon hard economic times, the town experienced high levels of unemployment. As one of the unionists had said in the 1874 dispute, they were "bound to the loom without any alternative." If they could not find work weaving carpets, they would have to leave Kidderminster. In fact, that was the rationale behind an emigration scheme promulgated by the new carpet weavers' union in the 1860s. It was evident to the men from the early days of the power loom that the alternative to carpet weaving was to seek work in another town or in another country. Indeed, in the 1895 dispute over the Royal Axminster looms the mayor advised the men to have their sons leave Kidderminster and seek employment elsewhere.[81]

THE CULTURAL PRODUCTIONS OF THE
LABOR DISPUTES

These industrial disputes between employers and male workers hinged on two interrelated issues. First, they concerned employers' attempts to lower production costs or to keep labor costs low, in order to deal with competition among manufacturers, and the male unionists' corresponding struggles to retain their wage levels and their employment. Second, they concerned the carpet manufacturers' tactic of hiring women rather than men. The male carpet weavers' union resisted losing their jobs to women or having women enter their trades. My descriptions of the disputes tell what happened, but they do not show how the various disputants interpreted the events. How people act depends on how they construct their experiences. What they do when faced with a threat to their livelihood is shaped by who are seen as enemies and who are seen as allies. In addition, their actions are influenced by what making a livelihood means to them. Scholars have often portrayed trade union demands as being concerned with so-called bread-and-butter issues, by which they mean short-term economic concerns. However, rarely have they explored the meaning of these bread-and-butter issues for the working people in question.

Letters and verse published in the *Kidderminster Shuttle* reveal how their writers understood the battle of economic relations in which they were participants. The writers employed symbolic representations whose meanings enjoyed wide currency and manipulated these cultural forms to produce a discourse about industrial relations in the carpet industry. For example, in the dispute over women working tapestry looms in 1874, the men's hostility to women's employment was evident in a letter published in the *Kidderminster Shuttle* and addressed to a Mr. Heverley, Cemetery-row, Kidderminster:

> mr heverley i dare say you thinks you are doing something Grand by sending your daughters to rob we men and our wifes and children of our dailey Bread But be carfull of What you are doing Because you and them will very liks get your Brains nock out so dont for get for we shant after saturday the first we get hold of will get something for it if we dont catch hold of them at the time we shal after it all quiet.[82]

In this letter the author blamed other working-class men rather than capitalists for causing their economic distress. Using another genre and defining a different enemy, Noah Cooke, a member of the carpet weavers' union who was known locally as the "weaver poet," published the following in the *Kidderminster Shuttle:*

The Lady Weaver

I'm a silly "Lady Weaver," and I'll use my best endeavour
To undermine the wages of the men;
Ay doing what I like I've brought about a strike,
And now I'll vex them with my little pen.
I've a perfect legal right to side with selfish might,
To bring reduction in the carpet trade.
The race for gain is keen, competition between,
And men's enormous wages can't be paid.
I have left a decent job, to do my best to rob
Poor men who wait for labor in the street;
I don't care what they say, I'll have my foolish way,
Our Masters say they'll mind they won't be beat.[83]

Cooke portrayed the conflict between capitalists and male workers as endemic in the industry, as rooted in the competition among manufacturers. He depicted competitive and greedy capitalists trying to enhance profits by lowering men's wages. However, he characterized women as frivolous class traitors who produced the strike by siding with capital against male labor.

In the 1880s Kidderminster experienced one of the most violent labor disputes in its history when Henry Dixon's firm hired women to make plush velvet using altered carpet looms. Noah Cooke wrote the following sardonic verse to interpret the bitter discord which eventually led city officials to call in troops to maintain order:

The Terrible Riots of Kidderminster

What shame that a master can't do as he likes
Without being menaced and harass'd with "strikes";
What's the use having power if 'tis to be curbed
And each good design by the rabble disturbed?
Because he begins making Medici plush,
Those tyrants of weavers bear down with a rush,
Demanding that Dixey shall follow their will,
And turn off the women that weave at their mill![84]

Here the weaver poet portrayed capitalists as a class enemy but offered the exclusion of women from the mills as the solution to the conflict.

The women, whose opportunities to work were limited to those low-paying jobs that the men refused to do, responded to an invitation to meet with the striking men in the dispute in 1874:

> I have the right to seek my labor at any price I like, and when and where I like; and the liberty I claim for myself I would gladly give for others. Then why should those *very big men* have their crowded meetings and throw off such big words from such little stomachs? Why should they meet and revile their betters? It is quite evident that the power loom weavers have no concern for any but self, or they would not bloc up the streets and the Marketplace puffing their dirty short pipes whilst women and girls have to do the hardest and heaviest work in the trade such as rug weaving, which requires both bone and muscle to perform it.[85]

In this letter the female writer depicted male carpet weavers as acting selfishly to reserve for themselves the best work while restricting women to the least desirable jobs. Like the threatening letter that blamed working-class fathers rather than capitalists for the economic plight of male breadwinners, the letter by the female carpet weaver located the source of the economic conflict in "the men"—the working men, not the capitalist men. Note also that the letter writer drew on the classic liberal (and male) discourse of equal rights and the principle of "freedom of contract" to justify her position.[86]

The employers generally reiterated that it was their "right" to decide whom to employ and to judge whether the work should be done by women or men. They argued that the male unionists should have nothing to say about the matter; hiring was the industrialist's decision.[87] Newspaper editorials such as the following from the *Birmingham Mail* supported the employers' claims to rights, although in their attempts to appear neutral they often softened their judgments of the male unionists for resisting:

> It may be accepted as an axiom that an employer has a right to get his work done as cheaply as he can, just as a workman has an equal right to get as much wages as he can. If women will work for less than men, the manufacturer is justified in employing them. . . . If cheap labor means cheap goods, the benefit is shared by the public, and no principle is sounder than that which says the injury of a class is of less concern than the benefit of the community.[88]

The writer went on to question whether the women had acted wisely in underselling men, but stated that the paper would not take a stand against free competition for employment. An editorial in a trade paper, the *Furniture Gazette,* urged the unionists to admit women into their union:

> We can of course sympathize with the men . . . but are not the women who are seeking work, the fatherless girls and the widows with children, and the poor young girls whose parents, from being ill-paid or out of work, are unable to support them, also deserving of our sympathy? . . . Place women on the same ground as men, and they will be in a position to demand equal rights with the men, to claim the same fair wages for the same amount of honest work, which they must do equally well or retire from the field.[89]

The journalist protected the idea of free competition for jobs but hinted that women should restrain themselves from underselling men in order to get jobs and that the men should admit women into their union. In effect, he was arguing for a gender-neutral labor market that would be primarily a male preserve and in which women would know their place and act accordingly.

However, the male unionists would not consider admitting women to their union. In fact, an organizer for the National Union of Working Women was in Kidderminster during the dispute with Brinton's in 1874 but postponed an effort to unionize the women because of anticipated hostility from the male weavers.[90]

CONCLUSION

This chapter has examined several skirmishes in a continuing battle between workers and industrialists over wages and jobs. Competitive pressures pushed employers to adopt the cost-saving strategies of hiring women rather than men and of altering carpet-weaving technology. The all-male carpet weavers' union fought a losing battle to preserve their jobs and wages. In the process, occupational segregation by sex was maintained, with one exception. After a fierce struggle, young men and women were hired in equal numbers to make plush velvet for draperies and were paid a "woman's wage" for doing the work. The men were driven to accept this because Kidderminster was a one-industry town and they had no alternative employment.

Verses, letters to the local newspaper, reports of speeches, and newspaper editorials show that the people of Kidderminster construed the disputes as conflicted class relations over jobs and wages. However, they did not agree on who caused the conflicts or on how they should be resolved. The variations in their interpretations of the strife and what should be done about it, coupled with the male unionists' refusal to invite women into their union, suggest that gender was significant to the way they experienced and understood class relations. The next chapter examines the gender content of the cultural productions of these disputes.

6

"Manliness, Virtue, and Self-Respect"

Gender Antagonism and
Working-Class Respectability

During the strike of 1874 by the Kidderminster carpet weavers' association objecting to Brinton's employment of women to weave tapestries, the editor of the industry's trade paper asked, "Men do not strike against their fellow workmen when the fields of labor become overfilled; why in the name of right and justice do they strike against women?"[1] The answer to this question is deceptively simple. The male weavers acted the way they did because their competitors were women, not men.

When employers were not contesting job segregation by sex, or when women and men earned the same wages, as in cotton powerloom weaving (the focus of the next chapter), then women and men cooperated in labor disputes. They often joined forces across occupational lines to battle for shorter hours or higher wages. For example, at Oldham in 1871 the entire work force in cotton-spinning factories (where women and men worked at sexually segregated jobs) engaged in industrial action to obtain a shorter work week, in what was known as the "Saturday half-holiday movement." When one employer locked the gates and barred the exits of his factory to prevent the workers from leaving at noon on a Saturday, male and female operatives joined together to resist. Women climbed over the walls to the outside, followed by the men on whose shoulders they had stood as they made their escape; both were assisted by crowds of men and women who had gathered outside the gates.[2]

However, when employers like Brinton in the carpet industry attempted to hire women in place of men, creating competition between them for jobs, hostility flared and men responded by striking against the women and excluding them from their union. Although skilled male workers engaged in numerous actions to restrict entry into their trade to protect their jobs, usually they did not exclude other men from their unions.[3] For example, when employers in Nottingham moved their lace machinery into the countryside in the 1880s in order to hire nonunionized rural men, city unionists responded by attempting to unionize the country workers.[4]

In either case, gender was not incidental to men's labor disputes. The conflicts between capital and labor over employment were not restricted to purely financial matters, although wages and jobs certainly were involved. Rather, gender was at the heart of these conflicts. At stake was not only the possibility that men would earn lowered wages because women's employment drove down wage scales, but what wage levels and employment itself signified to skilled working men— the definition of what it was to be a man. Gender was explicit in contests between workers and employers when women and men were in competition, and it was implicit in working men's struggles even when women were not directly involved.

THE RHETORIC OF
GENDER ANTAGONISM

A male unionist in the 1874 dispute with Brinton's asked, "Why should female labor be made scarce and men's labor be left idle?"[5] Unemployment, especially when it was the result of women replacing men in jobs and presented the possibility that an unemployed man would be supported by his wife and daughters, was the fear that drove carpet weavers to beg for jobs at women's wages when no other jobs were to be had. What else could the carpet weavers have meant in the violent dispute with Dixon's in the 1880s when they wheeled baby carriages in a procession through the town of Kidderminster alongside a wagon on which male weavers were doing laundry?[6] Such a dramatic depiction of the men's fear that the gender ordering of their lives would be toppled and that their masculine identities would be undone reveals what was taken for granted about gender distinctions in this time period: men were to be breadwinners; women were to take care of the day-to-day affairs of their households and remain economically dependent on men. Such an evocative display is reminiscent of Engels's report in 1845 of a letter written by a working man on meeting an old friend in Lancashire:

> but now t'world is turned up side down, Mary has to turn out to wark and I have to stop at home to mind Barns—and to Wash and Clean—Bake and mend, for, poar Lass—when she comes home at night, she is down up—thou nows Joe this is ard wark for one that want to Dow Different.—Joe sead, "I Lad it is ard Wark"—then poor Jack weept agane and sead that he wisht that he had never being Wead and that he never had being Born—but he did not think when Marred Mary that things would have comed to this, "I have meney a cry about it," said poor Jack.[7]

Although Engels himself believed that gender hierarchy in families was socially constructed, he suggested how people of the period might have reacted to such a letter in his comment, "Can one imagine a more senseless and foolish state of affairs than that described in this letter? It deprives the husband of his manhood and the wife of all womanly qualities."[8] Whether or not such beliefs about gender relations were widespread among working-class men when Engels first published *The Condition of the Working Classes in England* in 1845 is debatable. However, by 1877, when Engels's book was published in England, such beliefs pervaded working men's discourse. A letter to the *Kidderminster Shuttle* provides a graphic example from the 1894 dispute over who was to work Royal Axminster carpet looms:

> There are many cases where the father has no work at all. But the daughters or the mother weave Royal Axminster. What is the feeling of a man in this position? Has it not a tendency to reduce him and create a littleness when he is no longer the bread-winner of the family?[9]

Such rhetoric reflected the meaning of unemployment in the minds of these skilled working men at the same time as it legitimated their demands. A unionist declared at a strike meeting during the dispute with Dixon's in the 1880s:

> it was the duty of men to earn the living for the family, and it would not do to let women work on the looms to the exclusion of men, or they would place the men in an inferior position, and a man would cease to live in anything like comfort, so far as his conscience was concerned, if he saw his wife or daughters were the real bread winners of the family.[10]

He went on to argue that if plush velvet was to be made in Kidderminster, men should be employed to do it.[11]

In a letter responding to a Manchester newspaper article reprinted in the *Shuttle* which described how women and men in Lancashire worked together, "Medici" argued that men had the "care, anxieties, expenses and responsibilities of a home and family," while a girl had nothing like that to contend with. He said, "A person might do this [work with a female weaver], but not . . . until every vestige of manhood had left him, and he had assumed a total indifference towards those whom the law expects him to educate, foster and protect." [12]

Adding to the concern that adult male weavers would be idle while women were employed was the problem that there were not enough carpet weaving jobs for the number of lads who had apprenticed as creelers. As a unionist argued at a conference between the employers' association and the weavers' association during the 1884 dispute, "The manhood of many of the registered creelers could not be recognized, because they could not have a loom. They were, many of them, from 20 to 24 years of age and yet they were compelled to do youths' work." [13] This carpet weaver was reflecting the symbolic connection between adult manhood and being a carpet weaver. Tomkinson, the employer, turned the rhetoric about rearing sons to be men against the carpet weavers, claiming that allowing young men to work on these "women's machines" would not prepare them for manhood. He asked,

> in what position would a youth find himself, at man's estate, after having spent his whole time and the flower of his youth on such labor as the American loom demands—the strength of half a woman? . . . I hope you will not think I am giving you fatherly advice, but the question is, whether it is not better to bring youths up to a more arduous and skilled occupation—something more manly—than working on a loom that is specially adapted for female labor. [14]

To be a carpet weaver, a boy served his apprenticeship as a creeler, and then he was ready to assume "a man's estate." If there were no jobs to be had, the lad could not become a man, regardless of his age. This rhetorical ploy was used to argue that young men should be hired in place of women to weave plush. The unionist said that if Dixon would agree to that, the union would "regard the new work as an intermediate level between creeling and working on a tapestry loom or Brussels loom." [15] The carpet weavers were attempting to define a new step in the career ladder of a carpet weaver, and at the same time they were declaring a new stage in the male life cycle, equivalent to "young adulthood," so that young men need not remain boys. Historian Keith McClelland describes how the transition from apprentice to journeyman, or from being one of the "boys" or "lads" to being one of "the men," was marked by ritual celebrations among skilled male workers, much as other milestones in the life course are given public commemorations.[16] As sociologist Ava Baron argues, the concern over apprenticeship regulations expressed by many skilled workers may be understood as a generational aspect of gender.[17] Baron proposes that gender is shaped by work "at the site of production," in addition to being shaped by household and community relations.[18]

By the last quarter of the century, men achieved masculinity through work in two ways. They achieved it by doing physically demanding and/or difficult tasks, and/or by earning sufficient wages to support a family. A number of analysts of historical and contemporary work have noted how male workers construct their masculine identities using the kind of work they do as a crucial component. In her study of British printers, sociologist Cynthia Cockburn speaks of the "cross-valorization" of masculinity and manual labor.[19] Ava Baron's research on changes in technology in the American printing industry documents the connections between the kind of work to be done, the type of technology employed to do it, and notions of masculinity.[20] Sociologist Paul Willis suggests that modern-day manual work is inextricably bound up with definitions of manliness, and he reveals how schooling for working-class boys in Britain and the peer-group cultural forms they construct socialize them into the masculinized world of work.[21] In his ethnographic study of working men in an American chemical plant, sociologist David Halle proposes that the concept of "the working man" is an aspect of blue-collar workers' class identities.[22]

In the last half of the nineteenth century, the size of his wage packet linked a man's status at home and in the community with his masculinity at work. The connection between wage level and household status has most often been noted by historians of the family wage ideology in Britain and America. The demand for a family wage expressed the idea that an adult man ought to earn a sufficient wage to support his wife and children. Although the appeal for a family wage was widespread in the trade union movement of the late nineteenth century, it is doubtful that the majority of working-class families achieved it before the last years of the century.[23] As I argued in Chapter 4, financial hardship during at least some portion of the life cycle of most families would have demanded that other family members besides the head of household contribute to the household economy. Throughout the nineteenth century, the most skilled and secure working-class men comprised at best 20 percent of the body of working men.[24] Regardless of whether the family wage could have been achieved, from mid-century on arguments for it were central to skilled workmen's rhetoric about their economic discontent.

Scholars have debated why working men demanded the family wage and attempted to exclude women from the workplace because of it. Probably the best-known discussions of this issue for the British case are those by Heidi Hartmann and Jane Humphries.[25] Hartmann has suggested that organized male workers rejected women as coworkers in order to maintain dominance in the workplace and to command their wives' domestic services in the home. In Hartmann's thesis, men gained materially from an exclusionary strategy and the promulgation of a family wage ideal. Humphries has argued that unionists did not act selfishly by arguing for the exclusion of women from employment and for a family wage. Rather, women and children would be the indirect beneficiaries if women were excluded from the work force, because of the increased family wages earned by their husbands or fathers. She argues that the working-class family was strengthened and defended by working-class men and women as a buffer against the encroachment of capitalism in everyday life. For Hartmann, the argument for a family wage and the exclusion of women from the work force was a strategy that benefited working men, as men. For Humphries, the argument was a strategy that was intended to serve the working-class family and could be seen as a class strategy.

Examining the American case, Martha May has suggested that the demand for a family wage, and the exclusion of women from the work force, emerged first as a class demand for justice in the new industrial order and as a defense of the family.[26] In the twentieth century, however, gender privilege superseded class as the impetus for the family wage ideal. Supported by Progressive Era reformers and some employers as well as workers, the family wage became a cross-class gender issue. Although May recognizes that the argument for the family wage in the earlier period connected class and gender concerns, she believes the latter were subordinated to the former.[27]

These arguments fail to address the meaning of the family wage for the construction of masculinity in a parallel fashion to the way that the ideology of domesticity has been viewed to be at the center of the construction of nineteenth-century womanhood.[28] The evidence from disputes in the carpet industry, as well as in other industries in Britain from the middle of the nineteenth century to the start of the twentieth, suggests that the family wage ideology cannot be understood as either a class-based or a gender-based strategy. Rather, the family wage ideology was a vehicle meant to improve living conditions for working-class households and was constituted by gender and class simultaneously.

The demand for a family wage resonated with images of a "natural" division of labor between women and men in the family. It was used by men as a weapon to secure wages and jobs in the face of continuing threats by industrialists who sought to improve their competitive standing in the marketplace. It was premised on the idea that women should be at home raising families while men belonged in workplaces earning those families' livelihoods. Furthermore, just as the ideology of domesticity formed a cultural ideal for women, so too the ideology of male breadwinning that lay behind the demand for a family wage formed a cultural ideal for men. Wages and jobs were at the center of the disputes between workers and their bosses, but it was what wages and jobs meant to working-class men that was at the root of their strategies in these struggles.

MANLINESS AND WORK

Rhetoric about the "manly" nature of work or a worker's "manly" actions to change the conditions of his employment was common to male workers and their employers in numerous industries. For example, a member of the Brass and Metal Workers' Union complained about the demeaning effects of low wages paid to operatives and the subdivision of their work: "I am of the opinion that a man who turns the handle on a machine, or a man who pulls the lever in the interest of the community . . . ought to be regarded as a man, and be paid properly; machinery should be a blessing and not a curse."[29] Castigating nonunion men for playing into the hands of employers, W. J. Davis argued that the reason for joining the union was to improve, "not only the wage earnings, but there is such a thing as your manly independence in the workshop. There are regulations I know you rebel against, but have not the strength to throw over."[30]

Employers and their supporters frequently used the notion of manhood to question the legitimacy of the actions of opposing unionists.[31] In its editorial supporting Dixon's hiring of women to work plush, and demeaning the activities of the carpet weavers' union, the *Manchester Evening Mail* called the strike a "most unmanly strife" and the unionists' actions "selfish and unmanly intoleration," and suggested that the weavers should have gotten "a spark of common fairness into their natures, to say nothing of chivalry, and have withdrawn an opposition which it is discreditable on their part to offer."[32] Henry Dixon, the employer in the dispute, told his assembled workmen before they went out on strike: "I am truely sorry that before that resolution [the strike vote] passed . . . you had not the manly feeling to come to your employers to talk the matter over to them before going to the meeting."[33] Such statements by employers were simultaneously expressions of class position and exhortations about gender. Class relations were represented by gendered discourses and contained messages about both class and gender.

Employers also communicated their class position through statements about gender when they tried to portray their own actions in a favorable light. They justified hiring women by claiming that the work the women were to do was especially feminine. In the 1874 strike, Brinton said that he had purchased "women's machines," not "men's machines," to make tapestry. In the 1884 dispute, Dixon claimed that plush was a "woman's fabric," and he pointed out that it was not carpets that the women were making on the modified carpet-weaving machines. A letter to the *Kidderminster Shuttle* by someone who called himself Amicus Verus argued Dixon's case:

> Trade unionists may be right in trying to keep up their own wages, but they have no right to oppress women. Woman in all ages of the world has had to do with weaving. If in our day the more laborious and intricate kinds of weaving belong to men, the simpler, lighter kinds belong to the women. Plush is a woman's fabric; it would be absurd to see men employed upon it.[34]

The employers thus linked the sex of the employee with the kind of machine used, the nature of the task, and even the type of product that was made.

To vindicate their employment practices employers in the last quarter of the century might have argued a women's rights position or that the work was particularly suited to women's natures. Instead, they were careful to state that although women had a right to employment, men should be the breadwinners. At a meeting between the strike committee of the weavers' association and the employers' association during the dispute with Henry Dixon, one of the manufacturers argued:

> now women are coming forward in many walks of life—[in the] Post Office, in telegraph, in various public institutions of the country. Even in the universities themselves they found indications pointing towards some relief of the pressure still pressing upon women, and it was hoped the weavers wouldn't do something contrary to the spirit of the time. Far be it from him to suggest that women ought to take the bread out of the mouths of men. Nothing of the kind.[35]

When Mayor Tomkinson justified his hiring of women to work Royal Axminsters by claiming that the work was suitable only for women, he added that he could not displace the women he had hired,

> because it would leave some hundreds of girls without means of subsistence, and probably some would be driven to a life which we need not contemplate or discuss. As regards married women, foremen are instructed never to take on married women and never to continue to employ workers who had married except under special circumstances.[36]

(Note the implied claim to moral superiority in protecting and controlling women's sexuality.)

Editorials in trade and local newspapers also reflected current conceptions of masculinity and femininity in their comments about the disputes. The editorial writers walked a thin line in endorsing the employers' hiring practices while supporting particular notions of working-class masculinity espoused by weavers and shared by middle-class observers. An editorial in the trade paper *The Furniture Gazette* upheld Brinton's right to hire women to work his new tapestry looms in the 1874 dispute, but added:

> We have nothing here to do with the question of Home versus Workshop; of course every man worthy of his name would prefer that his wife should remain at home, devoted to domestic and social wants of its inmates, but no man can regulate the balance of sexes in his family, nor can he or his employer totally cope with competition so his earnings will be sufficient to keep his wife above the necessity of work.[37]

The *Kidderminster Shuttle*, while attempting to appear neutral in the dispute between the weavers' association and Henry Dixon over the employment of women to weave plush, argued that the material "is not carpet, but plush; and one of the simplest forms of weaving we ever saw. An able-bodied man would be ashamed to follow an employment so light and easy, requiring neither strength nor skill."[38] The editorial added, "Of course, when a man marries, it is a point of honor that he should keep his wife at home and away from the factory, but all women are not married, and girls and unmarried women have quite as much right as men to live, and to do the same kind of work too, if they are competent."[39] An editorial published a few weeks later elaborated on these themes, articulating the gender issues that were perceived to be at stake in the dispute over the making of plush:

> To every right thinking man there must be a sense of degradation in being dependent upon the manual labor of his wife for support, unless unavoidable calamity is the cause. We respect the weavers . . . for beginning to see that female factory labor is not conducive to the comfort and happiness of home. . . . If women's proper sphere is at home, provide a home for her and leave her free from the necessity of toiling in factories, workshops, or brickfields. To shut her out of the factory when she has no home provided for her, is beginning at the wrong end.[40]

WORK AND FEMININITY

Letters to the editor of the *Kidderminster Shuttle* by male weavers generally castigated the women who accepted employment that the men wanted by implying that women worked to earn money for frivolities. Working women responded by charging that the men squandered their money on liquor. In the last verse of "The Lady Weaver" Noah Cooke wrote disdainfully, "What is consequence to me if I can only get / A taller feather waving in my hat?"[41] "A Lady Weaver" replied, "it is better to spend [money] on a harmless feather than on drink."[42] At a speech at a business meeting of the weavers' association during the Royal Axminster dispute, a union official reported:

> People asked why the workmen didn't go to church—it was because, he was sorry to say, that some of the best pews in the church were rented by Axminster weavers [women] who were there in their "fal-de-dols" and finery whilst their fathers or brothers or other male relatives had no clothes to go to church in. When I saw the girls being marched through the streets to the cookery school, I often thought that at the modern rate of progress, the boys ought to be sent to the cookery classes instead of the girls—for the men in the future would have to stop at home to do

the cookery while the women went to work. It was said that many Axminster weavers had to keep old parents and widowed mothers but in the great majority of cases the money was simply thrown away, and instead of the carpet trade becoming the staple trade of the town, the milliners shops would become that.[43]

A letter from "An Experienced Female Weaver" retorted that if the girls looked well dressed, it was due "more to good management than to the amount of money they received." She went on to ask derisively if the homes of the young men who would replace the girls would benefit from their employment, or would it be "the publicans and tobacconists?"[44]

These letters to the editor of the *Kidderminster Shuttle*, the verse cited in the preceding chapter, and public speeches and demonstrations told of the contradictory connections between waged work and womanliness, as much by their silence on the subject as by their proclamations. The waged work a woman did could only detract from her femininity. Women could be truly feminine only if they "stopped at home."

At the same time, the insistence by some of the male weavers that women worked merely for "fal-de-dols" arose from two assumptions. First, they were playing with a commonly made association between women's love of finery and moral degradation, especially when the finery was purchased and worn by working-class women. As Mariana Valverde has argued, "the moral meaning attached to various kinds of clothes played a key role in the moral regulation of working-class women."[45] Love of finery was a key theme in middle-class political and scientific debates on the causes of prostitution.[46] The male unionists were drawing on these images as they battled with the women for employment in Kidderminster.

The second implication in these statements is that true women must work only for such frivolities; if they worked to serve family need they would be breadwinners, and that role was the sole preserve of men.[47] Responding to a letter in the newspaper arguing that women weavers had "common sense" and were responsible with their money, "Gil Blas" wrote:

> Most of these common-sensed girls (the ones who do not spend all their money on finery) have no time to be bothered with the domesticating philosophy of a well-meaning mother; no—the common-sensed girl has promised some of her like companions to attend a dance class, or a ball

at the Town Hall, or the Theatre, or she has to take a feather some-where to be dyed for which she paid 18s only a fortnight ago, and got it spoilt someway coming home when it was raining perhaps—or she is just off to try a new dress on.[48]

The ridicule and sarcasm in the statements by men that women would work while men did "the cookery" reveal the perceived sex-ually dimorphic qualities of housework and waged work. There were, to be sure, statements made about work that was "suited to women's natures," but there does not seem to be any implication in these state-ments that by doing the suitable work, a woman would enhance her femininity in the way a man could gain masculinity from his work. However, if a woman did the wrong kind of work, she would acquire masculine characteristics or would lose her "natural" feminine quali-ties. For example, a chain maker complained in a local newspaper how the women of the black country were "unsexed" to such an extent that when he was totally exhausted, his daughter could "still go on."[49] In an editorial printed in the *Kidderminster Shuttle* during the weav-ers' dispute with Dixon over hiring women to weave plush, the point was made that women should not work, but that to refuse them work was wrong:

> The factory system has not done very much for the elevation of women, and in many respects has unfitted them for domestic life. We do not object as much to the spirit of independence and self-reliance it has given them; but that it has tended to corrupt and brutalize their man-ners and characters. It is seldom taken into account how much the chil-dren of the laboring classes suffer from the fact that the mother has lost the bloom of femininity, and is often as hard, as harsh, and as masculine as the father.[50]

The message was quite clear that women had a less than legitimate relationship to paid employment, even if that employment was neces-sary for their own or their families' survival. The barbs thrown at working women for wasting their money on "finery" suggest that women could not justify their employment on the grounds that they wanted pleasures or luxuries. Men might waste their money on drink, but by doing so they did not risk their right to work. Women had a right to work only when family or personal need was extraordinary. However, this right placed the women who exercised it in a double bind: if they needed money to support a family they had the right to work, but then they became less feminine, for they had become bread-winners.

The rhetoric in these disputes between male workers and their employers reveals what was taken for granted about gender relations and definitions of masculinity and femininity. However, it would be incorrect to presume that these social constructions reflected long-standing traditions of work and family life among working-class people in Britain. The norm of the male breadwinner, the ideal of the family wage, and notions of working-class domesticity for women were products of midcentury, which probably spread rather slowly and came into general acceptance gradually.

BREADWINNING, DOMESTICITY, AND RESPECTABILITY

MEN AS HEADS OF WORKING HOUSEHOLDS

In the years before midcentury, honorable manhood was equated with possessing a skill and family headship. This notion of manliness did not require, nor was it related to, the ideal of full-time female domesticity. Prior to the industrial revolution and continuing into the nineteenth century, wives and children were expected to earn enough at least to maintain themselves.[51] Artisans in domestic workshops and their wives and older children worked together to produce the products by which the family earned its wage. In agricultural households, too, husbands and wives were partners in labor. In the early years of the nineteenth century, wives of skilled tradesmen such as shoemakers, tanners, curriers, tin-plate workers, and masons went on the tramp with their husbands.[52] These gender and work relations continued into the last quarter of the nineteenth century in some communities. For example, in certain framework-knitting communities in Nottingham-shire, census data show that, between 1851 and 1881, increasing numbers of wives were listed as employed.[53] Traditions of women's involvement in the household economy persisted in these communities. As factory production of hosiery displaced framework knitting, wives in 1881 stitched or seamed stockings or finished lace, now working as industrial homeworkers rather than as contributors to household production in domestic industry. For a man, being the head of a family and a skilled worker surely meant being independent of charity and poor relief. However, men were not expected to shoulder the full burden of economic responsibility for their families.

Wage and employment security did not characterize most of the skilled trades in the first half of the nineteenth century. The autobiographies of working-class men analyzed by David Vincent indicated "that constant financial insecurity was the lot even of those working men who had the good fortune to avoid recruitment into the ranks of the casual laborers or the factory proletariat, and spent their lives in seemingly prosperous and well protected skilled trades."[54] When their income proved inadequate to provide for a family, artisans might "take a shop for their wives to manage" while they continued at their regular employment.[55] In the early years of the nineteenth century, the wives of London tailors may not have assisted their husbands, who worked only on workshop premises, but they did work as necklace makers, embroiderers, mantua makers, milk sellers, and small shopkeepers.[56] At a testimonial dinner for William Gregory, who rose from his early years as a coal miner to become an important Nottingham lace manufacturer, Gregory is reported to have paid tribute to his wife, who had worked a stocking frame to help support the household, saying, "if she had not been an industrious and economic wife, he could not have succeeded as he had."[57] In a similar vein, J. B. Leno wrote in his autobiography that he owed much to his wife's help in his early days as a compositor: "How she labored at the press and assisted me in the work of my printing office, with a child in her arms, I have no space to tell, nor in fact have I space to allude to the many ways she contributed to my good fortune."[58]

In domestic industry, honorable manhood meant being a skilled worker and the head of the household's labor team.[59] The male head of household had access to the status of being a skilled worker because it was he and his older sons who would have been given formal training in the "mysteries of a craft." Domestic work and economic activity blended into one another for women and their daughters. Although they may have done the same work as their husbands, they were not considered to be skilled artisans. For example, in the domestic hosiery industry the husband and father directed the work of household members. The hosier paid him the wages due for the work done by the whole family working as a unit and held him responsible for the completed garment. Among handloom weavers, too, the head of household delivered the work to the warehouse and received the pay, although "in most cases the wife and children would have worked in activities such as carding and bobbin-winding, necessary to service the weaving of the father at the loom."[60] Men in industries like framework knitting might have thought of themselves as heads of their households and as artisans, but they would not have imagined themselves to be solely responsible for the economic well-being of their families. A vivid illustration is provided by Thomas Winters, a Chartist, trade unionist, and framework knitter, who testified in 1854 at Parliamentary Commission hearings on the knitting industry. Winters proposed that if the knitting performed by the family as a whole could be done solely by the adult man, the entire family would be better off

> because they are all laboring together for a certain sum; and that certain sum would then come into the hands of one person, and supposing that to be the case . . . it would give those other parties [women and children] an opportunity of getting employment elsewhere, and so of increasing the comforts of the family from that source also.[61]

There was no suggestion in this remark that women and children should not make economic contributions to the household budget. Even if by 1854 the idea of the male breadwinner as sole provider was beginning to spread among working men engaged in other occupations and living in other communities, the ideal would have clashed with the impoverished reality of the conditions of existence among framework knitter households. In such communities, dominated by a single industry dependent on women's work, it is unlikely that the ideals of domesticity for women and breadwinning for men could have had meaning.

Among skilled artisans, notions of skill and family headship were interconnected. Historian Sally Alexander has written: "In the minds of these different groups of male workers their status as fathers and heads of families was indelibly associated with their independence as workers through 'honorable' labor and property in skill, which identification with a trade gave them."[62] Labor was spoken of as the working man's "property," and it became part of the stock in trade of contemporary radical political debate.[63] The skilled artisan could pass on his labor and/or his trade to his sons as an inheritance.[64] David Vincent's analysis of working men's autobiographies shows the importance to a son of his father's ability to teach him his trade or to provide the funds necessary to apprentice him to another tradesman.[65] These autobiographies reveal the tight connection for the male child, in the years prior to midcentury, between family and future occupation. Security for a lad meant the success of the family economy headed by his father, and it was to his father that the growing male child would look for his only inheritance—a trade.[66] It is no wonder, then, that attempts by employers to replace men with women, or conditions of underemployment that forced women and children to be primary wage earners in their households, met with such resistance. As Vincent put it:

> The capacity to be involved in the socialization of a child was certainly an important value. The capacity to exercise influence over the child's occupational present and future was a different, though equally prized value. But the really destructive element of the factory system, and in particular the early mines and mills, was . . . it so destroyed his economic power that it prevented him from performing either role at any time.[67]

What was common to artisans working in domestic and in workshop settings was the idea of "property in skill"—skill as a source of honor, and the meaning of skill for men's status as heads of households.[68]

MALE BREADWINNING AND FEMALE DOMESTICITY

The twin ideals of domesticity and breadwinning developed out of and were in harmony with values which originated in preindustrial artisanal workshop culture.[69] Artisanal culture survived into the industrial age, and the values associated with it influenced the emerging proletariat, especially skilled workers.[70] At midcentury those values were linked to a defense of a traditional family structure. They evolved as part of a political language that the Chartists used to agitate for universal male suffrage. They were shaped by skilled male trade unionists as they resisted industrial transformation, especially when it was accompanied by the threat that men's skills would be degraded and their wages lowered by the introduction of women as cheap labor to do traditionally masculine work. And they were deployed in the 1840s by working men as a political strategy to agitate for a Ten Hours Bill in Parliament.

During the eighteenth and early nineteenth centuries, women were increasingly excluded from the workshop trades. As this happened, the differences between the work lives of artisans in domestic industry and artisans in workshops increased. Whereas artisans who worked in domestic units were incorporated into a community based on ties between families and neighbors, skilled workers in the workshop trades "appealed to a corporate, collectivist and solidarist idiom."[71] When men associated exclusively with one another, and especially when work was at the center of daily life and filled much of the time that people were awake, the conditions were ripe for the development of uniquely masculine work cultures.[72]

Artisans in all-male workshops reinforced their ties with one another by the elaboration of workshop rituals, associations outside the workplace such as, for example, the weekly celebrations of St. Monday, and in social gatherings at the public house.[73] As this masculine work culture developed, and as women and men came to spend less of their lives in daily proximity, the range of everyday experiences shared by women and men narrowed.[74] As historian Dorothy Thompson has put it:

> Since most working people of all levels spent the greater part of their time at work, the major preoccupations in their conversation and in their leisure were related to work and workmates. As long as the place of work was the home, women and children shared these preoccupations with the men to some degree, whether they themselves worked or not.[75]

As men's and women's work became increasingly separated physically in the years before midcentury, the ideal of the male breadwinner took shape. Male artisans banded together in response to the threat of degradation accompanying the drive for capital accumulation, using exclusionary tactics as a primary weapon. To preserve their status as skilled workers and as heads of households, artisans fought to preserve their jobs and their trades from the unskilled and from technological changes that threatened their craft and their livelihood.[76]

In some cases, whole communities became involved in protesting the changes threatening their livelihoods and their way of life. However, it was generally the skilled men of the community who articulated their grievances, using language that conjured up the images of artisan culture under threat of being dismantled. Male artisans thus created the public cultures of collective protest. Women were excluded by the rhetoric employed by the men of their communities, just as they were denied access to public rostrums.[77] Artisans fought for their rights as men who had "property in skill," who could claim their independence through pride in their work, their status as heads of households, and their ability to provide a future for their sons.[78]

Artisanal values influenced the attitudes and practices of the men who became the first adult male factory workers. The early mule spinners in the cotton industry defended their skill by attempting to control the pace and intensity of work and by restricting entry into their trade. The subcontracting system, wherein the mule spinner hired and paid his piecers, reinforced the relative privilege of their position among factory operatives. The combination of required strength, skill, and authority over other workers helped to maintain mule spinning as a solely male preserve.[79] They, and other skilled working men, retained the artisanal tradition of excluding women from their trades. It was among such men that the male breadwinner ideology developed in response to threats to their prerogative as skilled working men.[80]

As early as 1818, male mule spinners had been threatened by masters' attempts to introduce women spinners and had responded in several instances by burning the mill.[81] A union official wrote in the *Manchester Guardian*, "Girls . . . from 14 to 20 years of age [are] thus rendered independent of their natural guardians, who in many cases, indeed, become in consequence of this very employment, dependent upon their children."[82] The earliest unions in the cotton industry, dating from the 1790s, had included women members.[83] By 1829, however, they were becoming increasingly sexually segregated.[84] The Manchester union, for example, included no female members. A national meeting of male spinners in that year, organized by trade union leader John Doherty and held on the Isle of Man, adopted an exclusionist policy, restricting spinning to sons, brothers, or orphan nephews of spinners and all poor relations of mill proprietors. Women were encouraged to form their own unions. Doherty, who was also a Chartist and Ten Hours Movement activist, seemed consciously to be constructing the mule spinners' union in such a way as to reinforce the idea that male mule spinners were skilled workers. The explicit exclusion of women from the union in 1829 would have been part of that strategy.

Downward pressure on production costs continued as competition among capitalists increased, especially in such commodities as cotton textiles, which were produced for mass consumption. Employers threatened working men's jobs by attempts to substitute the cheaper labor of women for men. For example, in 1833 a particularly significant strike in Glasgow resulted in women and boys being hired to work self-acting mules, replacing the male mule spinners. These threats affected a number of industries during this time period. Earlier in the century, in 1810 and 1814, after the apprenticeship laws had been repealed, employers of male tailors had tried to introduce women into their workshops at half the male wage, and the tailors struck in response.[85] They struck again over the issue of women's employment in 1827 and in 1830. Many male unionists argued that "men had a greater right to a living wage than women, since they were family supporters."[86] Finally, in 1834 a major strike by nine thousand London tailors was lost, and large numbers of women were introduced into the striking workshops.[87]

Male workers responded to attempts to introduce women into their trades by excluding them from their unions and their workplaces and by bargaining for gender-segregated employment. These responses must be understood in the context of the way masculinity and skill were intertwined constructions. As historian Mariana Valverde has explained with regard to the mule spinners:

> Whether they saw the women workers as female and opposed their presence out of a desire to preserve male privilege, or whether they saw them as unskilled workers and harbingers of the decline of craft unions, is rather a futile question to ask. The point is that for the spinners masculinity and craft were completely intertwined. Even if gender struggle in the workplace was constructed primarily through the categories of craft unionism, it is no coincidence that women were seen as naturally unskilled and as belonging either in the home or in low-paid, non-craft occupations.[88]

Although the ideology of the male breadwinner and attempts by male unionists to exclude women from the workplace gradually became accepted by broad segments of the working classes and dominated labor politics during the mid-Victorian period, it would be mistaken to think that they gained preeminence without contest. Historian Barbara Taylor has documented the struggles between Owenite-influenced unionists who argued for equal wages for women and men and others who wanted the exclusion of women as the solution to the threat to their crafts.[89] One elderly journeyman tailor demanded in 1834:

if women are equal in the state of human existence, what right, would I ask, has any set of mechanics to deny them a right which they, the tailors, are at this moment claiming for themselves. Competition is the great, the only, the all-prevailing evil. Competition must be destroyed, and associated labor raised upon its ashes; all the rest must end in disappointment.[90]

But such voices arguing for sexual equality, rare even in the volatile 1830s, became fainter as the century advanced. Working-class leaders increasingly argued that women belonged not in the workplace but in the home. However fleeting was the articulation of an ideal of cooperation between men and women by some Owenites, its existence suggests that the twin ideologies of male breadwinning and female domesticity were forged through a struggle in which working-class leaders with particular ideas about the emerging social order gained preeminence in working-class communities.[91]

The articulation of the male breadwinner ideal and its corollaries, that women should remain out of the work force and that men should earn a family wage, informed the discourses of two important political movements of the 1840s: the Ten Hours Movement and Chartism. Both movements were collective responses to the economic, social, and political problems affecting the working class in the 1830s and 1840s. Recently, a number of social historians have noted that in the 1840s, the political rhetoric of these movements was colored by distinctively masculinist sentiments.[92] The twin ideals of male breadwinning and female domesticity were important symbols which contributed to working-class solidarity in these movements.

Short-time committees had been in existence among male cotton spinners since the second decade of the nineteenth century. However, sustained and organized agitation to reduce the hours of labor in textile factories began only in the early 1830s. It was in the 1840s that the short-time committees began to clamor to restrict women's employment. In 1842, the Short-Time Committee of the West Riding of Yorkshire presented a set of demands to influential members of Parliament and government ministers. Among them was a proposal to restrict young persons aged thirteen to twenty-one to a ten-hour day and a demand for the "gradual withdrawal of all females from the factories."[93] Members of the committee argued that it was an "inversion of the order of nature and of providence—a return to the state of barbarism, in which the woman does the work, while the man looks idly on."[94] The *Ten Hours Advocate* in 1846 proposed that factory hours for females should be restricted and that married women should be occupied with domestic duties: "We hope," it proclaimed, "the day is not distant, when the husband will be able to provide for his wife and family, without sending the former to endure the drudgery of a cotton mill."[95]

These sentiments appealed to middle-class reformers and aristocratic philanthropists. They were given legitimacy by the passage in 1842 of the Mines Regulation Act, which prohibited women from working underground in the mines. Given the groundswell of public opinion on the matter of women's employment generated by the hearings preceding the passage of the Mines Regulation Act, it is not surprising that, in 1844, women were equated with children as needing the protection of the state regarding the hours and conditions of labor. In the debate on the Ten Hours Bill in 1844, Lord Ashley argued that the women working long hours

> disturbs the order of nature, and the rights of the laboring men, by ejecting the males from the workshop, and filling their places by females, who are thus withdrawn from all their domestic duties, and exposed to insufferable toil at half the wages that would be assigned to males, for the support of their families.[96]

Note that Ashley equated the "order of nature" with the rights of working men. Increasingly, working women were perceived to be threatening that order by challenging the "rights" of men. Until mid-century, discourses about the necessity for protective labor legislation for women elaborated on the theme that for women to operate outside their "natural" domestic sphere threatened to destabilize the social order. Social order, then, was predicated on patriarchal control understood as a natural order.[97] We have seen, however, that the so-called order of nature was in fact created through political struggle.

The Chartist movement for universal male suffrage served to focus much of the discontent within the working class over the economic and social changes that were altering the familiar social landscape. Chartism was a mass movement involving thousands of people, especially in the industrial areas of the country.[98] It achieved momentum through the growth of a national working-class press and through a continuing tradition of public demonstrations of dissent. Although in the early years of Chartism, women were active in street demonstrations and other political protests, as the movement became more organized, as informal, community-based political gatherings were replaced by the formal political activity of men's delegations and committees, women became less visible, welcome, and/or comfortable as members.[99]

Possibly women withdrew from public prominence within Chartism in the 1840s as a consequence of a developing understanding, which they shared, about women's proper sphere of activity. Perhaps their relative silence contributed to that understanding. However that may be, the ideology of domesticity was articulated in Chartist rhetoric and was used as a political weapon. That rhetoric was explicitly preoccupied "with sexual/familial relations themselves, and in particular with their dislocation through the substitution of women for men as primary breadwinners."[100] As early as 1835, Chartist Francis Place wrote that "men should refuse to work in mills and factories which employ women," so that "the young women who will otherwise be degraded by factory labor will become all that can be desired as companionable wives, and . . . the men will obtain competent wages for their maintenance."[101] Chartists active in the factory reform movement in the 1840s frequently linked the campaign for universal male suffrage with the demand that married women be withdrawn from factory work. They continued to argue, as Place had, that woman's place was in the home and that men needed wages sufficiently high to support a dependent wife and children.[102]

The rhetoric of female domesticity and the family wage for men was partly a response to the threat that women posed in the labor market. However, that threat by itself does not explain the gendered content of this rhetoric. These ideals were capable of uniting men from diverse communities and occupational backgrounds into a common movement because they connected what seemed natural—a gender hierarchy with men at the helm—with the political demand for universal manhood suffrage. Symbolically key to the argument for suffrage was the idea that men held property in labor.[103] The Chartist political agenda to include working-class men in the body politic was justified by reference to that idea. In this important way, Chartism contributed to the formation of a new vision of masculinity and femininity, now linked with unequal political rights.[104]

The ideology of domesticity for women and breadwinning for men was a product of these complexly woven strands. It grew from artisanal values concerning skill and property in labor, was fed by the threat of degradation and the social disarray produced by capitalist industrial transformation, and came to full flower when men's jobs were threatened because women were hired. The politics of protest in the Ten Hours Movement and Chartism were responses to these experiences of working-class women and men. Gendered discourse shaped the ways that they understood their experiences. It is possible that Chartists and Ten Hours advocates appropriated middle-class rhetoric about domesticity. They may have done so because it was politically expedient and because it seemed to offer a way to restore the gender relations that had existed in the artisanal households of recent memory. However, the articulation of the ideology of domesticity and breadwinning, especially by the Chartist movement, was crucial in creating a new vision of male and female relationships and of proletarian family life.

MANHOOD AND WORKING-CLASS RESPECTABILITY

Chartist William Lovett in his *Social and Political Morality,* published in 1853, portrayed the home as a "private retreat from the harsh world of masculine endeavour, [and] extolled the female homemaker whose chief duty was to gratify the mind and console the heart of man by rendering his little household sanctum cheerful and attractive."[105] Lovett went on, "A man must indeed have lost all self-respect to allow himself and his offspring to be dependent on a wife's labor."[106] This idealization of home was to develop, if slowly, after midcentury, in response to a number of changes among skilled workers that affected working-class culture.[107] David Vincent has noted that it is only among "those autobiographers who were most preoccupied with the ideal of respectability that we see the beginning of a move to place domestic life on a pedestal, to see it as both the source and repository of all positive values and experiences of working class life."[108] London shipwrights, for example, held independence chief among their values; by *independence* they meant having a skill or trade "which would enable them to maintain themselves and their families by their labor at a decent level, above subsistence and with sufficient leisure to engage in respectable activities."[109]

The ideal of male breadwinning was slowly coming to mean being the sole family provider.[110] In an analysis of oral histories of working-class women born between 1890 and 1940, historian Elizabeth Roberts found that her respondents could not remember their mothers being employed. "Because it was generally . . . presumed that a woman only worked if there was inadequate income, many skilled men did not like their wives to be seen earning money—it reflected badly on their status as the breadwinner."[111] The idea that a man should earn sufficient wages so that his wife would not have to go out to work became a significant aspect of working-class respectability.

Social theorist Pierre Bourdieu has proposed that the whole gamut of behaviors and characteristics that make up life styles is the basis of classificatory systems over which individuals and groups struggle.[112] Clothing, manners, personal habits, household furnishings, and styles of speech articulate what he calls a "map of social space" which is read by people as a set of distinctions separating "us" from "them." Social identity is at stake in struggles over these expressive distinctions. Applying Bourdieu's ideas to nineteenth-century England helps us to see why symbols of respectability loomed large in working-class life, especially in the last quarter of the century. They were crucial signs of distinction in a society preoccupied with classifications and distinctions.[113] This obsession was intimately tied to class formation and the growth of working-class consumption.

Respectability became increasingly important to members of the working class in mid- and late-Victorian Britain.[114] It was a complex value system, held by a wide range of people from varying occupational groups, that had its roots in artisans' and skilled workers' notions of independence, the same working-class sources that originated the ideology of breadwinning for men and domesticity for women. It is not surprising, then, that the Victorian sense of respectability focused on the family and on self-help or self-improvement for working-class men.[115] Like the earlier artisanal values out of which Victorian working-class respectability grew, it was associated with economic independence for men, but the new version stressed domesticity (which meant economic *dependence*) for women.

Some aspects of respectability might have been displayed for effect only in the presence of a middle-class audience.[116] Even if "rough" and "respectable" elements might both have been aspects of the behavior of most working-class people, however, particular symbols of respectability increasingly became intrinsic aspects of working-class culture in the last half of the nineteenth century and were displayed for local, working-class consumption.[117]

The language of respectability was made up of emblems such as giving proper burial to a family member, having a freshly pressed Sunday suit to wear to church, and owning the appropriate items of front parlor decor.[118] The importance of the parlor to members of the working class has been noted by historian F. M. L. Thompson, who has called it "the cult of the parlor."[119] This was a particularly important symbol of respectability because to set aside a room to be used only for formal, ceremonial occasions required a four-room house and the money to pay for it.[120] As Thompson explains, "The essence of a parlor was the elevation of the front room to the status of a household shrine, a special room withdrawn from daily use and consecrated to special occasions."[121]

In the last half of the nineteenth century, the work-centered focus of skilled workers began to be replaced by one oriented toward the family and the home.[122] This change was associated with a variety of events including the shortening of the workday, growing geographical separation between home and workplace, increased spending power, and an increased division of labor between men and women in which women were no longer expected to earn money but, rather, were expected to remain at home to manage the money earned by their husbands.[123] The Education Acts of the 1870s, mandating school attendance, made it more difficult for women to go out to work and leave the household chores to older children and also reduced the likelihood of the children being able to contribute regularly to household income.[124] The withdrawal of both children and wives from visible and regular employment would have put an increasing responsibility on men to be "good providers."

As symbols of respectability increasingly focused on the home and full-time housewives came to be held responsible for keeping up the image of respectable home life, the role of breadwinner (now defined as being the sole adult provider) became part and parcel of masculine identity. The display of symbols of respectability signaled that a working man earned sufficient and regular wages and that he was capable of supporting his family by his own exertions. His respectable wife, meanwhile, could remain at home to care for the family, decorate and clean the front parlor, and press the suit he wore on Sunday. Because many of the symbols of respectability were visible, material possessions or were evident in public rituals such as weddings and funerals, they differentiated working-class people from one another. Respectability, then, was a gendered language of family status premised on a steady and sufficient family wage, earned by the male head of household.

The connection between the ideals of breadwinning for men and domesticity for women and working-class respectability was actively reinforced by middle-class "moral entrepreneurs" who promoted the idea that the employment of married women was a consequence of the profligacy of husbands. For example, at a coroner's inquest on the death of an infant girl in Ashton-under-Lyne in 1877, the coroner chastised the mother for working in the mill and "exposing the infant too early in the morning" when the mother took her "to nurse." Then the coroner summoned the father, and on learning that the father earned 19 shillings a week as a laborer, the coroner told the man that 19 shillings a week "properly spent is sufficient to keep you and allow your wife to be at home." He then said that the father "is morally responsible for the death of the child." When the father said that his wife went to the mill because "she said what I got wasn't enough," the coroner shamed him for blaming his wife.[125]

Employers, especially those who, like Hugh Mason, were prone to moralizing, also would have encouraged the connection between respectability and the twin ideals of domesticity and breadwinning. Mason was apparently shocked when he heard the infant mortality statistics for Ashton-under-Lyne in 1875, and he contrasted them with the rates for Oxford, the area in which he provided housing for his workpeople. "He commended the working men of Oxford for their manliness, virtue, and self-respect, and for their high regard for, and duty to, their children in themselves going to work, and the mother being allowed to stop at home." Mason added that he "hoped such a state of things would always exist, and if there was anything in the cottage which could be improved, it would afford him infinite pleasure to cooperate with them in bringing about, if it were possible, a better state of things."[126]

Working-class leaders, too, promulgated these ideals, linking them to the exclusion of married women from the workplace. At the Trades Union Congress in 1877, Henry Broadhurst argued for increasing the legal restrictions on women's work:

> It was [working men's] duty as men and husbands to use their utmost efforts to bring about a condition of things where their wives should be

in their proper sphere at home, seeing after their house and family, instead of being dragged into the competition for livelihood against the great and strong men of the world.[127]

The possibility that men could be replaced at work by women was a threat to a refashioned notion of masculinity that equated husband and family provider and linked these to community standing, to being a member of the respectable working class. As Barbara Taylor has put it, "The wage-earning wife, once seen as the norm in every working-class household, had become a symptom and symbol of masculine degradation."[128]

CONCLUSION

The letters to the *Kidderminster Shuttle* quoted earlier in this chapter reflect the symbolic linkage between gender identity and working-class respectability. The emphasis on male breadwinning, the complaints about lacking a Sunday suit proper for church attendance, the accusations of squandering money on drink all spoke simultaneously to gender and class standing. A letter to the *Women's Union Journal* in 1879 from a male unionist is illustrative of this symbolic connection:

> If a provident man like this takes up a seemingly hostile attitude towards his sisters, his cousins and his aunts employed in factories, it may be for reasons far from discreditable to him as a husband and father of daughters—reasons he might have quite apart from unionism. . . . Such a man might hold . . . that women should not be the rival of man, and that a man should support his wife entirely. Such a man might be made to feel the rivalry acutely while trying to keep his wife and daughters from the need of going to work like men. . . . Again if the rivalry gets too close, men will be unable to marry in any holy sense of home life, or even marry at all. . . . What sort of dispositions can we expect in children who have a father, a minder, but no mother to speak of—in fact three fathers, such a man might ask.[129]

Caliban, as the writer called himself, articulates in that letter how women's rivalry in the labor market affected men as men. He uses the images of adult manhood centered on the capacity to support a family. It may have been proper for older, unmarried daughters to be employed, especially in domestic work that would have trained them in the arts of "respectable household management." However, the husband was expected to support his wife or endanger his and his family's respectability.

Gender was implicit in the struggle between workers and employers in the nineteenth century, and it was central to some arenas of that struggle. A consequence was that workers' solidarity could easily be diffused by gender politics.[130] In addition, the connection between masculinity and working-class respectability promoted a working class divided along occupational lines.[131] Finally, that connection contributed to the association of femininity with domesticity, making the idea of the "working woman" anathema and the experience of wage earning for women a conflicted one.

7

"Brothers and Sisters in Distress"
The Cotton Textile Weavers of Lancashire

A placard posted throughout North Lancashire during the great strike and lockout in the weaving districts in 1878 was headed: "Good Name in Man or Woman is the Immediate Jewel of their Souls."[1] Borrowing lines from Shakespeare's *Othello,* strike leaders entreated cotton operatives to be upstanding members of their communities and suggested that women and men were equally important to the conduct of respectable labor politics. In Lancashire, where craggy hillsides were shadowed by the smokestacks of cotton mills and cloth manufacture dominated the economic and social landscape, male and female weavers lived and toiled together as kin and fellow operatives. Their family and work lives formed a seamless web of interdependent activities both inside and beyond the factory gates. Nowhere was this interdependence more evident than it was in labor politics.

Lancashire powerloom weaving was unique among the major industries in England in the nineteenth century in that men and women were not in competition for weaving jobs. From the time that men were first hired to work alongside women at powerloom weaving, employers had paid them the same piece rates that they paid women, and the sexually integrated weavers' unions insisted upon a standard piece rate for both men and women. Yet gender intruded on the seemingly equal positions of women and men in the labor force in many interconnected ways. Women's and men's work experiences were similar in important respects, especially in doing the same work and earning roughly the same pay. But their experiences also differed, because of the various ways that gender distinctions shaped work and family life.

Compared with the transformations in the labor process of cotton spinning and the exclusionary strategies of male mule spinners, which have been the subject of numerous studies, powerloom weaving and its sexually integrated work force have received little scholarly attention.[2] Yet, cotton powerloom weaving was virtually unique in being an occupation open to both women and men. At the same time it was vitally important to the economic and cultural life of Lancashire, where about 400,000 men and women worked in the cotton textile industry, about half of them in weaving sheds.[3]

Unlike spinning, which was rapidly transformed into a steam-powered industry, powerloom weaving was slow to dominate cloth manufacture. Technical difficulties, coupled with an oversupply of labor in the domestic handloom weaving industry, retarded the adoption of the power loom. Because spinning and carding had become mechanized and increasing amounts of yarn were available, the demand for handloom weaving rose. To meet the demand, women as well as men became cotton handloom weavers. The labor force in handloom weaving increased during the period that began around 1780 and ended with the French Wars.[4] From 1815 on, handloom weavers of both fine and coarse cloth experienced drastic reductions in their piece rates, primarily as a result of a decline in the demand for cotton cloth relative to the supply.[5] By that time, women were entering handloom weaving in large numbers. To make ends meet in weaving households, work was intensified, which in turn exacerbated the decline of piece rates for cloth.[6]

The power loom displaced the hand loom and became the primary mode of cotton textile manufacture between 1830 and 1850. By 1838 almost every spinning mill at Stockport and Hyde had a weaving shed; at Oldham, combined firms were in the majority.[7] During this period the wages of handloom weavers and powerloom weavers were in competition, although the fall in wages of handloom weavers was already well under way.[8]

The first "steam-weavers," both in England and in Scotland, were nearly all women.[9] Cotton weaving on the power loom began as a woman's occupation for a number of reasons, including the reluctance of male handloom weavers to enter the factory at all, and the low piece rates paid for powerloom weaving.[10] Since handloom weaving provided serious competition for manufacturers of powerloomed cloth, their factories could only survive if they kept their wages sufficiently low. According to historian Ivy Pinchbeck, "the level of wages originally was such that women's labor was more easily obtained than that of men."[11] In addition, manufacturers were anxious to employ women, in large part because they believed them to be less likely to form trade unions and cause trouble.[12]

In 1824 the only men employed in weaving departments were "dressers." According to Sidney Chapman, it was not until some years later that "the rising male generation began to be absorbed by the new industry."[13] Patrick Joyce estimates that it was during the 1840s that adult men entered powerloom weaving in significant numbers. By the time men entered cotton textile weaving, women were already preeminent in the industry, and their wages set the standard. Throughout the century, the rates paid to powerloom weavers fell below those paid to other male skilled workers. As a unionist commented, the "standard of comfort is reckoned in the double wage" in the weaving districts; but the joint income of husband and wife did not amount to more than the single wage of a mule spinner or an engineer.[14] Women weavers, however, made better wages than any other women workers in the country.

By the 1880s the manufacture of powerloomed cotton textiles dominated the towns and cities of North and Northeast Lancashire. Spinning was concentrated in South Lancashire and Cheshire, although the majority of firms in both the north and the south combined spinning and weaving departments.[15] The percentage of men who worked as weavers varied depending upon what other sources of employment were available. In districts where there were engineering firms or collieries, such as Oldham, Wigan, and Manchester, men had other opportunities for employment and could earn wages higher than were paid for weaving. In the regions of South Lancashire that specialized in the production of cotton yarn, men were either spinners or worked in jobs ancillary to spinning. But in those areas in which cloth manufacture was the staple industry—towns like Clitheroe, Burnley, Colne, Nelson, Blackburn, and Darwen—there were few alternatives, and so men as well as women became weavers.[16] The only occupations that were better paid and available in any number other than weaving were spinning (if there were firms that combined making yarn and making cloth) and the job of overlooker or "tackler."[17]

Low Moor, Clitheroe, in North Lancashire, was a hamlet about fifteen miles north of the great weaving center of Blackburn. Thomas Garnett and Sons' Low Moor Mill manufactured both yarn and cloth and was the primary source of employment for the residents of the village. Of the 279 employed males living in Low Moor in 1851 who worked in the local cotton mill, 68 were employed as piecers, 63 as weavers, 39 as spinners, and 20 as overlookers. The rest were employed in a variety of processes in small numbers.[18] There simply were not enough jobs as spinners or overlookers for the number of adult men who needed and wanted work.[19] Like the carpet weavers of Kidderminster who begged for women's jobs at women's rates of pay, men in the cotton-weaving districts became weavers because they had few other opportunities for employment.

Once women had become established as cotton weavers, men wanting jobs could not have demanded higher rates for themselves, or, as John Bright, whose factories in Rochdale employed women to weave cotton cloth as well as carpets, remarked, since women do weaving as well as men, "if men demanded more than women, women alone would be employed."[20] Because men were willing to work for the same rates that women were paid, employers could not play women off against men, especially since the weavers' unions insisted on a common piece-rate standard. At least until the end of the century, the industry remained sexually integrated, with about 40 percent male cotton weavers.

Unlike the other industries examined thus far in this book, women and men worked the same machinery, in the same factories, for the same piece-rate wages. Cotton weaving was not segregated by sex: men and women often worked side by side. Numerous aspects of cotton weaving provided the opportunity for male and female weavers to share experiences.[21] If they joined a trade union, they found both women and men as fellow unionists. William O'Neill, who lived in Low Moor, wrote in his journal that he and his daughter Jane together became members of the weavers' union in the winter of 1859.[22] The majority of weavers worked under similar structural conditions, then—but the extent to which their experiences were the same is arguable.

GENDER DIFFERENCES IN WEAVING

Although piece rates for weaving were set according to a single standard, men frequently earned more per week than did women.[23] Considering the industry as a whole, Sidney Webb and Beatrice Webb wrote:

> The great majority of the women will be found engaged on the comparatively light work paid for at the lower rates. On the other hand, a majority of the men will be found practically monopolising the heavy trade, priced at higher rates per yard, and resulting in larger weekly earnings.[24]

For example, at Wellington Mills in Ashton-under-Lyne, all of the broadloom weavers were men, whereas the more numerous narrow-loom weavers, who earned lower piece rates, were almost exclusively women.[25] Sarah Dickenson, secretary of the Manchester Women's Trades and Labor Council in 1914, believed that male trade unionists only pretended to care about women and would say some cloth was too heavy for women to weave in order to keep the better-paid work for themselves.[26]

In many mills, women and men were doing identical work; even so, men brought home more money than women.[27] In some factories men tended to work four or six looms and women tended to work two or four looms;[28] men tuned their own looms, but women generally had to wait in idleness for the tackler to adjust the looms; and men but not women were allowed by law to work overtime and during meals.[29] In Preston, male weavers' weekly wages ranged from 22 to 29 shillings, and females' wages varied from 21 to 27 shillings.[30] Even though opportunities for social mobility were extremely limited for both women and men in weaving towns, only men became overlookers, earning the best pay available in weaving sheds. Women were not encouraged either to tune their own machines or to apply for the post of overlooker.[31]

The weavers' unions had rules against men cleaning their machines outside of the legal factory hours, but even so many men worked overtime. The women often risked being penalized in order "not to be behind the pace-makers."[32] An official of the Darwen weavers' union commented that men's overtime work had the consequence of creating a "fictitious" production standard which employers then demanded of the women. He remarked that the women had "to strain every muscle to keep up the pace set by the men" who persisted in working during meal hours.[33]

What seems to have been at issue here was "rate busting" by men. Numerous studies of blue collar workers have shown that workers establish a relatively uniform production rate on the shop floor, and those who exceed that rate are subject to sanctions by their coworkers.

However, women weavers and the unions that represented them could not enforce a uniform pace of production. Men escaped the union's disapprobation for breaking the union's rules because they had the sympathy of male union leaders; after all, their wages were lower than those of other skilled workers, especially when compared with the wages earned by the spinners in their own communities. Working when women were prohibited from working, tuning their own looms, and, in some mills, working more looms than women or making a heavier grade of cloth, for which a higher rate was paid, than women made were ways for male weavers to gain a sense of masculine pride in being a weaver. In this way they could differentiate their work from women's work. To match the men's rate of production, women were forced to work at a faster pace than men.[34]

Overlookers represented the authority of employers in the weaving sheds; they often had the power to hire and fire.[35] They were the "aristocrats," both in the mills and in the communities that stretched beyond the factory gates. Not only were women weavers excluded from consideration for the job of overlooker, their experiences with overlookers differed from those of their male weaving colleagues. Because employers believed women could not tune their machines and women were discouraged from attempting to learn, more overlookers superintended women weavers than supervised men. This meant that individual women weavers were under closer and more constant supervision than were individual men. Women were frequent targets of a variety of forms of victimization from their overlookers. In many of the weaving districts, the overlookers were thought to be tyrannical and in some cases "much worse than the masters."[36] In many areas of Lancashire, including the Blackburn manufacturing district, women weavers were more subject than men weavers to being "driven" by the overlookers, who earned a percentage based on the output of the weavers who worked under them.[37] Thomas Birtwhistle, secretary of the East Lancashire Weavers' Association, believed "driving" was the reason that so few weavers could continue to work beyond the age of fifty.[38] In addition to the common practice of "driving" women, overseers often gave women extra allotments of difficult work to do that slowed their pace of production and reduced their weekly wages.

Sexual harassment is a contemporary term, but the behaviors that the term denotes certainly occurred in nineteenth-century mills. Some overlookers in weaving and in card and reeling departments of spinning mills were believed "to take advantage of the female employees under the cloak of their position."[39] Women feared the offending overlookers, knowing their employers would do nothing to help them. For example, in 1886 the Oldham Card and Blowing Room Operatives Union went on strike against the Henshaw Street Spinning Company because an overlooker had sexually harassed the female employees working for him. At first the employers refused to take any action against the man. It was only after he was convicted in court that the company officials discharged him; but they also refused to rehire any of the striking workers.[40] In Nelson the salacious advances of an overlooker led to a dispute that was settled in the female employees' favor only after local clergymen intervened by appealing to the employers to "recognize their duty in this matter . . . to make the moral conduct of their work-people the subject of nearer concern and of greater importance."[41] Mill managers also were guilty of abusing their authority by taking sexual liberties with the women who worked for them.[42]

There is some evidence that women were more subject to losing their jobs in cutbacks than were men. For example, whereas the male weaving work force at Low Moor Mill remained constant between 1851 and 1861, there was a 20 percent reduction in the number of women weavers during the same time period.[43] Because cotton weaving was the best-paid employment open to women and because they had access to a more limited number of jobs than did men, women who had families dependent on their wages were subject to a variety of forms of victimization. The very precarious economic position of women textile workers was especially evident during strikes and lockouts, when it was primarily women with children who sought relief from the Poor Law guardians.[44] In many districts unionists were persecuted by employers, and women were especially vulnerable to such victimization.[45] These various differences in the work experiences of the male and female weavers of Lancashire coexisted with the equal piece rates they earned and the similarities in the work they performed.

THE PARALLEL LIVES OF MALE AND FEMALE WEAVERS

Similarities between the life courses of male and female weavers coexisted with important gender differences that marked their life experiences. In Lancashire it was widely recognized and repeated to investigators such as Sidney Webb and to various Parliamentary Commissions that the wages a male weaver could make were insufficient to support a family. Thomas Birtwhistle told the Royal Commission on Labour in 1892 that a person who earned 28 shillings a week and who had no other family members at work could not save money and often got into debt over ordinary household expenses. He explained that it was the people with three or four grown-up sons or daughters who earned enough to save anything. Birtwhistle was describing the reality for the majority of weavers' households. In these households it was expected that family members should pool their wages in order to make ends meet and to put something aside for hard times. The weavers' secretary in 1892 could have been describing what the 1881 census of Low Moor, Clitheroe, had revealed about the households of those who worked at Low Moor Mill.[46] Of male weavers who headed households, 63 percent were married to weavers working at the mill. Only 29 percent of weaving husbands had wives who were full-time housewives. Not only did women weavers continue to work after they married, but they remained at their jobs after they had children and only left the mill when they had at least one child in the labor force. One-third of full-time housewives with children, compared with 70 percent of their counterparts who were weavers, lived in households in which none of the children were employed. In 61.4 percent of Low Moor households where there were children but none were in the labor force, both husband and wife were working in the mill. In contrast, in 73.9 percent of households where there was at least one working child, only the husband was in employment. Of all married women living with their husbands in Low Moor, 47.1 percent were employed.

For the majority in communities like Low Moor in which residents were virtually totally dependent on the local cotton textile mill for their employment, then, working in the mill was a family affair, and the earnings of more than one member of the family were necessary to meet household budgets. William O'Neill wrote eloquently in his journal about the economic interdependence of family members. After his wife had died, he and his daughter Jane moved to Low Moor, where both worked in the mill, he as a weaver, young Jane as a winder. On the last day of the year 1856, O'Neill wrote:

> I find that I am in rather better circumstances than I was at the beginning and Jane is also a great deal better, and if we should remain here

Table 1.   Age of Weavers in Low Moor by Sex, 1881

Age	Female		Male	
	N	%	N	%
0–14	10	6.3	9	9.5
15–19	30	19.0	22	23.2
20–24	33	20.9	15	15.8
25–34	33	20.9	21	22.1
35–44	32	20.2	18	18.9
45–54	14	8.9	4	4.2
55 and over	6	3.8	6	6.3
Total	158	100.0	95	100.0

Source: Calculated from 1881 enumerators' listings of households in Low Moor, RG 11/4035.

another year it is hard to tell what state we may be in if we live, but at any rate we must hope for the best. For so long as God gives us health and strength we are willing to work and do our best. For Jane is a good girl and as long as she remains with me she has nothing to fear. She has plenty of good clothes, more than she has ever had in her life before, and if nothing happens, I will have a new suit this next summer, and until then I will do my best.[47]

Such evidence suggests that family members led integrated lives at work as well as at home.

These men and women who made up the weaving work force resembled one another in age and marital status. The 1881 census data for Low Moor reveal demographic portraits of male and female weavers that were remarkably similar (see Table 1). Not only was the age distribution of male and female weavers similar, but the older age groups contained roughly equal proportions of women and men. This suggests that women remained weavers for about the same proportion of their lives as men—if not longer: in Low Moor 62 percent of all weavers were women, whereas 66 percent of weavers forty-five and older were women. In addition to the overall similarity in their age profiles, there was a similarity in the proportions of male and female weavers who were living with their parents: about 44 percent of female weavers, versus about 38 percent of male weavers. Moreover, roughly similar proportions of male and female weavers were single, married, and widowed (see Table 2). Only 8 percent fewer female

Table 2. Marital Status of Weavers in Low Moor by Sex, 1881

Marital Status	Female N	Female %	Male N	Male %
Single	68	45.9	34	39.5
Married	72	48.7	49	57.0
Widowed	8	5.4	3	3.5
Total	148	100.0	86	100.0

Source: Calculated from 1881 enumerators' listings of households in Low Moor, RG 11/4035; based on residents aged fifteen and older.

weavers than male weavers were married, although proportionately more male than female weavers were married than were single. These data show that the men and women who might have been working together in the sheds, and who could very well have attended union rallies, were similar in important respects. These similarities could have been highlighted by union leaders in their attempts to build solidarity among the workers. As we shall see below, however, union leaders used quite different referents in their rhetoric.

THE DIVERGENT LIVES OF MALE AND FEMALE WEAVERS

Although male and female weavers appear to have been remarkably similar according to these life course indicators, there were important differences between the working women and men of Lancashire in their lives as family members. As young children, boys and girls were assigned different household duties. Although boys and girls began working in the mills at about the same age, education was less valued for girls than for boys.[48] Girls were frequently kept out of school by their parents so that they could help at home. Officials took a dim view of boys who were not at school, but the absences of girls met with less disapprobation.[49] The education that girls in Lancashire received often was geared to preparing them for their future domestic responsibilities.[50] Parents believed that boys, but not girls, deserved special educational opportunities; some libraries were closed to girls.[51] From their earliest years, girls were encouraged by parents and teachers, as well as by sexually segregated recreational and educational activities in their communities, to look forward to a life of domesticity.

This was so even though much of their future lives would combine domesticity with mill work. Men's future responsibilities as fathers and husbands required no special preparation or definition other than as working men. As Elizabeth Roberts has written about growing up in Lancashire:

> the implicit lesson learned by all girls was that, fundamentally, whatever else a woman might do in her life, the ultimate responsibility for the daily care of the home and the family lay with her, and not with the male members of the household. While girls acted as apprentices to their mothers, or even as their substitutes, boys were more likely to be out of the house, doing the shopping, helping with the allotment, or accompanying the male members of the family on an expedition, like walks, fishing trips or food-gathering forays.[52]

Then as now, children's games and toys were differentiated by gender, and from the 1860s on, girls in school were required to study needlework and other aspects of housewifery.[53] In these ways the ideal of domesticity for women and the Victorian notion of separate spheres pierced the very different reality of life in Lancashire mill towns. These different "gender tracks" both reproduced and reflected the reality of the double shift for women and the single shift for men.

Evidence from both the Victorian and the Edwardian period reveals that some men whose wives worked full-time helped them with their onerous and exhausting domestic chores. One Preston man's father prepared Sunday dinner, and he would "clean-up and wash-up."[54] Others helped their wives by tending young children or doing the cleaning, especially if there were no older children who could alleviate the pressures of keeping a household going. Yet, most of the evidence we have suggests that the burdens of domesticity were not shared equally.[55] Whether women worked in the mill or not, they cooked, laundered, cleaned, and managed the household finances. And they combined work in the mill with the lion's share of caring for and feeding their younger children. Harry Pollitt remembered how his mother cared for him and his sister:

> My sister and I were carried out of our bed at 5:30 every workday to be left in the care of Granny Ford for 4s a week, until it was safe to leave us in bed to look after ourselves, and that wasn't very long. Mother came rushing home from Benson's in the breakfast half-hour to give us our breakfast.[56]

Mothers wrapped babies in their shawls and took them to child minders early in the morning. When the dinner buzzer sounded, they hurried home to feed their young ones. Sometimes their infants were brought to the weaving sheds, "and they began to suckle their infants while friends put steaming pints of tea at their sides and whatever it was they had brought to eat." [57] If comments by contemporaries and their descriptions of how working women cared for their young children are accurate, they suggest that although husbands and wives in weaving households contributed almost the same amount of income to the household coffers, responsibility for children fell more heavily on mothers than on fathers. It was probably the case that husbands whose wives were working full-time did more housework than wives who worked in the mills part-time or were at home full-time. However, men's contributions to housework and child care did not come near to equaling that of their wives.

Generally, working mothers relied on the older children who were not yet working in the mill to watch the younger ones. It is no wonder that many Lancashire workers resented the Education Acts, which removed older children from the home, making working women's lives that much more difficult or even preventing mothers of very young children from working. At a rally during the great strike and lockout of 1878, a male weaver from Preston complained that the Education Act deprived the family of wages that the mother might earn (presumably because the older children could take care of the younger ones while the mother worked). He said, "Where there is a family of six children under twelve and the father is receiving only £1 a week, it was hard living. If that family had a child nine or ten years of age, the mother was perhaps able to earn 12s or 14s a week for support of the children." [58] The same weaver also objected to prohibiting children under the age of fourteen from working full-time. When a child could enter the labor force as a full-time worker, then the mother could withdraw from wage earning and devote herself fully to her family.

Census data from Low Moor, Clitheroe, in 1881 show that the majority of women worked until at least one child had entered the labor force. Women's factory work, especially in North Lancashire, was adjusted to the family life cycle. Mothers of one or two children were as likely to work as wives with no children living at home. [59]

This evidence suggests two important aspects of working-class life in the weaving districts of Lancashire. First, wage earning and family relations were intimately and intricately intertwined, especially for women and children. Second, a major difference between male and female powerloom weavers concerned how working in the mill was tied to the family life cycle. Men began work at the same age as women and remained in employment until they found other jobs, retired, or lost their jobs. In contrast, women continued at the weaving sheds until at least one of their children could replace their contribution to the household income.

Aggregate data from census materials, however, should not blind us to the differences among women and among men as they moved between home and work. Some mothers continued to work until they retired, like men. Some women never became mothers, and others never married. Like widowed women and like men, these single women would have continued to work in the sheds until they grew too old to go on working. A few men could afford to have their wives leave work when they married, just as some others had wives who continued at the mill for most of their married lives. Also, as I have indicated, there were both similarities and differences in the lives of women as a group and men as a group. They had the same or very similar jobs and pay rates and spent about the same proportion of their lives working in the sheds. But they differed in the timing of work and family life, as well as in their respective responsibilities when they combined the two. In addition, women workers in the mills often underwent more trying experiences at work than their male comrades.

Like scholars who attempt to capture the vast diversity that makes up the human experience in order to create a story about it, union leaders had to fashion their appeals for solidarity with particular images of workers in mind. They may not have examined the statistical makeup of the weaving community that they represented, but they painted word portraits of them in their public speeches. It was partly through those speeches that the members of the working class were identified and made into political subjects, abstracted from the varied daily existences which formed the reality of their lives.

GENDER AND TRADE UNION POLITICS

A strike by the Blackburn weavers, followed by a lockout of nearly all the cotton operatives in North Lancashire, lasted almost three months in the spring of 1878. The preceding fall, employers, who were organized into a massive and powerful employers' association that included master spinners and cloth manufacturers, had proposed a 5 percent reduction in the piece rate. After negotiation with the representatives of the weavers' and spinners' unions, they decided to delay taking action until the spring. In late March the employers' association announced that the piece rates would be reduced 10 percent, leaving the operatives no room for negotiation. Weavers struck at mills in several communities, but the bulk of the strike activity was in the Blackburn district. Claiming that the Amalgamated Weavers had plotted to concentrate the strike in Blackburn and to keep the mills in other towns operating at the reduced rate in order to raise funds to support striking workers, the employers' association proclaimed an industrywide lockout that affected all workers in the cotton industry of North Lancashire.

Strike leaders and trade union activists faced two problems concerning the rank and file in the labor dispute of 1878. They had to promote solidarity and perseverance, especially because out-of-work funds were minimal. As the strike wore on, the workers and their dependents were increasingly hard pressed, and many people had to appeal to the Poor Law authorities for help. In addition, union leaders were concerned that any behavior which was not "respectable" would hurt their cause.[60] They had to encourage restrained behavior and speech on the part of the strikers and to convince the industrialists that they could negotiate honorably.

In examining the role of women in the 1878 strike, we must recall that the male union leadership had been steeped in the culture of paternalism. In addition, the extension of the franchise to urban workers in 1867 had both rewarded their restrained behavior and, for the first time in history, given working-class men in the factory districts some political clout. They used their new political influence to secure laws that benefited the trade unions. The 1871 Trades Union Act gave legal protection to trade union funds, and the Criminal Law Amendment Act of 1875 legalized peaceful picketing. Political rights for working men and the continuing denial of those rights for women were an important backdrop to the strategies adopted by the union leadership in the 1878 strike.

Women weavers were active in the three major labor disputes that occurred in the last half of the nineteenth century in the weaving districts of North Lancashire. Ann Fletcher and Margaret Fletcher traveled around Lancashire giving fiery speeches during the bitter strike and lockout in Preston in 1853–1854.[61] The *Preston Chronicle* identified one of the Fletchers as a strike committee delegate.[62] It was rare for women to play so formal a role in strike activities, and I have found no evidence that women occupied positions on speakers' platforms or were on unionwide strike committees in the two major labor disputes that occurred later in the century.[63] However, they attended rallies and meetings in large numbers; they participated in street demonstrations; and they voiced their opinions from the crowd.

In the strike and lockout that affected all of North Lancashire in 1878, women's presence at strike meetings and rallies was noted by the press. For example, the *Blackburn Standard* reported that a meeting of the card and blowing-room hands, held at the Britannia Inn in Blackburn to consider what to do about the employers' announcement of a wage reduction of 10 percent, drew a large number of workers, including many women.[64] At Burnley three thousand operatives met, and the press reported "a fair muster of operatives of the gentler sex."[65] At a major strike rally held in Blackburn, with the crowds spilling out from Exchange Hall onto Blakey Moor, "many ladies were present."[66]

The women not only attended these meetings and rallies, they spoke from the audience, and sometimes they were active in persuading others to their point of view. For example, at a meeting in Darwen called to consider a strike vote, a male weaver moved to accept a 5 percent reduction unconditionally. When the chair asked if anyone would second the amendment, a female weaver proclaimed, "Nobody will second it." When the motion to strike was put to the crowd, it carried "amidst deafening shouts and whistling, with female voices being heard above the rest."[67] Toward the end of the dispute, women were active in deciding whether or not to go along with the decision of the strike leaders to end the strike.[68] Finally, in debates about how strike funds ought to be distributed, women argued, as one did at a Padiham meeting, "if there was any money in the union, it should be for those who had a lot of children, but no 'brass' to support them."[69] However, women rarely, if ever, made formal speeches about the dispute. When they participated from the audience, they spoke briefly. Sometimes they were oppositional, often by commenting on the proceedings from the crowd without being recognized by the chair. For example, in a rancorous discussion between the union leaders and the striking workers when the leadership was trying to get the workers to vote to end the strike, a woman was heard to say from the crowd, "I've not popped all my clothes yet." Her comment produced laughter from those around her.[70]

The employers' association instituted the lockout early in May, knowing full well the sorry financial state of the weavers' unions, whose fiscal affairs were reported in the local newspapers. In many communities only small percentages of the weavers were unionized; in Blackburn, for example, only one-third of the weavers were union members. This made the unions financially weak although the workers, whether unionists or not, remained loyal to the strike. The operatives continued to appeal to the employers to negotiate and to submit the dispute to arbitration, but to no avail. In spite of repeated urging by the strike leaders for people to remain calm, street demonstrations were held. Eventually riots erupted and spread from one village and town to the next. Troops and specially commissioned policemen, reinforced in one case with a private army of coal miners hired by an employer, were brought in to quell the insurrections. The national labor press called the conflict a "civil war,"[71] and a local newspaper carried the headline "Barbarism in Cottondom."[72]

The rioting began when the strikers in Blackburn learned that the employers' association had refused to see the strike committee. The newspaper accounts of street demonstrations and brawls and the descriptions of those who were arrested suggest that the primary instigators and participants were young people. Many were in their twenties, and some were much younger; it was rare for the police to arrest anyone over the age of thirty. Only occasionally was an adult woman or man charged with an offense. These primarily youthful protagonists included not only young men but young women, not only boys but girls. In Preston several hundred young men and women marched down Church Street singing "Rule Britannia": "Britons never shall be slaves."[73] The previous day three young female weavers had been arrested and charged with "outrage" for taking part in a demonstration during which an employer was "hooted," graffiti was chalked on his cab, and his partner was pelted with lumps of dirt and apples. Two of the women were twenty-two, and the third was a seven-year-old half-timer.[74] In Burnley a young woman was arrested for striking a police officer and kicking him with her clogs. In sentencing her the magistrate said, "It must be distinctly understood that women will be dealt with in future in the same way as the men, for their experience told them [the magistrates] that in these disturbances they were generally as bad as the men, if not worse."[75] Elsewhere women were charged in court with stone throwing, and some were accused of having participated in burning and vandalizing the house of Raynsford Jackson, a Blackburn employer who was the chair of the employers' association.[76] The *Blackburn Standard* reported of the latter incident: "a collection of half-dressed Irishwomen who accompanied the mob appeared to be chiefly instrumental by their yells and execrations in keeping up the excitement, and in hounding on those around them to further deeds of violence."[77] The press took special note of women's behavior. For example, at Darwen a crowd of people attacked a school in which police had been billeted. The newspaper reported, "Large, flinty stones were hurled through the windows . . . and it is not a little remarkable that women took a prominent part in the rioting."[78] A similar event in Accrington in which "youth and young women" participated produced the following comment from the press: "The young women delighted in the row as much if not more than the men."[79]

Although women came to meetings and supported this and other strikes, they participated from the sidelines and were portrayed by the press as being among the frustrated crowds hurling stones and epithets. Only men were the strike leaders. Only men spoke from the platforms in open-air mass meetings and the fronts of the meeting halls. Men formed the strike committees. Men led the local unions and composed the leadership of the Amalgamated Weavers' Association. Women remained steadfast in their resistance to the employers' demands and united with the men against their bosses in labor disputes, but the union leadership had difficulty recruiting them to membership, which, to judge by the leaders' own statements, generally weakened the unions' position vis-à-vis capital.[80] It was not until late in the century, and then only in very small numbers, that women assumed positions of leadership in the unions in areas where women were the majority of the work force. However, throughout the period they participated when their economic interests were at stake, but they did so shouting their comments from where they stood beneath the platforms and clustered in groups at the edges of the assemblies. They brandished stones and staves in the streets and spoke from the sidelines, behaving in ways that challenged the union leadership, because they had no voice in formal protest and resistance.

By examining the rhetoric used by men during the strike, we can understand both the nature of women's participation during disputes and over specific grievances and their limited involvement in the weavers' unions more generally. Of course women's economic interests were at stake in labor disputes, and it was those economic interests that were the focus of strike rhetoric. However, for a strike, especially one in which large numbers of people were not union members, to succeed, loyalty must be generated. Women's attendance at strike rallies and meetings and their loyalty during the difficult weeks of the lockout were actively solicited by the strike leaders. At almost every meeting across the breadth of Lancashire, including at rallies held in South Lancashire where strike leaders spoke to raise money, the chair and/ or the presiding union officials specifically addressed the audience as "working women and working men," "brothers and sisters," "ladies and gentlemen." For example, at a rally in Ashton called to garner financial and moral support for their comrades in the north, the president of the Preston Weavers' Union said to the assembled crowd that he knew he would have the support of "his brother and sister operatives."[81] At Burnley in the early days of the strike, the chair of a crowded meeting of operatives addressed the audience as "Ladies and Gentlemen."[82] It was commonplace for women to be included in invitations to meetings announced on placards.[83]

Strike leaders used gender-inclusive language that recognized women workers as important participants in the conflict. However, they also made numerous speeches and comments during the strike that placed male workers in the center of the struggle and constructed women as at best marginal and at worst a problem for the union. For example, the men reinforced the idea that it was unusual, and perhaps lacking in respectability, for women to speak up in public. At a Burnley meeting that was crowded with both women and men, the chair asked, "Is there any gentleman in the body of the hall, or a lady either, for all that, if they think proper, who wishes to make any remarks in support of this resolution or otherwise? If they do they will have an opportunity of doing so."[84] Given this ambivalent invitation, it is not surprising that Annie Brown began her letter to manufacturers which was printed in a local newspaper with the demurral that she hoped she would not be thought "bold or unladylike." In her letter she portrayed the working class as victims, using imagery that was iconographically female. She referred to workers as "poor unfortunates," "poor creatures," "poor slaves"; and she wrote of "man" and "gentlemen" to question the honor and worthiness of the employers. For example, she argued that to reduce wages without running short time would "do no good, and would be an act unworthy the name of man."[85]

The men who spoke in public meetings during the strike frequently used the terms *manly* and *manliness,* most often to exhort their fellow workers to bravery and honor. They expressed their entreaties in military metaphors.[86] Historian Elizabeth Faue has analyzed how men in the American labor movement of the twentieth century used such metaphors to build solidarity. She has written: "The metaphors of struggle, even political struggle, are the metaphors of war and battle; and war is not female."[87] Faue's analysis fits the public culture created during the Lancashire strike of 1878. For example, early in the dispute the strike leaders described it as a "contest between capital and labor" with the operatives and employers being in the same position "as the two late contending armies in the East. The Employers were the Russians, and the operatives were the Turks."[88]

Using the language of respectable resistance, the leadership linked their pleas for restraint and decorum with manliness. They identified bravery and honorable battle with masculinity, to condemn the street disturbances and vandalism as illicit forms of worker resistance. For example, a placard urging calm and civil order after the riots in Padiham proclaimed: "As a body of operatives we have entered upon the present struggle voluntarily, and therefore, we ought to fight fairly and manfully . . . and suffer rather than submit to the harsh terms held out for acceptance."[89] The following placard was posted at Darwen in the wake of riots and street disturbances there:

> Every factory worker who conducts himself peacefully proves himself a man! Every factory worker who conducts himself in any other way injures his own cause, and degrades his own class. . . . Be peaceful and firm in both language and conduct and success will be more certain.[90]

The notice was signed by John Brennan, secretary of the card-room operatives' strike committee, which primarily represented female workers. These entreaties deployed masculine imagery and stressed the leaders' ideal of respectable manhood. By implication they linked with womanhood the disorderly behavior threatening their authority.

The language of respectable labor relations echoed with tones of patriarchy when it appealed to families as the ultimate source of control and restraint. For instance, strike leaders at Padiham urged families to keep their children at home and "fight manfully not with brick-bats and staves."[91] The most eloquent of the pleas for order that focused on women and men in their roles as parents was issued by the Amalgamated Weavers' Association after the rioting and was signed by its secretary, Thomas Birtwhistle, and the presidents of the affiliated associations of Blackburn, Preston, and Darwen:

> "Good name in man or woman is the immediate jewel of their souls." To the Operatives of North and North East Lancashire—Brothers and Sisters in distress—We address you once more as men laboring under a sense of the deepest responsibility for every word now said by us in this grave crisis. . . . riots have existed. This vagabondism we disclaim and condemn. . . . Security is the twin sister of industry. Without peace labor can never enjoy plenty. There is not a man amongst you who would grant to a ruffian with a brickbat what he had previously denied to persuasion and reason. We know it is not the fair average Lancashire man or woman who has done the mischief. . . . Fathers and sons, remember in the midst of these new dangers your lads may be easily tempted. Mothers and daughters, we ask your help to restore peace. In conclusion, we appeal to you fellow-workmen to assist . . . in restoring peace and order in the disturbed districts.[92]

This appeal was framed in gender-inclusive language, but was focused on familial authority based on a division of responsibility between fathers and mothers. The slogan that "security is the twin sister of industry" was an entreaty to restore orderly relations between labor and capital. The statement that "there is not a man amongst you who would grant to a ruffian with a brickbat what he had previously denied to persuasion and reason" used "man" to symbolize the conduct of rational and respectable labor relations.

Even though women and men in cotton weaving earned roughly equal wages, and they often lived together as husband and wife, trade union leaders used family-wage rhetoric in addition to battle imagery to inspire solidarity. A male unionist exhorted the assembled operatives in Burnley "to be united, and to remember that they were struggling not only for themselves, but for their wives and families. If they had to face the inevitable let them acquit themselves like men."[93] Like the carpet weavers who fought to retain their wages and their jobs in the face of competition from lower-paid women workers, the male cotton weavers legitimated their struggle by appealing to the ideal of the male breadwinner. Shortly after the employers informed the weavers' unions that wages would be reduced by 10 percent, union leaders from Preston, Blackburn, and Burnley issued a memorial to the employers' association, pleading, "We beg to remind you also that men with families of small children feel keenly the high rents and dear provisions."[94] At a mass meeting in Clitheroe, Thomas Sutton exhorted those gathered to unite and be strong. He asked:

> how had those men who had large families, and we the only ones working in the house, to sustain themselves at the reduced rate? One man could not make £3 a week and he did not advocate the employment of both man and wife in the mill. A man ought to be able to earn sufficient to keep his wife at home, and then they would be more healthy and comfortable and would help diminish the quantity of cloth in the market.[95]

The strike leaders also drew on the ideal of men as breadwinners and protectors to persuade the rank and file to end the strike and return to work at the 10 percent reduction. At a mass meeting at Blakey Moor in Blackburn, which drew an estimated crowd of between fifteen thousand and twenty thousand people, the chair told the assembly that the strike had gone on long enough and it was their duty to end it: "If they [the rank and file] were prepared to let their wives go and beg from door to door and to let their children run wild about the street, he was prepared to clothe his children and keep up the struggle."[96]

As strike leaders and male operatives drew on the popular images of masculinity in their public rhetoric, they often linked their demands and these masculine images to the "working mother" problem that was part of the larger discourse on motherhood that was taking shape during this period. A speaker at a meeting at the Mackenzie Arms in Bamber Bridge referred to the mortality rates in Preston, which were higher than elsewhere:

> The authorities were now trying to establish nurseries for wives to take little ones to be looked after. There was nothing that would touch a father's feelings more than to know that his wife had to leave their little ones with some unnatural mother, who would not look properly after them. . . . when a woman got married she ought to stop at home and attend to house duties, but this could not be done if the masters reduced the wages.[97]

In Ashton, a town in South Lancashire, where almost all the weavers were women, at a meeting called by strike leaders to raise funds Thomas Banks, the president of the Preston weavers' association, said:

A great deal of misery at home and over-production in the mills was caused by weavers allowing their wives to go to the mill, and ... if it were at all possible ... keep the wives out of the mill. Let them suckle their infants at home, for a great deal of infant mortality was caused by the neglect of the mothers who had to attend their work at the mill and could not give their children the attention they required.[98]

Banks used the link between working mothers and infant mortality in a commentary on class relations. He argued that mothers worked at the mill and their children died because "the husbands could not earn enough money in the mill to keep their wives and children."[99]

We do not know the responses of working women to these orations in the meeting halls. Given the arduousness of their daily lives and the difficulties of caring for infants under the conditions in which they lived and worked, we can only surmise that the speakers' family-wage rhetoric and images of domesticity touched a sensitive nerve. However, we do not know either how they saw their lives as workers and as trade unionists or how this rhetoric affected their interpretation of their life experiences. What does a married woman worker hear when she is told that she *should not be* a worker? What does a married man who shares the burden of economic support for his family with his wife hear when he is told that she should not have to work, but instead should be at home taking care of their children?

These representations constructed workers and the working class as masculine and marginalized women. Although strike leaders recognized that females and males were present at public meetings and demonstrations, men were the subjects of their discourse and women were usually mentioned only in contexts that stressed the desirability of their absence as workers. Public rhetoric that made men central and women peripheral to the workplace portrayed working women as outside working-class politics.

When strike leaders called for a family wage and glorified motherhood, portraying it in opposition to paid employment, they did not offer a view of the problems these working women faced that might have drawn them into union affairs. Family wage rhetoric was silent on the subject of women as *workers*. Unionists did not speak, for example, of the double shift and their overwork in the home, nor did they demand direct assistance from employers or the state in rectifying the problems that beset working mothers.[100] Unionists accused working wives of helping to cause the excessive production of cloth which contributed to the economic problems of the industry. However, they usually failed to mention the overtime voluntarily done by men during meal times, or the "driving" by overlookers, whose loyalty to the strike was believed to be critical. They merely reiterated that married women should not work and husbands should earn enough to support them.

The concept of womanliness in the Lancashire weaving communities focused on motherhood and marriage more than it did on women's identity as weavers and as workers. In the construction of masculinity in Lancashire, men's workplace relations and their participation in the labor force as male heads of households were emphasized. In spite of the fact that women weavers ostensibly earned the same wages as men and were even reputed to make better weavers, especially on the finer goods, it was their family status that defined them.

Like homeworkers whose wages were essential to their households, women powerloom weavers were construed as secondary wage earners.[101] This is ironic in several ways. In the first place, many married women continued to work as weavers after they had children, because their households depended on their wages for economic survival. Thus, childbearing alone did not distinguish women and men as workers; what differentiated them was the double shift for women but not for men. In the second place, the growing imbalance in the sex ratio in the nineteenth century as young women increasingly outnumbered young men meant that many women would remain single and would be self-supporting for their entire lives. Finally, male weavers rarely were able to support a household without the contribution of at least one other full-time worker.

In spite of the centrality of women's wages in weaving households, however, men as a class were construed to be the primary wage earners whose wages were only being supplemented by their wives. Such a portrayal interpreted their experience as men married to weavers as temporary and unimportant for their identity as men. It denied the actual dependence of men on their wives' earnings.[102] It glossed over the reality that male weavers were not breadwinners in the same way as their fellow spinners. In Low Moor, for example, only 29 percent of married male weavers had wives who were housewives, in comparison to 42 percent of spinners.[103] The rhetoric presented as an ideal a family form that was unattainable by the majority of weavers. It played with aspiration and manipulated a primary symbol of Victorian respectable manhood—that of the breadwinner and family provider—for its emotional charge.

Rhetoric that placed men at the center and women on the periphery of the working class was not unique to the strike of 1878. Speakers in the Preston strike and lockout of 1853–1854, including Ann Fletcher and Margaret Fletcher, urged married women to remain out of the labor force and advocated a family wage for men.[104] The promotion of the family wage by these particular women is not what is noteworthy. It was the meaning of the family-wage demand, not necessarily the sex of its promoters, that was important. What is remarkable is that the Fletchers went around the country giving public speeches during a time when women appeared less and less often in public and were uninvolved in the formal proceedings of working-class organizations.[105] Ironically, it was just such oratory that encouraged their disinterest.

During a districtwide weavers' strike in 1884 the all-male Weavers' Committee (composed of some of the same men as in the dispute six years earlier) issued a circular addressed "To the Trades of the United Kingdom and the Public Generally." It requested assistance in their struggle against yet another reduction in weavers' wages.[106] They justified their request in the following way:

> The trade to which we belong is of an exceptional character, such a large number of women and children being engaged therein, whose intentions are to leave it as they grow up, especially the females after getting married. In consequence, this class scarcely ever enter our societies or make any provision for emergencies, and a still further number as in most trades, neglect that duty to themselves and brother workers.[107]

Male trade unionists generally blamed women for the weakness of integrated unions representing large numbers of women. Such blaming contributed to a discourse about women workers that emphasized, not what they had in common with male workers, but their differences. The belief that women made bad trade unionists was widely promulgated and contributed to women's apparent reluctance to take an active part in integrated unions such as the weavers' associations.[108]

GENDER DIVISIONS WITHIN TRADE UNIONISM

Major spokesmen of the trades union movement of the day were less than enthusiastic about women workers. Labor leader George Howell, who headed the influential Parliamentary Committee of the Trades Union Congress in the last quarter of the century, wrote:

> Women are essentially weak, in an industrial as well as physical sense, as those know who are acquainted with the facts of actual life. Some of the causes of this weakness lie deep and hidden in human nature, others are not far to seek. The fact, however, is patent; woman needs protection.[109]

Henry Broadhurst expressed his support for increasing legislative restrictions on women workers to the Trades Union Congress, where women unionists were present for the first time:

> It was a well-known fact that women . . . were unable to do anything to help themselves unless someone stretched out a helping hand to them. . . . Much good has been done by Mrs. Paterson, and other ladies, in forming and maintaining unions, but they would never be able to lift woman to her proper sphere unless they had some restrictions put upon the greed of those who would work their mothers or sisters like dogs or slaves for the sake of gain.[110]

The next year, when a proposal advocating that women be hired as factory inspectors was discussed, Broadhurst argued against it:

> One of the reasons why he had doubted the wisdom even of inviting ladies to the Congress as delegates was not because he did not like their company, but because he feared that under their persuasive eloquence the Congress would at some time or other be led into the illogical position that men could be placed in and would vote for a proposition which they would not entertain in their clearer and more rational moments.[111]

Women were continually portrayed by such leaders and the labor press as mothers or potential mothers first and as workers second, if at all. *The Bee-Hive* in 1873 was eloquent on the subject of "Mothers":

> The woman who should be most honoured, most loved in this world, is she who brings up a dozen children loving one another thoroughly. She may not be great-minded; she may be a little inclined to scandal; only let her so manage with her children that they shall unostentatiously love one another, and it may be truly said to her—"thou hast not lived in vain."[112]

The *Cotton Factory Times* printed the following verse in 1891:

How sweet it is when toil is o'er
To sit upon the hearth once more
To whistle, sing, and sweet converse,
With the sweetest queen in universe,
In homely way.[113]

Even Lady Dilke, a vociferous advocate of the women's trade union movement, wrote that it seemed "natural" for men to earn more than women:

> For man is properly regarded and paid as the breadwinner, who is answerable for the maintenance of others besides himself, whilst the woman's labor, however constant and fruitful, is only looked on as something by which she may supplement his earnings. . . . we know that women are not in a position at present to demand equal payment nor would they be supported by public opinion. They are not, as a rule, the breadwinners; nor as a rule can they work as hard or as long as men.[114]

However, many women publicly disagreed with these categorizations of them; they argued a different point of view at congresses and in the press. To John Ruskin's letter in the *Women's Union Journal* that asserted that men should protect women and not allow them to work at all, "a woman unionist" responded:

> If it is desirable that the women should become so much plastic clay in the hands of the men, to be moulded to whatever form they choose, that women should be degraded into slaves, for what slavery is worse than that of the mind, then it is desirable that women should look to men for their support.[115]

The male unionist who called himself Caliban wrote to the *Women's Union Journal* that women work in factories with "the inherited tendency to lean" on men for support, and "they cannot be taught" political economy, trade, commerce, or market rates of wages to make them good unionists.[116] "One Who Cannot Be Taught" wrote in response:

> Wilt thou, O superior being, who lookest down with such tender pity from thine height upon the creatures born but to cook and nurse, wilt thou believe in such a monstrous creation as a working woman who actually had the audacity to take that kind of teaching, nay more, carried her presumption to such startling lengths that she obtained the first prize in political economy at the Society of Arts against all her male competitors.[117]

Although some women spoke out in their own defense as workers and as unionists, male trade union leaders experienced difficulty in attempting to organize large numbers of women and to motivate their active participation in union affairs. Trade union leaders of the day accounted in a variety of ways for women's reluctance to become active unionists. Some believed the domestic duties of women prevented them from coming to meetings;[118] others believed women were out having fun in the evenings rather than either doing domestic chores or attending union meetings. Some presumed the women themselves thought men were better leaders; these claimed that women would not vote for other women.[119] According to the president of the Bolton and District Weavers' Association, it was the mothers of young weavers who were the stumbling blocks to their participation.[120]

Other interpretations suggested that it was difficult for individual women to enter men's domains. A woman weaver from Chorley responded to social investigator B. L. Hutchins's questions about women's activism by saying that "the men would not welcome them."[121] A weaver from Nelson who wanted to become a dues collector said that the Nelson Weavers' Institute had no women's room; she tried going to the institute, "and the men stared at her but made no difficulty."[122] The secretary of the Ashton society reported that women objected to the possibility of being the only woman on the committee and would not stand for election.[123] The secretary of the Burnley and District Weavers, Winders and Beamers remarked that the indifference of women might result from the fact that they had had no good women speakers to rouse them.[124] Sarah Dickenson, head of the Manchester Women's Trades and Labor Council, believed that it was better for women to be organized separately from men, because the men looked out for their own interests and did not concern themselves with women's needs.[125]

Surveys of trade unions conducted by Sidney Webb from the 1890s through 1914 show that women were more likely to be leaders in those associations that had very few men. For example, in 1894 weavers and winders in the Oldham district (predominantly female) elected a woman president, a forty-seven-year-old winder who had been employed for twenty-seven years.[126] By 1914 the Weavers' Committee at Wigan was entirely made up of women; and at Glossop, where 81 percent of the weavers in the union were women, four women sat on the committee, and women had acted as canvassers both in the sheds and at the weavers' homes.[127] However, even at that late date no women held positions of leadership in the Amalgamated, and the male secretaries of weavers' societies at Rochdale, Nelson, and Chorley, where male weavers were more numerous, complained that women left the organizational work of the union to men.[128]

It was not being female that made women reluctant unionists, nor did their presumed lack of enthusiasm for unionism result simply from the fact that the majority of women married and had children. Rather, unionists were made, not born, and those who spoke for the unions needed to encourage women's participation through public rhetoric and action. To enter the working men's world of labor politics in this period was, in the words of historian Joanna Bornat, "to be something of a rebel."[129] It is no wonder that Annie Brown, who during the 1878 strike wrote the only strike-related letter published in a newspaper of which I am aware, began it by saying: "I trust you will not think it bold or unladylike in me if I say a few words on the wage?"[130] It has always been difficult to stand alone.

Given the constraints, it is surprising to find that there were women who took the risk to their jobs and reputations to become active union organizers. For example, in Leicestershire in December of 1874, Mrs. Mason founded the Seamers and Stitchers Union, an organization of women homeworkers. Within a few months, Mrs. Mason, with her colleague Mrs. Fray, had enrolled three thousand women members in Leicester and twenty-seven surrounding villages. They accomplished this by walking from one house and one village to the next, often traveling up to twenty miles a day in ground covered with snow. At the Women's Trade Union League annual meeting, Mrs. Mason said, "We were over our shoe tops in snow and our clothes froze on us, but we did not care for that. We were in earnest and determined to find them [the homeworkers] all out."[131] Ann Ellis, a founder and principal spokesperson for the (sexually integrated) Dewsbury and District Heavy Woollen Weavers Association in Yorkshire, was fired from her job after having given an exceptionally strong and passionate public speech.[132]

It would be a mistake to view the heroism of women like Mrs. Mason and Ann Ellis in isolation from the context in which they acted. Certainly some exceptional people have stepped out of the multitude to imperil their lives and livelihoods in the service of others. The ranks of followers have swelled and the leaders who accepted the perils of organizing workers and collecting dues and strike funds have flourished when they have had support. But organizing efforts are successful when leaders address the experiences of the rank and file and portray them so that they legitimate their experiences as subjects of political action. It is surely no coincidence that Mrs. Mason and Mrs. Fray of Leicester, themselves homeworking seamers, stepped forward when they did to form a union among the most unlikely of potential trade unionists: homeworkers. They began their work in the same year and as a part of the same women's union movement that had been begun by Emma Paterson, who founded the Women's Protective and Provident League in July 1874. The league was established by bourgeois feminists to promote trade unionism among working women and was supported by a number of well-known and highly respected philanthropists and intellectuals, including Arnold Toynbee and Harriet Martineau.[133]

It is likely that the women unionists were given added encouragement by the activities of suffragists. Lancashire working women's involvement in the suffrage movement provides an interesting comparison to their reported lack of enthusiasm for trade unionism. As Jill Liddington and Jill Norris's study of the suffrage movement in the factory districts has told us, a special suffrage campaign was launched in Lancashire around the turn of the century.[134] Between 1900 and 1906 that campaign became increasingly successful in attracting the support of working women. A petition to the House of Commons, eventually signed by fifteen thousand women cotton workers, was launched in Blackburn:

> That in the opinion of your petitioners the continued denial of the franchise to women is unjust and inexpedient. In the home, their position is lowered by such an exclusion from the responsibilities of national life. In the factory, their unrepresented condition places the regulation of their work in the hands of men who are often their rivals as well as their fellow workers.[135]

The campaign was successful in stimulating women's active support for the vote because it spoke directly to the realities of their lives at home and at work. It construed those realities in a way that stimulated gender consciousness and promoted activism on behalf of the vote. Also, the campaign was successful because some of its leaders came from the ranks of women's trade union organizations, and they built on the foundation already begun by women trade unionists.

I am not arguing that male unionists consciously conspired to discourage women from being active unionists. However, the evidence that I have analyzed suggests that unexamined ideas about gender difference and a masculinized construction of work stymied working men in soliciting women's active involvement in union organization. Ideas about what it meant to be woman and what it meant to be man blinded working-class leaders to different ways of articulating the interests of women and men. At the same time, however, union men were exerting their dominance over women workers in labor politics, and their words and actions were expressions of power.[136]

CONCLUSION

The rhetoric of trade union leaders at congresses, in the press, and in labor disputes shows why the women weavers of Lancashire were more reluctant than men to be unionists and to participate actively once they had joined. It suggests why during disputes they spoke from the sidelines and expressed their inchoate resentments by hurling apples and rocks rather than by making formal speeches. Union solidarity was premised on masculine values, especially that of respectable manhood centered on the image of the male provider, and was secured by men who pitched their appeals to other men. When it was particularly important for the unions to make certain they had the women with them, they could act with unity. They made a cross-gender alliance possible by insisting on equal rates of pay, and they furthered that alliance in strikes by recognizing in their public speeches that women were present. Their rhetoric in strikes such as the one in 1878, however, created an alternative path for those who were not specifically included in their discourse. They implied that if respectable, orderly combatants were manly, then women were disorderly and might behave accordingly.

The very discourses used by labor leaders to produce restraint, then, may have contributed to its opposite, leading women to express their enthusiasm for workers' causes in ways that threatened male leaders' authority.[137] At best, union leaders' messages were mixed, and their assumptions about sexual difference unwittingly helped to weaken the union. Public oratory which made men central and women peripheral to the workplace portrayed working women as on the sidelines of working-class politics. But, ironically, the marginalization of women and its consequences were at the very heart of those politics.

8

Conclusions and Afterthoughts

Gender distinctions were woven into the fabric of industrial capitalism, and the development of industrial capitalism had an impact on what it meant to be a man and what it meant to be a woman. These meanings and the divisions between women and men in which they were articulated colored working-class life. They created different experiences for women and men of the working-class, and ideologies of gender influenced how those experiences were interpreted.

Gender distinctions were expressed in the division of labor that led women and men to do different jobs in manufacturing. They were articulated in an ideology of family life that portrayed men as those who were answerable for the economic well-being of the family and women as those charged with the care of children and the upkeep of the household. These representations were embedded in employer hiring and managerial practices and were at the center of the public policies that circumscribed the ways that working-class men and women made their livelihoods. However, the representations belied the extent to which most men were frequently economically dependent on their wives and children and most married women frequently combined their domestic responsibilities with economic contributions to their households. Single and widowed women had to be self-supporting or the sole support of others, or they had to make substantial economic contributions to the households in which they lived. Because women as a category were low-waged workers and primarily were hired to do work defined as unskilled, women without men were forced to subsist on earnings that did not cover the costs of maintaining themselves. Because many men worked at jobs that did not pay enough fully to support a family, and lurches in the economy could further reduce their earnings or even throw them out of work altogether, married women had to contribute to the support of their households. Women with babies and young children found it hard, but often necessary, to combine waged work with child care.

The language of gender represented women as childbearers and dependents and men as breadwinners. It constituted the labor market as a domain in which jobs were designed for men. Women's employment, especially the employment of married women and women with children, became problematic. Since wages were constructed as individual earnings and were not adjusted to the numbers of people dependent on them, men with families were forced to struggle under oppressive circumstances. Both women and men had difficulty meeting their family and workplace obligations. In addition, women often were accused of undermining male workers, and their economic pursuits stigmatized their husbands. Men's unemployment became symbolic of a character failing. Unemployment, which generally depended on the state of trade in the developing capitalist economy, became a symptom of masculine dishonor.

These gender constructions and the practices in and through which they were articulated affected class dynamics. Women and men often were thrown into competition; workers fought with one another as well as with their employers in their struggle for a livelihood. Even in cotton powerloom weaving, where men and women did the same work for equal piece rates, the gendered construction of men as workers and women as mothers weakened their sexually integrated unions. Because what it meant to be a man became bound up with being the primary breadwinner who could maintain his wife and young children at home, conflicts between male workers and capitalists were fueled by gender even when women were not competitors.

Gender distinctions were intrinsic to the dynamic of labor politics, but they operated in particular ways under differing circumstances. Employers who were forced to cut their labor costs to remain competitive often attempted to do so by hiring women to do work that men had been doing. Generally, male workers resisted their employers' initiatives and attempted to exclude the women. However, in the very rare situations when men were hired to work at jobs in which women were already preeminent, the only way men could get hired was to agree to work at women's wages.

Only rarely did jobs become sexually integrated. This happened when men had very few alternative opportunities for work. Job openings were limited, for example, when they lived in one-industry towns. These were the circumstances under which the Kidderminster carpet weavers' union eventually agreed to allow men to work with women to make plush for draperies. Similar conditions promoted job integration in the more significant case of cotton powerloom weaving in Lancashire. Otherwise, gender divisions and job segregation by sex were continually being reproduced through the struggles between workers and industrialists. Employers usually created sexually segregated employment, but occupational segregation also was recreated as a consequence of disputes with their male workers. Jobs were either "masculinized" or "feminized." They were rarely done by both women and men at the same time and in the same workplace.

Even in those exceptional instances where women and men worked side by side at the same jobs, gender distinctions affected their working conditions. Because men were thought to be the breadwinners, even when both women and men in the household were employed, men often were given privileges at work that were denied to women. These privileges fed male pride and helped to redress the threat that doing "women's work" posed to their manliness. A woman's chief identity was that of a wife and mother, regardless of her actual job commitments. In effect, although her job may have been a source of pride, it was still viewed as secondary to, or even as a detraction from, her femininity. When these meanings were elaborated in labor politics they had the consequence of keeping working women in subordinate roles in those trade unions to which men also belonged.

This study has identified several primary instruments of gender in working-class formation in the last half of the nineteenth century. Chief among these was working-class respectability, which developed as a supreme value among the working classes during the course of the century. To be respectable required that a man earn enough to support his wife and that he conduct himself at work and in the community in ways that were considered "manly" or honorable. Family respectability, and the respectability of family members, was premised on a male breadwinner whose wife could devote herself to the arts of domesticity. Respectability expressed intra-class distinctions and was a vehicle in cross-class relations, but it was also a gendered cultural form. Respectability and manliness were closely intertwined. A woman's respectability was subordinate to the man's: for a married woman it meant managing the household finances, making them stretch to accommodate the visible emblems of respectability that could be purchased in the marketplace, and it involved practicing the arts of domesticity, and for all women it was linked to their sexuality.

Respectability was centered on the family and on its connection, through men, to the workplace.

The rhetoric of the family wage, which made its appearance both in labor disputes where women and men were in competition for jobs and in disputes where there was no such competition, may be understood as part of this larger quest for respectability. The family-wage ideal was based on a vision of a strict, gender-based separation of economy and domesticity that masked their actual interdependence. The demand for a family wage was founded on an ideal of masculinity that required a man to be the sole support of his family. It was premised on the desirability of his wife being a full-time homemaker and mother. It rested on a contradiction between waged work and domesticity that was buttressed by public policy as well as by popular belief. Ultimately, the family wage, never fully achievable by male members of the working classes except perhaps for the most skilled artisans, was the bedrock of respectability and was a major ground of contention between employers and male workers, serving as a potent club in labor disputes.

Finally, during the last half of the nineteenth century a maternalist rhetoric developed among the bourgeoisie and was incorporated by leaders of the trade union movement. Maternalism was a construction that represented all women as mothers or potential mothers and gave women the primary responsibility for the health and welfare of children. Women were responsible for the care of their children, and men were admonished by the bourgeoisie for being bad husbands if their wives had to earn wages and were not at home to carry out their domestic duties.

Although women have entered the labor force in large numbers since World War II, and it is now acknowledged that both women and men are wage earners, the legacy of the nineteenth century lives on. Women in Britain and the United States are still juggling the demands of wage earning and the responsibilities of child care with little assistance from the state or communities in which they reside. Most jobs are still structured as though they were to be held by men, by people, that is to say, with minimal responsibilities for families and by people who do not bear children. When accommodations are made to women's presence in the labor force and jobs are restructured, two job tracks tend to emerge, with women in one kind and men in another. Job segregation by sex persists into the present and is continually being recreated. Rather than a reevaluation of the workplace to take into account the diversity of people who are actually working there and to shape work life to make the connections between work and family easier, women's jobs are still defined as different. They are the special case, just as women's machines in the nineteenth century were specially constructed when an employer wanted to replace men with women. The norm or the model of the worker was and still is a masculine one. Issues about "fetal protection" in the workplace resonate with maternalist ideology and reflect the continuation of gender distinctions, especially the incompatibility between women or motherhood and employment, that developed in the nineteenth century.

The evidence presented in Chapter 7 points to the power of gender distinctions and the pervasiveness of gender in labor politics regardless of the relatively equal positions of women and men in the paid labor force. But it also suggests that politics articulated in ways that speak to the difficulties faced by all workers, acknowledging the different needs of different workers while privileging no special group as "the norm," may create unity from diversity. However, this path has not often been followed, and it may not result in long-term solidarity. Alliances are always fragile, and alliances that acknowledge differences along with common purposes may be especially difficult to achieve. However, alliances that suppress crucial differences to create uniformity are always in danger of being undermined and subverted by what has been repressed.

Public policies and private negotiations between women and men must recognize that the differences between women's and men's experiences, produced at home and in their communities, as well as in the workplace, are constraining. Ultimately, change will depend on the creation of a society in which gender distinctions do not translate into superordinate and subordinate relations. An equitable society will acknowledge multiplicity, and the standards for jobs and for self-worth will not be based on the values and experiences of a single segment of the population.

I have shown how people's livelihoods were limited by the multiple ways that gender influenced the development of industrial capitalism and how gender ideologies and gender relations were changed by that development. The portrait I have drawn resembles a spider's web of interacting forces, all of which had gender distinctions built into each of them, but in ways that varied over time. This complexity is the reason that change has been so slow, coming in fits and starts, forward and retrograde movements. In recent years, conscious efforts at reform have been targeted at particular issues. Access to jobs, pay scales, child care, and parental benefits have each been the subject of political action. As soon as limited reform begins to make changes in one area—for example, through affirmative action programs—other problems have come to the surface as gender divisions have persisted.

Giving women and men the same or equivalent jobs for the same pay alone is not likely to remove gender inequality and occupational segregation, especially if those jobs continue to be structured, as they were in the nineteenth century, as though the people doing them could not have babies. (If decent wages were earned for doing them, though, at least the wage workers' lives would be improved.) At the same time, creating jobs that, in theory, can be structured to suit the people holding them will not change the distribution of women and men in those jobs unless other changes occur. If the highest social and economic rewards continue to be reserved for employment structured the old way—for men—then the distribution of women and men in these different jobs is likely to reproduce the gender divisions that have been so persistent. Until responsibility for the care of dependents has been reexamined and redefined as one to be shared by the community, as well as more equally between women and men, then gender hierarchies will continue to be recreated. As long as gender distinctions that result in structured inequalities are accepted as "natural" and are not made a focus of politics, business will go on as usual.

In the nineteenth century, working-class women, as a group, were more disadvantaged than working-class men, as a group. They earned less money and faced more difficult circumstances in their jobs, in addition to the trying conditions under which they fulfilled their familial responsibilities. However, working-class men did not get off easily. What I have tried to illuminate in this book is that gender affected class relations in ways that impaired the collective efforts of men and women to live their lives.

The approach I have taken suggests two points that are important for understanding how and why gender has been crucial to class relations. First, gender shapes all social relations, through a cultural process distinguishing male from female. Second, production and reproduction are linked in ways that are fundamental to the character of class relations.

GENDER AS A CULTURAL PROCESS

The reason for the persistence of occupational segregation over time has remained a mystery. Jobs were sexually segregated before the development of capitalism, and they continue to be segregated in "advanced capitalism," as well as under state socialism.[1] Sexual segregation has persisted through depressions and recessions as well as in times of economic expansion. This has been so because of the way that gender operates.

Gender is a cultural process distinguishing females and males in all social relations, including economic or production relations. Employers and workers have been gendered, and the jobs they have done have also become gendered. Historically, economic relations were created by gendered people who brought to their interactions particular understandings of economic issues that were influenced by their having been gendered. Another way of saying this is that gender shapes all social relations and social practices through the ways it constitutes social agents as men and women. It shapes social action by providing interpretations and constituting meanings that guide the actions of social agents. Economic practices, production relations, are shaped by these meanings. Gender, then, is an important aspect of the cultural construction of class relations.

The role of gender became clearest when employers' strategies deviated from the path of "strict economic rationality"—from making the most money most efficiently. For example, employers instituted marriage bars when it was not in their financial interests. Industrialists went to elaborate lengths and expense to design facilities (separate stairways and tearooms, for example) and to create management plans that reflected their gender ideology. Even during World War II, employers in Britain were reluctant to hire women to work in traditionally male industries.[2] At times it was in their financial interests to hire women to do one kind of work and men to do another. However, this did not mean that gender distinctions were irrelevant to their behavior. For example, homework was a flexible and low-cost hiring strategy geared particularly to married women. In many ways homework in the nineteenth and twentieth centuries and part-time work now are similar. Both kinds of work are designed for women. Sociologist Veronica Beechey points out the gender structuring of part-time work by noting that when employers want flexibility with a male work force, they adopt different forms of work organization.[3] The question "why women here and men there" is not really answered by the argument that employers acted rationally.

Gender distinctions are embedded in all power relations and result in practices that have given men power over women. At least in Western societies, men and the jobs, tools, ideas, and ways of thinking associated with them have had higher status than women and the things associated with them. As historian Joan Scott has pointed out, gender has been an important way of signifying relations of power.[4] When these material and ideological representations of gender have come to be contested—for example, when women have begun to do work previously associated with manliness—men have struggled to maintain or recreate distinctions, especially those that gave them status and power. Women have often yielded, because, as Cynthia Cockburn has put it, if they do not they "become unlovable."[5] Most often the meanings of gender are so entrenched that they have become part of what everyone, including women, knows to be true.

In contending that the development of industrial capitalism was gendered by means of cultural processes, I am disputing the value of "dual systems" analyses of the relationship between class and gender. All versions of dual systems analysis picture two autonomous but interacting structures, one through which men benefit as men and the other through which capitalists benefit as capitalists. According to dual systems theorists, the interaction of these systems produces gender hierarchies at work and in the family. A primary problem with dual systems theories is their emphasis on structures rather than on the historical development of patterns of social relationships. Structures do not interact; only people interact. History happens through human agency—which is how gender was involved in the development of industrial capitalism from the start.

In arguing that gender was an aspect of the cultural constitution of class relations, I am not saying that gender is "purely" ideological whereas class is "material." Gender distinctions are expressed in ideologies that portray the ways in which women and men are supposed to differ. But they are also articulated in the sexual segregation of jobs, machines, and household responsibilities and in unequal political rights and activities. In turn, these practices create gender. Gender distinctions are built by human agents into practices that control women's sexuality and that have given advantages to men in sexual as well as economic relationships. In turn, those practices create gender difference and inequality, as well as representing gender distinctions and disparities of power.

Gender and class differ conceptually as well as in how they work to create social structures. Gender creates distinctions between males and females. Class gives some people (capitalists) economic clout over others (workers). This study has shown that the content of class relations is gendered and the content of gender distinctions and gender relations is "classed." Class and gender relations are constructed simultaneously.[6] I illuminated these interacting processes at several different points in the book. For example, I argued that the ideals of male breadwinning and female domesticity emerged, in part, as working men struggled against capitalists who were threatening their livelihoods, and through the political organizations they created to combat those threats. These new meanings of gender difference became integral to working-class families' efforts to establish their respectability by differentiating themselves from other women and men of the working class. New visions of masculinity and femininity fortified and amplified divisions among members of the working class. Capitalists, too, were influenced by class and gender simultaneously. Through paternalistic practices that manipulated familial forms and sentiments, industrialists honed their class position and linked it to a sense of their own manhood as they attempted to shape class relations.

Class relations, however, are not constituted solely by gender, nor is gender shaped only by class. Gender and economic relations are culturally constituted by race and ethnicity, as well as by and through other possible social identities. As Joy Parr has put it:

> Never did class and gender, either singly or in conjunction, map the whole of social existence; both personally and collectively, understandings and obligations were also framed in religious faith, ethnicity, and nationality. None of these roles was assumed sequentially. A man was not by day a worker and by night a man, Saturdays a husband and Sundays a Baptist. Women who were mothers were mothers at the mill and at home, at the laundry line, and on the picket line.[7]

LINKING PRODUCTION AND
REPRODUCTION

This book has shown that working-class livelihoods were limited by gendered class relations. In addition, through cultural analysis it has revealed that the different meanings of work and wages for women and for men were shaped by their lives outside the factory gates, and especially in their families and households.

People did not engage in economic relations only to survive as individuals. Social life has not been organized around people living entirely alone, although in contemporary Britain and the United States increasing numbers of people are residing alone. In all societies people have created cooperative relations to sustain life on a day-to-day basis, as well as intergenerationally, although how those relations have been organized has varied considerably. The increasing number of people living in solitary residences is something to be explained, not to be taken as prototypical of all human existence. Yet, we have conceptualized production and reproduction as totally separated fields of social life, despite the connections between them in people's lived experiences.

The paid and unpaid activities that sustain people on a daily basis and intergenerationally in England were coordinated by people residing in households.[8] They improvised ways of making a livelihood that were shaped by both gender and class simultaneously.[9] John Benson has shown how men as well as women have pieced together a variety of means to contribute to household subsistence.[10] Feminist historians such as Ellen Ross and Elizabeth Roberts have uncovered the ways that women manipulated goods, budgets, diets, and a variety of wage-earning activities in the service of family subsistence.[11] Studies such as these have profound implications for how we understand gender and work. These studies, with this one, have shown that women and men of the working class created ways to survive with the needs of their families in mind, but gender very much affected their style and substance, as well as the extent to which they were bound to the service of their kin.

Although women and men improvised ways of earning wages, making ends meet, and rearing and caring for children and ill or aging parents, they did not necessarily do so without argument. Evidence of woman battering and other forms of family violence, the poorer diets of women and children relative to men, and records of visible family squabbles do not testify to untroubled, harmonious lives in working-class households.[12] Also, as this study has confirmed, the solutions were not equitable between women and men: the sheer amount of time demanded toward insuring family survival was greater for wives than for husbands. Yet, whether or not there was equanimity in their decision making and whether or not the consequence was an equal allocation of responsibilities, husbands and wives, parents and children coordinated their efforts for subsistence.

We cannot fully understand the nature of the interactions between capitalists and workers if we restrict our attention to "the point of production." When we do this we assume that people live in order to produce. We are reifying an abstract understanding of social life by ignoring the links between economic relations and family relations. For the same reason that we cannot ignore the question of gender because people are gendered and their lived experiences are gendered, we cannot ignore the observation that work and home life were connected in people's lived experiences. Historian Keith McClelland has written about the meaning of work for working-class men in the nineteenth century:

> When trade-unionists and others contemplated the potential terrors of scarcity of jobs they were well aware that they spoke not just as individuals, nor even as part of a collectivity of workers within particular trades and industries, but, usually, as men who had dependents. These men knew that they lived with the constantly gnawing possibility that any gains in wages or conditions of work might be short-lived and melt away as quickly as snow in summer.[13]

Family lives, even for men, were far from incidental to their behavior as workers, just as their behavior as workers was crucial to their lives as family men.

The rhetoric of working-class domesticity and preoccupation with respectability, coupled with biased census counts of the number of married women working, has often been misconstrued by sociologists and historians as the reality experienced by the majority. This emphasis has inadvertently contributed to the idea that free choice determines whether or not women work, and that when they do earn wages, women adjust wage earning to their primary obligations as wives and mothers. Extrapolating from the observation that married women rarely worked continuously throughout their lives and that their employments often were "makeshift," scholars have frequently portrayed working-class women's income earning as subordinated to the demands of housekeeping and child rearing. In contrast, men's intermittent work has been seen by scholars to be caused by dislocations in the economy. Yet, this study has suggested that, on the contrary, women often had to make their familial responsibilities fit their wage earning. It has also shown that the behavior of men in the workplace was informed by their responsibilities as heads of households.

By neglecting the myriad ways that working-class men and women pieced together a livelihood and the reasons that such strategies were necessary, scholars have continued to reinforce the idea that women's involvement in the labor force must be viewed within the context of their family lives, whereas men's employment must be viewed from the perspective of their workplace obligations.[14] By constructing an understanding of women's employment as structured by family concerns that bear little or no relationship to class relations, scholars have perpetuated the idea that family relations have nothing to do with class relations and class formation. Yet Leonore Davidoff and Catherine Hall have shown, and my analysis of paternalism has suggested, that family ties and familial ideology were crucial to middle-class formation just as they were to working-class formation and to the relations between the classes.[15]

The middle classes understood family life to be separate from the world of commerce, a different kind of order. In contrast to industry, which was seen as a volatile and competitive world in which conflict characterized social relationships, the family came to symbolize the harmony of mutual interests. However, familial harmony was believed to emanate from a sense of reciprocal obligation predicated on a hierarchy of power and a strict division of labor between women and men. The Victorian family was envisioned as a patriarchal formation in which the father, as head of the family, had responsibility for the welfare of wives and children and guided them with firm but caring authority.

This elite image of family life, characterized by mutual obligation and a gender and age hierarchy, became a model for paternalist industrial management. Its purpose was to mollify class relations by recreating capital and labor as an interdependent, cooperative unit. Paternalism was predicated on a gender and power hierarchy in which the head of the enterprise—the male employer—who made and enforced the rules, was both a benefactor to his dependents—his male and female employees—and their educator.

A number of years ago, historian Joan Kelly proposed that there are several interconnected sets of social relations, not two separate spheres of social life, the private (family, sexuality, and affectivity) and the public (work, politics, and productivity).[16] More recently, sociologist R. E. Pahl has shown that although work may be subdivided analytically into productive and reproductive tasks, what distinguishes them as one or the other varies historically and culturally.[17] His is a broad view of work that encompasses waged and unwaged activity both in and outside the household. This book, as well as the recent historical studies of nineteenth-century England by Judy Lown and nineteenth- and twentieth-century Canada by Joy Parr, suggest that the way forward in the analysis of class and gender relations is to focus on the multiple links between production and reproduction, employment relations and family relations.[18] Theoretically, this path will not be easy. History and sociology as disciplines have been carved up in ways that mimic and perpetuate the ideology of separate spheres. Our theoretical sights have been narrowed by giving primacy to production in the story of history.

If we start from observations of lived experience rather than from abstract ideas about what has been important in that experience, we will create stories that are complex but inclusive. These stories will reveal the multiple realities experienced by men and women. They will illuminate how these multiple realities were interpreted in public, political rhetoric. They will suggest how working-class politics were created: who was included, and who was excluded; which of the multitude of possible interests were identified and accentuated, and which were repressed. Then our historical recreations will retain images of the interconnected influences that shaped how working women and men made their livelihoods and lived their lives.

Notes

CHAPTER 1

1. See E. P. Thompson, *The Making of the English Working Class* (Harmondsworth, 1968; reprinted Harmondsworth, 1980).

2. For a recently published series of essays discussing Thompson's contributions to class formation theory, see Harvey Kaye and Keith McClelland, eds., *E. P. Thompson: Critical Perspectives* (Cambridge, England, 1990). For a recent assessment of Thompson's importance for sociological studies and a discussion of problems in his conception of class, see Anthony Giddens, *Social Theory and Modern Sociology* (Palo Alto, 1987), chap. 9. Also see Craig Calhoun, *The Question of Class Struggle* (Chicago, 1982).

3. Neil Smelser, *Social Change in the Industrial Revolution* (Chicago, 1959). For critiques, see Michael Anderson, "Sociological History and the Working-Class Family: Smelser Revisited," *Social History* 6 (1976): 317–34; John Foster, *Class Struggle and the Industrial Revolution* (London, 1974), 302–3; Calhoun, *Question of Class Struggle*, 191–96. A path-breaking work which challenges the determinist idea that family structure varies in a uniform way with industrialization and urbanization is the research of Michael Anderson, *Family Structure in Nineteenth Century Lancashire* (Cambridge, England, 1971). However, nowhere in this important study was either Chartism or the long and bitter Preston strike of 1853–1854 mentioned. The work of historical demographers associated with the Cambridge Group for the Study of Population and Social Structure has been crucial in our understanding of family structure. See the important work of Peter Laslett, *The World We Have Lost* (London, 1965); and the essays in Richard Wall, Jean Robin, and Peter Laslett, eds., *Family Forms in Historic Europe* (Cambridge, England, 1983). However, the work of such scholars lacks attention to politics. For work that combines a class-centered perspective with the study of family formation, see David Levine's insightful studies, *Family Formation in an Age of Nascent Capitalism* (Cambridge, England, 1977) and *Reproducing Families: The Political Economy of English Population History* (Cambridge, England, 1987). For a feminist critique of the family history literature, see Rayna Rapp, Ellen Ross, and Renate Bridenthal, "Examining Family History," *Feminist Studies* 5 (1979): 174–200.

4. For example, Jane Humphries argues that the working-class family resisted the devastation of industrial capitalism and was crucial in unifying the working class. See "Class Struggle and the Persistence of the Working Class

Family," *Cambridge Journal of Economics* 1 (1977): 241–58. However, Humphries does not analyze gender divisions within the family nor the meanings of gender and family relations. In the 1970s the domestic-labor debates among feminist scholars addressed the question of how domestic life could be related to class analysis. For a review of those debates see Maxine Molyneux, "Beyond the Domestic Labour Debate," *New Left Review* 116 (1979): 3–27. Recent work on working-class masculinity in Britain has linked gender ideology and men's working-class politics: see Harold Benenson, "Victorian Sexual Ideology and Marx's Theory of the Working Class," *International Labor and Working Class History* 25 (1984): 1–23; Wally Seccombe, "Patriarchy Stabilized: The Construction of the Male Breadwinner Wage Norm in Nineteenth-Century Britain," *Social History* 11 (1986): 53–76.

5. Eric Hobsbawm, *Labouring Men* (London, 1964), and *Worlds of Labour* (London, 1984); Patrick Joyce, *Work, Society and Politics* (Brighton, Sussex, 1980). See especially Hobsbawm, *Labouring Men,* chap. 15; *Worlds of Labour,* chaps. 12, 13, 14. Also see Royden Harrison, *Before the Socialists* (London, 1965). For a highly contested approach see Foster, *Class Struggle and the Industrial Revolution.* There are numerous critiques of Foster's work. Gareth Stedman Jones examines the connections between changes in the labor process and the nature of workplace struggle and suggests that the decline of radicalism was due to changes within capitalism itself: see *Languages of Class: Studies in English Working-Class History, 1832–1982* (Cambridge, England, 1983), chap. 1. Also see A. E. Musson, "Class Struggle and the Labour Aristocracy, 1830–1860," *Social History* 1 (1976): 335–66; Calhoun, *Question of Class Struggle,* 23–32. Calhoun focuses his critique on how Foster defines class, that he discounts the importance of trade union struggles, and that he never establishes a causal relation between class consciousness and community solidarity. For debates about the labor aristocracy, see H. F. Moorhouse, "The Marxist Theory of the Labour Aristocracy," *Social History* 3 (1978): 64–65, 86; H. F. Moorhouse, "The Significance of the Labour Aristocracy," *Social History* 6 (1981): 229–33; Gregor MacLennan, "The Labour Aristocracy and Incorporation: Notes on Terms in the Social History of the Working Class," *Social History* 6 (1981): 71–81; Michael Shephard, "The Origins and Incidence of the Term Labour Aristocracy," *Bulletin of the Society for the Study of Labour History* 37 (1978): 51–67. For a study that explores Joyce's thesis about reformism in the cotton districts see Neville Kirk, *The Growth of Working Class Reformism in Mid-Victorian England* (Urbana, 1985).

6. For an excellent critique of the continuing gender-neutrality of social history and a strong argument for the importance of gender relations in social history, see Gisela Bock, "Women's History and Gender History: Aspects of an International Debate," *Gender and History* 1 (1989): 7–30.

7. For the United States, see Alice Kessler-Harris's landmark volume *Out to Work: A History of Wage-Earning Women in the United States* (New York, 1982). For Britain, see Sally Alexander, "Women's Work in Nineteenth-Century London: A Study of the Years 1820–1850," in Juliet Mitchell and Ann Oakley, eds., *The Rights and Wrongs of Women* (Harmondsworth, 1976),

and Jane Lewis, *Women in England 1870–1950* (Bloomington, Ind., 1984). For a comparative approach, see Louise A. Tilly and Joan W. Scott, *Women, Work and Family*, 2d ed. (London, 1987; reprinted London, 1989).

8. The resurrections for the English case include Alice Clark, *Working Life of Women in the Seventeenth Century* (London, 1919; reprinted London, 1982); Ivy Pinchbeck, *Women Workers and the Industrial Revolution, 1750–1850*, 3d ed. (London, 1981); Clementina Black, ed., *Married Women's Work* (London, 1915; reprinted London, 1983); Barbara Drake, *Women in Trade Unions* (London, 1920; reprinted London, 1984). For the United States, see Edith Abbott, *Women in Industry: A Study in American Economic History* (New York, 1910; reprinted New York, 1969), and Julia Cherry Spruill, *Women's Life and Work in the Southern Colonies* (Chapel Hill, 1938).

9. See my historiographic essay " 'Gender at Work': Sex, Class and Industrial Capitalism," *History Workshop* 21 (1986): 113–31. The point about the modes and timing of women's wage earning is made especially clearly in Tilly and Scott, *Women, Work and Family.*

10. Heidi Hartmann's essay on occupational segregation, to which I am profoundly indebted, stimulated a generation of research and debate. See Heidi Hartmann, "Capitalism, Patriarchy and Job Segregation by Sex," *Signs* 1 (1976): 137–69. More recent work includes Nancy Grey Osterud, "Gender Divisions and the Organization of Work in the Leicester Hosiery Industry," in Angela V. John, ed., *Unequal Opportunities: Women's Employment in England 1800–1918* (Oxford, 1986); Harriet Bradley, *Men's Work, Women's Work: A Sociological History of the Sexual Division of Labour in Employment* (Cambridge, England, 1989); Sylvia Walby, *Patriarchy at Work* (Minneapolis, 1986); Sylvia Walby, ed., *Gender Segregation at Work* (Milton Keynes, 1988); Judy Lown, *Women and Industrialization* (Cambridge, England, 1990). For the United States see Ruth Milkman, *Gender at Work: The Dynamics of Job Segregation by Sex During World War II* (Urbana, 1987); Mary Blewett, *Men, Women, and Work: Class, Gender and Protest in the New England Shoe Industry, 1780–1910* (Urbana, 1988). For Australia see Ann Game and Rosemary Pringle, *Gender at Work* (Sydney, 1983). For Canada see Joy Parr, *The Gender of Breadwinners: Women, Men, and Change in Two Industrial Towns* (Toronto, 1990).

11. See the work of Cynthia Cockburn, *Brothers: Male Dominance and Technological Change* (London, 1983), and *Machinery of Dominance: Women, Men and Technical Know-How* (London, 1985); Ava Baron, "Contested Terrain Revisited: Technology and Gender Definitions of Work in the Printing Industry, 1850–1920," in Barbara Wright et al., eds., *Women, Work and Technology: Transformations* (Ann Arbor, 1987), and "Questions of Gender: De-skilling and De-masculinization in the U.S. Printing Industry 1830–1915," *Gender and History* 1 (1989): 178–99; Keith McClelland, "Some Thoughts on Masculinity and the 'Representative Artisan' in Britain, 1850–1880," *Gender and History* 1 (1989): 164–77.

12. Those who have contributed to the view that gender is an aspect of all social relationships include Joan Acker, "The Problem with Patriarchy," *So-

ciology 23 (1989): 235–40, and "What Happened to the Paradigm Shift? Making Gender Visible," in Phyllis A. Wallace, ed., *Sociological Theory and Feminism* (Beverly Hills, 1989); Ava Baron, "Gender and Labor History: Learning from the Past, Looking to the Future," in Ava Baron, ed., *Work Engendered* (Ithaca, 1991); Veronica Beechey, *Unequal Work* (London, 1987); Blewett, *Men, Women and Work;* Alice Kessler-Harris, "Gender Ideology in Historical Reconstruction: A Case Study from the 1930s," *Gender and History* 1 (1989): 31–49; Mary Ann Clawson, *Constructing Brotherhood* (Princeton, 1989); Cynthia Cockburn, "The Relations of Technology: What Implications for Theories of Sex and Class?" in Rosemary Crompton and Michael Mann, eds., *Gender and Stratification* (Cambridge, England, 1986), 74–85; R. W. Connell, *Gender and Power* (Palo Alto, 1987); Leonore Davidoff, " 'Adam Spoke First and Named the Orders of the World': Masculine and Feminine Domains in History and Sociology," in H. Corr and L. Jamieson, eds., *The Politics of Everyday Life: Continuity and Change in Work, Labour and the Family* (London, 1990); Leonore Davidoff and Catherine Hall, *Family Fortunes: Men and Women of the English Middle Class, 1780–1850* (London, 1987); Sandra Harding, *The Science Question in Feminism* (Ithaca, 1986); Alison Scott, "Industrialization, Gender Segregation and Stratification Theory," in Crompton and Mann, eds., *Gender and Stratification,* 154–89; Joan W. Scott, *Gender and the Politics of History* (New York, 1988); Mariana Valverde, "The Making of a Gendered Working Class," *Labour/Le Travail* 22 (1988): 247–57. See Scott, "Industrialization, Gender Segregation and Stratification Theory," 154. For a discussion of the marginalization of feminist analysis and its consequences for sociological theory generally, see Judith Stacey and Barrie Thorne, "The Missing Feminist Revolution in Sociology," *Social Problems* 32 (1985): 301–16.

13. Baron, "Gender and Labor History," makes a similar point. Also see Connell's *Gender and Power,* a major contribution to the development of a theory of gender. Also see Acker, "What Happened to the Paradigm Shift?"; Stacey and Thorne, "The Missing Feminist Revolution in Sociology." Weak theorizing has contributed to the marginalization of feminist thinking in sociology.

14. The description of the hosiery industry that follows is taken from a more complete account of the sexual division of labor in this industry in my article "Gender Segregation in the Transition to the Factory: The English Hosiery Industry, 1850–1910," *Feminist Studies* 13 (1987): 163–84. For an analysis of the relationship between women's work in the domestic hosiery trade and the development of knitting as a factory industry, see my "Protoindustry, Women's Work and the Household Economy in the Transition to Industrial Capitalism," *Journal of Family History* 13 (1988): 181–93. For other studies of this industry see Joy Parr, "Disaggregating the Sexual Division of Labour: A Transatlantic Case Study," *Comparative Studies in Society and History* 30 (1988): 511–33; Osterud, "Gender Divisions and the Organization of Work in the Leicester Hosiery Industry"; Bradley, *Men's Work, Women's Work;* and Harriet Bradley, "Technological Change, Management Strat-

egies, and the Development of Gender-based Job Segregation in the Labour Process," in David Knights and Hugh Wilmott, eds., *Gender and the Labour Process* (Aldershot, 1986), 54–73.

15. *Nottingham Daily Guardian,* 3 July 1861, 3.

16. As Ludmilla Jordanova has written, "Gender stands as a putatively natural fact. It has been deemed a part of nature. . . . We now perceive more readily that what appears natural is in fact a social-cum-cultural construct" (*Sexual Visions: Images of Gender in Science and Medicine Between the Eighteenth and Twentieth Centuries* [Hemel Hempstead, Hertfordshire, 1989], 4–5). In a private communication Susan Porter has suggested that this "taken-for-granted" aspect of gender is the reason it has been so "hidden from history."

17. This point is central to the contemporary theory of symbolic interaction, which has been based on the writings of George Herbert, *Mind, Self and Society* (Chicago, 1934), and Herbert Blumer, *Symbolic Interaction: Perspective and Method* (Englewood Cliffs, 1969). It is central to the idea of "practical consciousness" in the theory of Anthony Giddens: see *The Constitution of Society* (Berkeley and Los Angeles, 1984). Moreover, it is also fundamental to some versions of historical materialism, especially to the writings of Raymond Williams: see *Marxism and Literature* (Oxford, 1977).

18. Stuart Hall has written, "The 'deep-structure' of a statement . . . is the network of elements, premises and assumptions drawn from the long-standing and historically elaborated discourses . . . which now constitute a reservoir of themes and premises on which people draw for signifying new events" ("The Toad in the Garden: Thatcherism among the Theorists," in Cary Nelson and Lawrence Grossberg, eds., *Marxism and the Interpretation of Culture* [Urbana, 1988], 73, 35–74).

19. See Lynn Hunt, *Politics, Culture and Class* (Berkeley and Los Angeles, 1985). Kenneth Burke conceived of human action as rhetorical: see Kenneth Burke, *On Symbols and Society* (Chicago, 1989), and the introduction by the volume editor, Joseph Gusfield.

20. Numerous scholars emphasize the importance of examining the cultural productions of politics, including rituals: see Sean Wilentz, *Chants Democratic* (New Haven, 1984); David I. Kertzer, *Ritual, Politics and Power* (New Haven, 1988). For an analysis of political discourse in class formation, see William H. Sewell, *Work and Revolution in France* (Cambridge, England, 1980). For an analysis of how gender affects class formation through political discourse, see Joan W. Scott, "On Language, Gender, and Working-Class History," *International Labor and Working-Class History* 31 (1987): 1–13. For an exceptionally insightful cultural analysis of public policy, see Joseph Gusfield, *The Culture of Public Problems: Drinking, Driving and the Symbolic Order* (Chicago, 1981). The work of political scientist Murray Edelman also stresses the symbolic aspect of political practice: see his *The Symbolic Uses of Politics* (Urbana, 1984), and *Constructing the Political Spectacle* (Chicago, 1987).

21. Stuart Hall, "The Rediscovery of 'Ideology': Return of the Repressed

in Media Studies," in M. Gurevitch et al., eds., *Culture, Society and the Media* (London, 1982), 56–60; Paul Smith, *Discerning the Subject* (Minneapolis, 1988); Ernesto Laclau and Chantal Mouffe, "Post-Marxism Without Apologies," *New Left Review* 166 (1987): 79–106.

22. Scott, *Gender and the Politics of History*. For the debates see the article by Scott, "On Language, Gender, and Working-Class History," and responses to her article by Christine Stansell, Bryan D. Palmer, and Anson Rabinbach in *International Labor and Working-Class History* 31 (1987): 1–36. For a wide-ranging critique of discourse analysis see Bryan Palmer, *Descent into Discourse* (Oxford, 1990), and the review by Jane Caplan, "The Point Is to Change It," *The Nation* (13/20 August 1990): 173–75.

23. Stansell, "A Response to Joan Scott," 28.

24. Some of the best work being done in theorizing ideology comes from scholars interested in film and the media. See the work of Theresa de Lauretis, especially *Alice Doesn't: Feminism, Semiotics, Cinema* (Bloomington, Ind., 1984), and *Technologies of Gender* (Bloomington, Ind., 1987). Also see Hall, "The Rediscovery of 'Ideology,' " and "The Toad in the Garden."

25. As a prime example, Thompson's *The Making of the English Working Class* was criticized for giving too much weight to culture. Thompson, however, believed that productive relations determined the experiences that were mediated by culture. See Lynn Hunt's introduction to Lynn Hunt, ed., *The New Cultural History* (Berkeley and Los Angeles, 1989), 4. This point is at the center of William H. Sewell's critique of Thompson in "How Classes Are Made: Critical Reflections on E. P. Thompson's Theory of Working-class Formation," in Kaye and McClelland, eds., *E. P. Thompson: Critical Perspectives*, 50–77. For an exposition of the problems in the idealism/materialism dualism see Marshall Sahlins, *Culture and Practical Reason* (Chicago, 1976). Also see Maurice Godelier, "The Ideal in the Real," in Raphael Samuel and Gareth Stedman Jones, eds., *Culture, Ideology and Politics* (London, 1982), 12–37.

26. Jordanova, *Sexual Visions*, 5–6. Also see Williams, *Marxism and Literature*, 38–44.

27. An important aspect of Marx's work was to show that the independence of economic history from human agency was illusory. See Karl Marx and Friedrich Engels, *The German Ideology* (London, 1965), 54. Also see the discussion of this point by Philip Abrams in his *Historical Sociology* (Ithaca, 1982), 38–43.

28. Raymond Williams, *Politics and Letters* (London, 1979), 141.

29. For the idea that analytically, but not empirically, the economy is the ultimate cause of social processes, see Louis Althusser, *For Marx* (London, 1969).

30. See the essays in Nelson and Grossberg, eds., *Marxism and the Interpretation of Culture*. Also see Laclau and Mouffe, "Post-Marxism Without Apologies."

31. For an analysis of the ideal/real dualism, see Godelier, "The Ideal in the Real." The problem I am raising has also been discussed as the dichotomy

between subjectivity and objectivity, the problem in the base/superstructure distinction and in economic reductionism. In an early article Sandra Harding argued that the material base in Marxist thought has been restricted to economic relations; she suggested that the problem for feminists is to locate the material base of gender relations in personality or character formation. See "What Is the Real Material Base of Patriarchy and Capital?" in Lydia Sargent, ed., *Women and Revolution* (Boston, 1981). The dilemma in Marxism that I am raising has been phrased by Sahlins, *Culture and Practical Reason*, as the relation between productive acts and the symbolic organization of experience. When this problem is considered as the opposition of objectivity and subjectivity it may be seen as gendered; that is, as associated with the meanings of masculinity (objective, rational) and femininity (subjective, emotional). For an analysis of the gendered construction of economic and social thought see Davidoff, " 'Adam Spoke First,' " and Carole Pateman, *The Sexual Contract* (Stanford, 1988).

32. An example is Harding's "What Is the Real Material Base?"

33. Hartmann, "Capitalism, Patriarchy and Job Segregation by Sex"; Heidi Hartmann, "The Unhappy Marriage of Marxism and Feminism: Towards a More Progressive Union," in Lydia Sargent, ed., *Women and Revolution* (Boston, 1981); Walby, *Patriarchy at Work*. Sahlins, *Culture and Practical Reason*, argues that Marx's materialism is based on a naturalized notion of human needs and that his problematic suffers from a view of humanity no different from the utilitarians'.

34. Michèle Barrett is usually identified with the former position and has been criticized for lacking a theory of ideology. See the response to her critics in the introduction to *Women's Oppression Today*, revised ed. (London, 1988), xvi–xvii. The second position is associated with Johanna Brenner and Maria Ramas, "Rethinking Women's Oppression," *New Left Review* 144 (1984): 68–69, and Humphries, "Class Struggle and the Persistence of the Working-Class Family." For a brilliant exposition of the social construction of bodies, see Connell, *Gender and Power*.

35. See especially Williams, *Marxism and Literature*. Also see his arguments in *Politics and Letters*. Williams used the term *practical consciousness* to connote the idea that thought is part of action. Anthony Giddens also has used the concept to refer to the "reflexive monitoring" by human beings of their activities: see *The Constitution of Society*, and his recent critique of post-structuralism, with its focus on "the subject" rather than on "agency," and discussion of the importance of practical consciousness for human action in "Structuralism, Post-structuralism and the Production of Culture," in Anthony Giddens and Jonathan Turner, eds., *Social Theory Today* (Stanford, 1987).

36. The Marxian concept of "mode of production" was not meant to single out "the economy" as a distinct sphere of activity, although exactly how economic relations are interconnected with political and cultural relations has been the subject of continuing debate among Marxist scholars. See the work of Karl Polanyi for a critique of the "economistic fallacy": *The Great Trans-*

formation (Boston, 1957). See the discussion of Polanyi's work by Fred Block and Margaret R. Somers, "Beyond the Economistic Fallacy: The Holistic Social Science of Karl Polanyi," in Theda Skocpol, ed., *Vision and Method in Historical Sociology* (Cambridge, England, 1984). For a view similar to the one adopted here, see Derek Sayer, *The Violence of Abstraction: The Analytic Foundations of Historical Materialism* (Oxford, 1987). Also see Sharon Zukin and Paul DiMaggio, Introduction to Sharon Zukin and Paul DiMaggio, eds., *Structures of Capital: The Social Organization of the Economy* (Cambridge, England, 1990), and Fred Block, *Postindustrial Possibilities: A Critique of Economic Discourse* (Berkeley and Los Angeles, 1990), esp. chap. 1.

37. In Pierre Bourdieu's language, they become "doxa": see *Outline of a Theory of Practice* (Cambridge, England, 1977).

38. Williams writes, "just as all social process is activity between real individuals, so individuality, by the fully social fact of language . . . is the active constitution, within distinct physical beings, of the social capacity which is the means of realization of any individual life" (*Marxism and Literature,* 41).

39. Numerous scholars who stress the importance of cultural practices that establish the dominance of particular worldviews trace their ideas to Gramsci: see Antonio Gramsci, *Selections from the Prison Notebooks* (New York, 1971). For a clear exposition of these ideas, see Williams, *Marxism and Literature,* 108–14. Joan Cocks uses both Gramsci and Raymond Williams in developing her ideas about oppositional gender politics: see Joan Cocks, *The Oppositional Imagination* (London, 1990).

40. By structures I mean, following Connell, the constraints on practices and the possibilities giving rise to practices: see R. Connell's *Which Way Is Up? Essays on Class, Sex and Culture* (North Sydney, Australia, 1983), 39.

41. This is similar to the idea of practical consciousness elaborated by Giddens: see *The Constitution of Society,* 41–45.

42. See Joan Scott's definition of gender in *Gender and the Politics of History,* chap. 2. Also, as legal scholar Martha Minow points out, distinctions or differences are usually based on an unstated point of reference that is considered to be the norm. Women are different in comparison to the unstated male norm. She writes, "The unstated reference point promotes the interests of some but not others; it can remain unstated because those who do not fit have less power to select the norm than those who fit comfortably within the one that prevails": see Martha Minow, *Making All the Difference: Inclusion, Exclusion, and American Law* (Ithaca, 1990), 51–78.

43. Connell argues a similar point: he suggests that gender works on the body through transcendence and negation: see his *Gender and Power,* 78–82, and *Which Way Is Up?* 68–69. This is also the point made so forcefully by de Lauretis, in her *Technologies of Gender,* 6–11. De Lauretis argues, using Althusser's definition of ideology as the imaginary relation of people to the "real relations in which they live," that gender is a primary instance of ideology. For Althusser's original statement about ideology, see Louis Althusser, "Ideology and Ideological State Apparatuses (Notes Towards an Investigation)," in *Lenin and Philosophy* (New York, 1971).

People use anatomical sexual differences rather than other physical characteristics such as eye color or hair color as a basis for distinctions between types of people because females and males are positioned differently in society in uniquely clearly patterned ways. This is Pierre Bourdieu's important insight about the genesis of *habitus,* the structuring mechanism of practices. Bourdieu insists that classificatory systems reflect the systematic location of people in social space. For a clear exposition of this point, see Pierre Bourdieu, "Social Space and Symbolic Power," *Sociological Theory* 7 (1989): 18–22, and Bourdieu, *Outline of a Theory of Practice.* Bourdieu's theoretical project is to account for both structure and agency by developing a reflexive sociology. Anthony Giddens's prolific theorizing also is concerned with reflexivity and the unity of structure and agency: see his *Central Problems in Social Theory: Action, Structure and Contradiction in Social Analysis* (Berkeley and Los Angeles, 1979), and *The Constitution of Society.* For a comparison of the two theorists and a critique, see Connell, *Gender and Power,* 94–95. Connell, in *Which Way Is Up?* 76, makes a point similar to mine.

44. Mary Poovey, *Uneven Developments: The Ideological Work of Gender in Mid-Victorian England* (Chicago, 1988), 6.

45. Davidoff and Hall, *Family Fortunes.* Also see Susan Kent, *Sex and Suffrage in Britain 1860–1914* (Princeton, 1987), esp. chap. 1.

46. Michel Foucault, *The History of Sexuality.* Volume 1: *An Introduction* (New York, 1980).

47. Baron has shown how masculinity among printers was constructed through the contrast between adult male workers and apprentices: see "Questions of Gender."

48. Pierre Bourdieu, *Distinctions: A Social Critique of the Judgement of Taste* (Cambridge, Mass., 1984).

49. My concern here primarily with class and gender is not intended to deny that race/ethnicity, age, sexuality, nationality, and other social positions are complexly interwoven in an individual's identity.

50. For the ways that fraternal organizations simultaneously affected the construction of masculinity and served as a class resource, see Clawson, *Constructing Brotherhood.*

51. See Benenson, "Victorian Sexual Ideology"; Mariana Valverde, " 'Giving the Female a Domestic Turn': The Social, Legal and Moral Regulation of Women's Work in British Cotton Mills, 1820–1850," *Journal of Social History* 21 (1988): 619–34.

52. For a theoretical discussion of the relationship between the state and gender, see Jane Jenson, "Gender and Reproduction: Or, Babies and the State," *Studies in Political Economy* 20 (1986): 9–46. For an insightful analysis of state formation as an aspect of the development of capitalism, see Philip Corrigan and Derek Sayer, *The Great Arch: English State Formation as Cultural Revolution* (Oxford, 1985).

53. Ira Katznelson, "Constructing Cases and Comparisons," in Ira Katznelson and Aristede R. Zolberg, eds., *Working-Class Formation: Nineteenth Century Patterns in Western Europe and the United States* (Princeton, 1986),

6. See also David Stark, "Class Struggle and the Transformation of the Labor Process," *Theory and Society* 9 (1980): 96.

54. For an analysis of this problem in the work of E. P. Thompson, see Sewell, "How Classes Are Made."

55. This point is made especially clearly by Geoff Eley, "Edward Thompson, Social History and Political Culture: The Making of a Working-class Public, 1780–1850," in Kaye and McClelland, eds., *E. P. Thompson: Critical Perspectives*, 12–49, esp. 24–26.

56. Thompson's formulation attempted to dissolve Marx's distinction between class in itself (class position) and class for itself (class consciousness). Scholars interested in class formation are still debating the utility of the original distinction: see, for example, Katznelson and Zolberg, eds., *Working-Class Formation*.

57. See Katznelson, "Constructing Cases and Comparisons."

58. Eley, "Edward Thompson, Social History and Political Culture," 26.

59. This point is made especially clearly by Jane Jenson, "Paradigms and Political Discourse: Protective Legislation in France and the United States Before 1914," *Canadian Journal of Political Science* 22 (1989): 238. Also see Scott, *Gender and the Politics of History*, 57. However, I disagree with Scott's belief that it is only through discourse that class is created.

60. This point is one that Pierre Bourdieu has emphasized: see Bourdieu, "Social Space and Symbolic Power," 23.

61. Calhoun makes a similar point: see *Question of Class Struggle*, 229.

62. For an outstanding analysis of the unevenness of capitalist development in England and of the proliferation of labor-intensive production processes, see Raphael Samuel, "Workshop of the World: Steam Power and Hand Technology in Mid-Victorian Britain," *History Workshop Journal* 3 (1977): 6–72. For the connection between women and labor-intensive processes, see Alexander, "Women's Work in Nineteenth-Century London." For studies of tailoring, see James A. Schmiechen, *Sweated Industries and Sweated Labor: The London Clothing Trades, 1860–1914* (Urbana, 1984); Jenny Morris, "The Characteristics of Sweating: The Late Nineteenth-Century London and Leeds Tailoring Trade," in John, ed., *Unequal Opportunities*, 95–124; Barbara Taylor, *Eve and the New Jerusalem* (New York, 1983); Shelley Pennington and Belinda Westover, *A Hidden Workforce: Homeworkers in England, 1850–1985* (London, 1989).

63. For more general discussions of the course of industrialization in Britain, see Sidney Pollard, "Labour in Great Britain," in Peter Mathias and M. M. Postan, eds., *The Cambridge Economic History of Europe*. Vol. 7, Part 1: *The Industrial Economies: Capital, Labour and Enterprise* (Cambridge, England, 1978); A. E. Musson, *The Growth of British Industry* (London, 1978); Sir John Clapham, *An Economic History of Modern Britain*, vol. 1 (London, 1939); C. R. Harley, "British Industrialization Before 1841: Evidence of Slower Growth During the Industrial Revolution," *Journal of Economic History* 42 (1982): 267–89.

CHAPTER 2

1. Ruth Milkman uses the phrase "images of gender" to describe how gender influenced employers' hiring practices: see Ruth Milkman, *Gender at Work: The Dynamics of Job Segregation by Sex During World War II* (Urbana, 1987).

2. Michael Burawoy has proposed that there are two aspects of the processes of production that are central to class relations: the labor process, "the coordinated set of activities and relations involved in the transformation of raw materials into useful products," and "the political apparatuses of production, understood as the institutions that regulate and shape struggles in the workplace": see his *The Politics of Production* (London, 1985), 872. In this chapter I am distinguishing hiring practices and the allocation of jobs to people, an aspect of the labor process, from managerial strategies, the regulation of employer-employee relations. I argue that gender was involved in both.

3. The interaction between worker resistance and employer strategies is examined in Chapter 5.

4. For discussions of the social construction of skill, see Anne Phillips and Barbara Taylor, "Sex and Skill: Notes Towards a Feminist Economics," *Feminist Review* 6 (1980): 56–79; Cynthia Cockburn, *Brothers: Male Dominance and Technological Change* (London, 1983), and *Machinery of Dominance: Women, Men and Technical Know-How* (London, 1985); Diane Elson and Ruth Pearson, " 'Nimble Fingers Make Cheap Workers': An Analysis of Women's Employment in Third World Export Manufacturing," *Feminist Review* 7 (1981): 87–107.

5. See Samuel Cohn, *The Process of Occupational Sex-Typing* (Philadelphia, 1985). In explaining why the General Post Office feminized clerical work but the Great Western Railway did not, Cohn argues that in contrast to the railroads, the post office's costs were concentrated in a highly labor-intensive work process. He suggests that employers in industries in which labor costs were high relative to other costs substituted women for men in their work forces. Such an explanation assumes that women workers were simply low-waged workers, who had no other special characteristics making them more or less appealing as a source of labor to employers. Only employers who were not under pressure to economize on their labor costs could afford to hire men, who were more costly. However, the theory of economic interests does not explain why employers hired men when they did not have to economize on labor costs—when their costs were "buffered," to use Cohn's term.

6. Leonore Davidoff and Catherine Hall, *Family Fortunes: Men and Women of the English Middle Class, 1780–1850* (London, 1987). For the United States, see Mary Ryan, *Cradle of the Middle Class: The Family in Oneida County, New York, 1790–1865* (Cambridge, England, 1983). Mary Poovey has argued that the domestic ideal helped "depoliticize class relations" in mid-nineteenth-century Britain: see her *Uneven Developments: The Ideological Work of Gender in Mid-Victorian England* (Chicago, 1988). Catherine Gallagher

analyzes the way the idea of separate spheres contributed to "the condition of England" debates: see *The Industrial Reformation of English Fiction, 1832–1867* (Chicago, 1985).

7. This does not mean that men were paid a family wage, that is, a wage high enough to support a wife and dependent children. The large majority of families in the working classes survived only by pooling income from husband and either wife or children or both: see Lynn Hollen Lees, "Getting and Spending: The Family Budgets of English Industrial Workers in 1890," in John M. Merriman, ed., *Consciousness and Class Experience in Nineteenth-Century Europe* (New York, 1979), 169–86. See also Michele Barrett and Mary McIntosh, "The 'Family Wage': Some Problems for Socialists and Feminists," *Capital and Class,* 1980, no. 11: 51–72. John Holley argues that skilled workers in Scotland did earn a "family wage," which he defines as "a wage high enough to keep a whole family at a passable living standard without the wife or very young children having to work." However, he defines a family wage as enough to keep families above "grinding poverty," and he found that even among skilled workers in the woolen industry, the head's income comprised no more than 57 percent of all family income. Among skilled paper workers, heads earned 44 percent of all family income, and unskilled heads earned only about 30 percent of their families' subsistence: see "The Two Family Economies of Industrialism: Factory Workers in Victorian Scotland," *Journal of Family History* 6 (1981): 57–69.

8. If the workers were unionized, then union demands to raise rates and opposition to lowering rates also figured into employer decisions.

9. For an exceptionally clear and insightful discussion of women's "customary wage" see Alice Kessler-Harris, *A Woman's Wage* (Lexington, Ky., 1990), 6–32.

10. Edward Cadbury, M. Cecile Matheson, and George Shann, *Women's Work and Wages* (London, 1906), 133.

11. See the studies by Alice Clark, *The Working Life of Women in the Seventeenth Century* (London, 1919; reprinted London, 1982); Ivy Pinchbeck, *Women Workers and the Industrial Revolution, 1750–1850,* 3d ed. (London, 1981); and the more recent work of Maxine Berg, *The Age of Manufactures, 1700–1820* (London, 1985).

12. For evidence, see Ann Kussmaul, *Servants in Husbandry in Early Modern England* (Cambridge, England, 1981), 37. Kussmaul's data are based on a sample of Quarter Sessions assessments from the sixteenth to the eighteenth century. The median ratio of maximum male to maximum female wages was 1 to 0.60; Barbara Hanawalt reported that a statute of 1388 decreed that "female laborers and dairymaids should earn 1s. less a year than plowmen": see her *The Ties That Bind* (Bloomington, Ind., 1986), 151. Dairymaids on Bishop Worcester's estate earned less than male servants, according to R. H. Hilton, *The English Peasantry in the Later Middle Ages* (Oxford, 1975), 103. See also Chris Middleton, "The Familiar Fate of the 'Famulae': Gender as a Principle of Stratification in the Historical Organisation of Labour," in Raymond E. Pahl, ed., *On Work* (Oxford, 1988). Middleton's figures were based

on those compiled by Thorold Rogers, *Wages of Agricultural Labourers*, vol. 2 (London, 1866), 576–83. See also Chris Middleton, "Women's Work and the Transition to Pre-industrial Capitalism," in Lindsey Charles and Lorna Duffin, eds., *Women and Work in Pre-Industrial England* (London, 1985).

13. Berg, *The Age of Manufactures, 1700–1820*, 152.

14. Ivy Pinchbeck, *Women Workers and the Industrial Revolution*, 144.

15. The work of Chris Middleton is important in showing the development of occupational specialization and the association of men with tasks that were considered more skilled and women with unskilled or less specialized work. In addition to the references cited in note 11 above, see "The Sexual Division of Labour in Feudal England," *New Left Review* 113–14 (1979): 147–68; "Peasants, Patriarchy and the Feudal Mode of Production in England: A Marxist Appraisal," *Sociological Review* 29 (1981): 105–54. See also Michael Roberts, "Sickles and Scythes: Women's Work and Men's Work at Harvest Time," *History Workshop* 7 (1979): 3–28, and his essay on gender and the meaning of work in the early modern period, " 'Words They Are Women, and Deeds They Are Men': Images of Work and Gender in Early Modern England," in Charles and Duffin, eds., *Women and Work in Pre-Industrial England*. Barbara Hanawalt has found that peasant women were more likely to be doing work in or close by their houses, whereas men spent time away from household units: see her *The Ties That Bind*, and her "Peasant Women's Contribution to the Home Economy in Late Medieval England," in Barbara Hanawalt, ed., *Women and Work in Preindustrial Europe* (Bloomington, Ind., 1986). Alice Clark's analysis of precapitalist and preindustrial women's work suggests that women's involvement in family production was important, but it also reinforces the picture drawn here. Prior to industrial capitalism, women engaged in a variety of trades, but usually as wives and daughters rather than as skilled artisans: see Alice Clark, *Working Life of Women in the Seventeenth Century*.

16. Diane Hutton, "Women in Fourteenth Century Shrewsbury," in Charles and Duffin, eds., *Women and Work in Pre-Industrial England*, 96.

17. See Clark, *Working Life of Women in the Seventeenth Century*. Clark argues that women's skilled work declined as a consequence of the decline of domestic industry and the substitution of an individual wage for a "family wage," here defined as the wage a family would earn by working together to manufacture a product.

18. For a brief review of this legacy, see Harriet Bradley, *Men's Work, Women's Work: A Sociological History of the Sexual Division of Labour in Employment* (Cambridge, England, 1989). The reasons for the continuation of women's low wages into the industrial period are complex, and an analysis of why and how this tradition persisted is beyond the scope of this inquiry. By the period of this study, employers hired women expecting to pay them less for the same work than they paid men. Women, whose choices of jobs were limited, rarely protested, nor could they often afford to protest. There was a labor surplus in England, and jobs were at a premium. For an analysis of the development of manufacture prior to the industrial revolution and of the com-

plex ways that women's and men's employment were shaped, see Berg, *The Age of Manufactures, 1700–1820.*

19. The machine-made lace industry was an outgrowth of the framework knitting or hosiery industry in Nottingham. The industry split off from its origins in hosiery during the nineteenth century. Once steam power was applied to the making of lace, the industry industrialized rapidly. By 1861 lace making was carried out entirely in factories.

20. *Parliamentary Papers* 22 (1861): 529.

21. Ibid.

22. *Parliamentary Papers* 15 (1843): 584.

23. Roy A. Church, *Economic and Social Change in a Midland Town: Victorian Nottingham 1815–1900* (London, 1966), 7.

24. Machines could be purchased on a lease-option plan. Only widowed women who had inherited money could have purchased them. Therefore, even the possibility that women would buy and run them was so limited as to be virtually nonexistent.

25. Katrina Honeyman, *Origins of Enterprise* (Manchester, 1982), 155.

26. *Parliamentary Papers* 22 (1861): 96.

27. Ibid., 11.

28. Ibid., 12.

29. For an analysis of the ways that the jobs of boys and girls were differentiated in the silk industry, see Judy Lown, *Women and Industrialization* (Cambridge, England, 1990), 53–56.

30. The issue of how and under what conditions boys were apprenticed to trades formed a continuing source of dispute in a number of trades. I take up the meaning of the differentiation between boys' work and men's work in Chapter 6. For an examination of the issue of apprentices in the American printing industry, see Ava Baron, "Acquiring Manly Competence: The Demise of Apprenticeship and the Remasculinization of Printers' Work, 1830–1915," in Clyde Griffen and Mark C. Carnes, eds., *Meanings for Manhood: Constructions of Masculinity in Victorian America* (Chicago, 1991).

31. Mary Freifeld, "Technological Change and the 'Self-acting' Mule: A Study of Skill and the Sexual Division of Labour," *Social History* 11 (1986): 319–43. Freifeld argues that the transition from the common mule to the self-actor did not deskill the work of the spinner. The job remained male because women were not hired as mule spinners and piecers during the period just prior to the introduction of the self-actor. Therefore, they were deprived of a tradition of learning craft skills.

32. Often they had to wait many years until a mule spinner was needed. In a number of areas a surplus built up of young men trained to be spinners. As William Lazonick has noted, capitalists exploited the oversupply of big piecers first by creating an apprenticing system, hiring the big piecer to work a pair of mules but paying him less than the minders were paid. This was successfully fought by the operatives' unions. As the oversupply of piecers and minders grew at the end of the century (caused in part by the introduction of ring spinning, which was done by women), industrialists introduced the join-

ing system, in which the minder was downgraded and the big piecer upgraded to equally paid positions. Interestingly, in areas where weaving or coal mining offered young men alternative occupations to piecing, spinners were forced to accept the joining system in order to recruit young men into the occupation. See William Lazonick, "Industrial Relations and Technical Change: The Case of the Self-Acting Mule," *Cambridge Journal of Economics* 3 (1979): 248–49.

33. Unlike in the hosiery industry, where women were hired to mind circular frames under the supervision of men who were in charge of repairing and tuning the women's machines, in cotton spinning, technical responsibilities were often left in the hands of the minder rather than given to the overseers. For the hosiery industry, see Sonya O. Rose, "Gender Segregation in the Transition to the Factory: The English Hosiery Industry, 1850–1910," *Feminist Studies* 13 (1987): 163–84. In cotton the long-term connection between a minder and a particular pair of mules meant that the minder knew the peculiarities of his machines and was better able to make the adjustments necessary in running them than could the overseer. William Lazonick has written, "The long-run effect of such minder control over the technical adjustment and tuning of the mules was to create a situation where no two pair of mules worked in precisely the same way, thus making each minder less dispensable for the successful operation of his particular pair": see William Lazonick, "Production Relations, Labor Productivity and Choice of Technique: British and U.S. Cotton Spinning," *Journal of Economic History* 41 (1981): 501. It is not simply that minder control over the work process and technical know-how were related, but that career routes were charted in the spinning mill so that it was only men who had technical expertise.

34. *Parliamentary Papers* 30 (1876): 199. The act of 1878 that consolidated the factory and workshops acts and reduced the hours of labor of women, children, and young persons to nine, permitted boys under the age of eighteen to work at night, although they were not permitted to work overtime.

35. Report by B. L. Hutchins in British Association for the Advancement of Science Committee on the Economic Effect of Legislation Regulating Women's Labour, Coll. 486, 2/4, p. 11, at the British Library of Political and Economic Science. (Hereafter British Association for the Advancement of Science Papers.)

36. Judy Lown shows, for example, how women's job choices in the Courtauld silk mills were extremely limited, whereas the few men who stayed on at the mills could move up career ladders to better, higher-paying jobs: see her *Women and Industrialization,* 54.

37. A number of scholars have noted the connection in numerous industries among technology, mechanical competence, skill, and masculinity: see Ava Baron, "Contested Terrain Revisited: Technology and Gender Definitions of Work in the Printing Industry, 1850–1920," in Barbara Wright et al., eds., *Women, Work and Technology* (Ann Arbor, 1987); Cockburn, *Machinery of Dominance;* Cockburn, *Brothers;* Erik Arnold and Wendy Faulkner, "Smothered by Invention: The Masculinity of Technology," in Wendy Faulkner and

Erik Arnold, eds., *Smothered by Invention: Technology in Women's Lives* (London, 1985), 18–50.

38. This type of deskilling is similar to what was espoused by the principles of scientific management. The idea, made very clear by Harry Braverman, was that it was cheaper for the employer to deskill the work process, pay for a few expensive managers or supervisors, and have the large majority of the work force paid for unskilled work: Harry Braverman, *Labor and Monopoly Capital* (New York, 1974). Braverman shows that this system is economically advantageous to employers. However, it was always women, not men, doing the repetitive, semi-skilled work of machine minding and men, not women, supervising them.

39. His Majesty's Stationery Office, *Women in Industry* (London, 1930), cmd. 3508, p. 20.

40. Cockburn, *Machinery of Dominance*, 40. Even *to master,* often used to mean "to become competent or skilled," is inherently gendered. Along with its gendered sense, it resonates with domination. One dictionary defines the verb as "to become master of; overcome; to become skilled or proficient in the use of," and the noun *master* is defined as "a male teacher." *Webster's New Collegiate Dictionary* (Springfield, Mass., 1977).

41. B. L. Hutchins, *Women in Modern Industry* (New York, 1915), 201.

42. Diane Elson and Ruth Pearson make this point very clear: see their "Nimble Fingers Make Cheap Workers."

43. See especially Barbara Taylor, *Eve and the New Jerusalem* (London, 1983).

44. Ava Baron has reported that the issue of the design of technology was contested in the American printing industry. The version of the linotype that was eventually adopted, however, was the one that was most closely associated with masculinity: see Ava Baron, "Contested Terrain Revisited."

45. See Cockburn, *Machinery of Dominance;* Cynthia Cockburn, "The Relations of Technology: What Implications for Theories of Sex and Class?" in Rosemary Crompton and Michael Mann, eds., *Gender and Stratification* (Cambridge, England, 1986), 74–85.

46. Joy Parr, *The Gender of Breadwinners* (Toronto, 1990); Sonya Rose, "Gender Segregation in the Transition to the Factory."

47. *Kidderminster Shuttle,* 9 February 1895, 5.

48. *Kidderminster Shuttle,* 24 October 1874, 5.

49. Ken Tomkinson, "Lottie Mary Cooper," in *Characters of Kidderminster* (Kidderminster, 1977), 136.

50. Ibid.

51. Rose, "Gender Segregation in the Transition to the Factory."

52. British Association for the Advancement of Science Papers, Coll. 486, 2/7, pp. 10–12.

53. See British Association for the Advancement of Science Papers, Coll. 486, 2/9, p. 15; Barbara Drake, *Women in the Engineering Trades* (London, 1917), 8–9.

54. Webb Trade Union Papers, sect. A, vol. 67, p. 37. For a demonstration

of how employer costs led to the "feminization" of a formerly male occupation, see Samuel Cohn, *The Process of Occupational Sex-Typing*.

55. *Parliamentary Papers* 30.1 (1876): 151.

56. British Association for the Advancement of Science Papers, Coll. 486, 2/6, p. 37.

57. *Parliamentary Papers* 29.2 (1876): 250.

58. *Parliamentary Papers* 30.1 (1876): 253.

59. British Association for the Advancement of Science Papers, Coll 486, 2/6, p. 54. Chamberlain maintained in this interview that women would make great mathematicians and physicians, as well as better confidential clerks and managers than men.

60. Ibid.

61. British Association for the Advancement of Science Papers, Coll. 486, 2/6, p. 37.

62. *Parliamentary Papers* 29.2 (1876): 258.

63. British Association for the Advancement of Science Papers, Coll. 486, 2/6, p. 42.

64. Note no. 1 accompanying B. L. Hutchins's report on "Paper Making London and Elsewhere" in the British Association for the Advancement of Science Papers, Coll. 486, 2/4, p. 44.

65. British Association for the Advancement of Science Papers, Coll. 486, 2/6, p. 27.

66. British Association for the Advancement of Science Papers, Coll. 486, 2/3, pp. 32–33.

67. The decline of paternalism is associated with the development and proliferation of limited liability companies. In Lancashire, paternalistic managerial practices were not found in the last part of the nineteenth century in Oldham, where limited liability companies dominated: see Patrick Joyce, *Work, Society and Politics* (Brighton, Sussex, 1980). Richard Whipp has described the paternalistic strategies of employers in the pottery industry of the early twentieth century: see his "The Art of Good Management: Managerial Control of Work in the British Pottery Industry, 1900–25," *International Review of Social History* 29 (1984): 359–85.

68. Michael Burawoy argues that paternalism developed as a managerial strategy when workers had lost control over the production process, upon what Marx had termed the "real subordination of labor": see *The Politics of Production*, 98. Also see Joyce, *Work, Society and Politics*, who makes a similar argument, documenting paternalism in cotton textile factories. For an argument that paternalism was due as much or more to employer vulnerability than it was to loss of control over work, see Richard Price, "Conflict and Cooperation: A Reply to Patrick Joyce," *Social History* 9 (1984): 217–24. The extent to which workers lost control over the labor process after the invention of the self-acting mule, however, is a matter of active scholarly debate. Mary Freifeld argues that the self-actor did not deskill spinning: see Mary Freifeld, "Technological Change and the 'Self-acting' Mule," *Social History* 11 (1986): 319–43; William Lazonick, "Industrial Relations and

Technical Change," and "Production Relations, Labor Productivity and Choice of Technique," *Journal of Economic History* 41 (1981): 491–516.

69. John Seed has described how the Unitarians of Manchester in the 1930s, in their efforts to reform the working classes to the discipline required by industrialism, set up Domestic Missions whose missionaries gave detailed reports on the poverty and suffering of the masses: see John Seed, "Unitarianism, Political Economy and the Antinomies of Liberal Culture in Manchester, 1830–50," *Social History* 7 (1982): 1–25.

70. Reinhardt Bendix, *Work and Authority in Industry* (New York, 1956), 13. He argues that employers extended a "traditional" mode of securing legitimacy, a style of management which had characterized economic relations from precapitalist and preindustrial times into the industrial era.

71. See Bendix, *Work and Authority in Industry*. Recent contributions to the literature on paternalism in England include David Roberts, *Paternalism in Early Victorian England* (London, 1979); Joyce, *Work, Society and Politics;* Seed, "Unitarianism, Political Economy and the Antinomies of Liberal Culture in Manchester, 1830–50,"; H. I. Dutton and J. E. King, "The Limits of Paternalism: The Cotton Tyrants of North Lancashire, 1836–54," *Social History* 7 (1982): 59–74, and Lown, *Women and Industrialization.*

72. See Lown, *Women and Industrialization.*

73. A. S. Turberville, *John Bright—His Character and Career* (Swindon, 1945), 16.

74. Leonore Davidoff and Catherine Hall, *Family Fortunes: Men and Women of the English Middle Class, 1780–1850* (London, 1987).

75. Joyce, *Work, Society and Politics,* 136.

76. Davidoff and Hall, *Family Fortunes,* chap. 2.

77. See Joyce, *Work, Society and Politics.*

78. Pierre Bourdieu, *Distinctions: A Social Critique of the Judgement of Taste* (Cambridge, Mass., 1984).

79. Dutton and King suggest that paternalism was sharply limited before midcentury in part because of economic insecurity and that aspects of paternalism such as company outings coexisted with a lack of benevolence on the part of most manufacturers: see Dutton and King, "The Limits of Paternalism." However, John Seed has shown the importance of a developing Unitarian liberal culture among manufacturers in Manchester that stressed "the gentle discipline of kindness" and direct personal involvement between the middle classes and the poor: see his "Antinomies of Liberal Culture," 22. Also see Catherine Gallagher's analysis of the "family-society" polarity in mid-Victorian British literature, *Industrial Reformation of English Fiction,* especially part 2.

80. For a discussion of the transformation of the idea of dynasty among the English bourgeoisie, see F. M. L. Thompson, *The Rise of Respectable Society: A Social History of Victorian Britain, 1830–1900* (London, 1988), 212. See also Robert Gray, "Languages of Factory Reform," in Patrick Joyce, ed., *The Historical Meanings of Work* (Cambridge, England, 1987), 158.

81. Gallagher, *Industrial Reformation of English Fiction.*

82. My argument about the categorization by the bourgeoisie of people in the working classes draws on the insights of Edward Said, *Orientalism* (New York, 1979). For the idea of discourse used here and in Said's work, see Michel Foucault, *The Order of Things: An Archaeology of the Human Sciences* (New York, 1973). For an analysis of the development of culture, see Raymond Williams, *Culture and Society* (London, 1958). Eric Hobsbawm has remarked on the outpouring of such bourgeois cultural representations: see *Worlds of Labour* (London, 1984), 177–78.

83. For an analysis of industrial novels, see Raymond Williams, *Culture and Society* (London, 1958); Catherine Gallagher, *Industrial Reformation of English Fiction*.

84. Raymond Williams notes that the fear of mob violence is expressed in such disparate novels as Dickens's *Hard Times*, George Eliot's *Felix Holt*, and Charles Kingsley's *Alton Locke:* see his *Culture and Society*, 94–109.

85. Elizabeth Gaskell, *North and South* (London, 1854–1855; reprinted London, 1970), 232.

86. Ibid., 233, 234.

87. The similarity between the way paternalist employers (and those bourgeoisie who commented on working-class life) portrayed the working classes as "other," and the construction by colonizers of the colonized, or, in Edward Said's formulation, the European construction of Orientalism, is striking. By constructing the working classes as "a different species," they oppositionally defined themselves and their "natural" superiority. This gave them the license to control that which was defined as opposite to their idealized image of their own moral superiority. See Edward Said, *Orientalism*.

88. Michael Burawoy has suggested the connection between paternalism and other managerial practices such as production games and securing consent to the "rules of the game": see his *Manufacturing Consent* (Chicago, 1979) and *The Politics of Production*.

89. See Edward Cadbury's testimonial to the sound business sense of managerial practices that produced harmonious labor relations and happy, productive workers: *Experiments in Industrial Organization* (London, 1912).

90. Patrick Joyce, in his important work on paternalism, argues that paternalistic practices were crucial in creating deferential workers in the last half of the nineteenth century: see Joyce, *Work, Society and Politics*. See also Richard Price, "Conflict and Cooperation: A Reply to Patrick Joyce." Price argues that paternalism was a reflection of the vulnerability of employers and a consequence of the bargaining between capital and labor. Bernard Elbaum and his colleagues have spoken about "terrains of compromise" fostered by styles of labor-management relations: see Bernard Elbaum et al., "Symposium: The Labour Process, Market Structure and Marxist Theory," *Cambridge Journal of Economics* 3 (1979): 227–30. See also the important case studies and theoretical analyses by Michael Burawoy in *Manufacturing Consent* and *The Politics of Production*.

91. Cadbury, *Experiments in Industrial Organization*, xvii.

92. Gareth Stedman Jones has discussed bourgeois public concern with

sweating and poverty in London in the last decades of the nineteenth century as having been a response to the fear of "the residuum": see *Outcast London* (Oxford, 1971; reprinted London, 1984).

93. Illuminated address dated 4 October 1879, Muniments Room, Brinton's Inc., Kidderminster.

94. See, for example, *The Preston Chronicle of Lancashire Advertiser,* 11 May 1878, 6.

95. Joyce, *Work, Society and Politics,* 136. For the American case, see Philip Scranton, "Varieties of Paternalism: Industrial Structures and the Social Relations of Production in American Textiles," *American Quarterly* 36 (1984): 235–57.

96. See Joyce, *Work, Society and Politics,* 180.

97. For example, see Patrick Joyce's description of the factory celebration by Richard Edleston when his son was born, in *Work, Society and Politics,* 183.

98. *Ashton-under-Lyne News,* 30 March 1872, 6.

99. Ibid.

100. Minutes of the Thomas Mason and Sons Oxford Mills Workpeople and Tenants Committee, 3 August 1881, Tyneside Local History Library.

101. Copy of letter dated 15 February 1886, in Minutes of the Thomas Mason and Sons Oxford Mills Workpeople and Tenants Committee.

102. Joyce, *Work, Society and Politics,* 183–86.

103. How widespread "respectable" trade unionism was is still subject to debate. In such trades as brick making, where employers attempted to undermine craft control, trade unions engaged in organized violence: see Richard Price, "The Other Face of Respectability: Violence in the Manchester Brickmaking Trade 1859–1970," *History Workshop Journal* 23 (1987): 110–32.

104. The extent to which moderation or reformism on the part of trade unionists was related to employer initiatives, or employer initiatives were responses to "respectable dissent," is still not clearly understood: see Neville Kirk, *The Growth of Working Class Reformism in Mid-Victorian England* (Urbana, 1985); Richard Price, "Structures of Subordination in Nineteenth-Century British Industry," in Pat Thane, Geoffrey Crossick, and Roderick Floud, eds., *The Power of the Past: Essays for Eric Hobsbawm* (Cambridge, England, 1984).

105. A major point in Patrick Joyce's argument is that in contrast to workers in Lancashire, where paternalist factories proliferated, workers in Yorkshire, where paternalism was not the dominant managerial style, more readily participated in radical politics: see Joyce, *Work, Society and Politics.* Also see Price, "The Other Face." Eric Hobsbawm has argued that it was in the thirty years following the collapse of Chartism that industrial capitalism "became the common and accepted way of life of the labouring classes" (*Worlds of Labour,* 181). In spite of his critique of Patrick Joyce's thesis, Neville Kirk suggests that conflict and class pride coexisted and operated within the context of an overall acceptance of the system: see Kirk, *Growth of Working Class Reformism,* 26.

106. The description of the Cadbury factory community that follows is drawn from B. L. Hutchins's report on her visit to the works, British Association for the Advancement of Science Papers, Coll. 486, 2/6, pp. 16–17.

107. Cadbury, *Experiments in Industrial Organization*. Unless otherwise indicated, the descriptions that follow of the Cadburys' employment practices and Edward Cadbury's prescriptions for good factory management are taken from Cadbury's book.

108. Ibid., 255.

109. British Association for the Advancement of Science Papers, Coll. 486, 2/2, p. 4.

110. Ibid., 4.

111. David Lowe and Jack Richards, *The City of Lace* (Nottingham, 1983), 36.

112. Quotation from an article about Corbett, "A Salt Town," *Kidderminster Shuttle*, 26 September 1874, 7.

113. *Webb Trade Union Papers*, letter to B. L. Hutchins dated July 1891, sect. A., vol. 48, 174–75.

114. *Kidderminster Shuttle*, 26 September 1874, 7.

115. "Mr. Hugh Mason on the Sanitary State of Ashton and Oxford Mills," in *The Bee-Hive*, 4 March 1876, 5.

116. Report by B. L. Hutchins on Paper Making in London and Elsewhere, British Association for the Advancement of Science Papers, Coll. 486, 2/4, note no. 7, p. 3.

117. Michel Foucault has argued that such interest is a site for the play of power to control people's minds and bodies: see *Discipline and Punish* (New York, 1979); *The History of Sexuality*. Volume 1: *An Introduction* (New York, 1980). Foucault does not make it clear that this "play of power" emanated from one class and spread to another. Antonio Gramsci's ideas about hegemony and middle-class ideological domination in what he calls civil society are particularly suggestive: see Antonio Gramsci, *Selections from the Prison Notebooks* (New York, 1971). Together the ideas of Foucault and Gramsci provide insight into bourgeois social and moral reform movements beginning in the last quarter of the nineteenth century in England and Progressive Era reform in the United States.

118. British Association for the Advancement of Science Papers, Coll. 486, 2/8, p. 33. Although many employers were adopting marriage bars, others subcontracted work through middlewomen or, sometimes, middlemen to married women, who labored under conditions that could not be adequately regulated or controlled by the state until the Trades Boards Act was passed in 1909 after an almost twenty-year campaign against sweated labor. Some manufacturers who practiced the minor paternalism of the marriage bar or the more major paternalistic practices that recreated the family in work also benefited from sweated labor. Some probably rationalized their practices as fostering the domestic ideal by offering married women paid work in homes rather than factories. Others shielded themselves from the knowledge of the

sweated conditions of homeworkers' labor by subcontracting the work instead of directly employing homeworkers themselves.

119. Jane Lewis, *Women in England 1870–1950* (Bloomington, Ind., 1984), 146–49.

120. British Association for the Advancement of Science Papers, Coll. 486, 2/5, p. 15.

121. British Association for the Advancement of Science Papers, Coll. 486, 2/8, p. 44.

122. British Association for the Advancement of Science Papers, Coll. 486, 2/2, p. 25.

123. The argument that the widespread exclusion of married women from paid employment was in the interests of capital, to create a "reserve army of labor," is likewise unsatisfactory. As studies by Ruth Milkman and Irene Breugel have shown, the sex-typing of jobs generally prohibited employers from using women as a reserve army of labor even in depressions. It was only under extraordinary economic and social conditions that married women provided a supply of labor that resembles what is usually meant by the concept of the reserve army of labor: see Ruth Milkman, *Gender at Work* (Bloomington, Ind., 1987); Irene Breugel, "Women as a Reserve Army of Labour: A Note on Recent British Experience," *Feminist Review* 3 (1979).

124. From notes dated 17/2/02, British Association for the Advancement of Science Papers, Coll. 486, 2/6, pp. 16–17.

125. Joyce, *Work, Society and Politics*, chap. 5.

CHAPTER 3

1. Joseph Gusfield has argued that laws may be seen as a system of communications; they may be analyzed semiotically. Laws thus possess a mythical property, and their imposition is public ritual: see Joseph Gusfield, *The Culture of Public Problems: Drinking-Driving and the Symbolic Order* (Chicago, 1981), esp. chaps. 5 and 6. In this chapter I suggest that both public policies and the debates that produce them may be understood in this way.

2. This suggests that the state has the appearance of being a neutral arena. However, although those who create and administer laws may not officially or even unofficially represent particular economic or gender interests, they build into public policies unquestioned assumptions about gender and class relations. Because the state provides an arena for competing (but unequal) claims about the social order, state-level politics contribute to ideological hegemony: cf. Antonio Gramsci, *Selections from the Prison Notebooks* (New York, 1971), esp. 260–63. Gramsci argues that the state includes "hegemony protected by the armour of coercion" (263).

3. Carol Smart, *Feminism and the Power of the Law* (London, 1989), 4. Also see Zillah R. Eisenstein, *The Female Body and the Law* (Berkeley and Los Angeles, 1988), 6–22.

4. For a similar interpretation of gender and public policy, see Jane Jenson, "Paradigms and Political Discourse: Protective Legislation in France and the

United States Before 1914," *Canadian Journal of Political Science* 22 (1989): 235–58.

5. Philip Corrigan and Derek Sayer, *The Great Arch: English State Formation as Cultural Revolution* (Oxford, 1985), 22.

6. Diana L. Barker, "Regulation of Marriage," in Gary Littlejohn et al., eds., *Power and the State* (London, 1978), 254.

7. The state's varied efforts to deal with illegitimacy or bastardy and with prostitution are other examples of laws regulating sexuality and gender relations that also were concerned with economic relations.

8. Philip Corrigan and Derek Sayer propose that "States ... *state;* the arcane rituals of a court of law, the formulae of royal assent to an Act of Parliament, visits of school inspectors, are all statements. They define, in great detail, acceptable forms and images of social activity and individual and collective identity; they regulate, in empirically specifiable ways, much—very much, by the twentieth century—of social life. Indeed, in this sense 'the State' never stops talking" (*The Great Arch,* 3). This insight is fundamental to the argument of this chapter. Nancy Fraser has proposed that discourses about politics in capitalist societies have concerned where the limits of the political are to be drawn. She argues that what is "political" has been defined against what is "economic" and what is "domestic": see Nancy Fraser, *Unruly Practices: Power, Discourse and Gender in Contemporary Social Theory* (Minneapolis, 1989), chap. 8, especially 166–71.

9. Corrigan and Sayer suggest that state formation is *"moral regulation:* a project of normalizing, rendering natural, taken for granted, in a word 'obvious', what are in fact ontological and epistemological premises of a particular and historical form of social order" (*The Great Arch,* 4).

10. My analysis is very similar to one formulated by Jane Jenson in "Gender and Reproduction: Or, Babies and the State," *Studies in Political Economy* 20 (1986): 9–46. Also see Jenson's "Paradigms and Political Discourse."

11. For the history of the Poor Law Amendment Act and the treatment of poverty in nineteenth-century England, see Sidney Webb and Beatrice Webb, *English Poor Law History. Part 2: The Last Hundred Years* (London, 1929); Sidney Webb and Beatrice Webb, *English Poor Law Policy* (London, 1910); H. L. Beale, "The New Poor Law," *History* 15 (1931): 308–71; Eric J. Hobsbawm, *Industry and Empire* (Harmondsworth, 1969), 228–30; Derek Fraser, *The Evolution of the British Welfare State* (London, 1973; 2d ed. London, 1984); Pat Thane, *Foundations of the Welfare State* (London, 1982), 10–50; Michael E. Rose, *The Relief of Poverty 1834–1914* (London, 1972; 2d ed. London 1986).

12. Michael Rose, *The Relief of Poverty,* 10.

13. For a description and discussion, see E. P. Thompson, *The Making of the English Working Class* (Harmondsworth, 1968; reprinted Harmondsworth, 1980), 242–58.

14. Frank Perkin, *The Origins of Modern English Society, 1780–1880* (London, 1969), 190.

15. Beale, "The New Poor Law," 14.

16. Hobsbawm, *Industry and Empire*, 229.

17. Earlier notions of independence stressed self-employment rather than wage labor: see Christopher Hill, "Pottage for Freeborn Englishmen: Attitudes to Wage Labour in the 16th and 17th Centuries," in *The Collected Essays of Christopher Hill* (Amherst, Mass., 1985).

18. Pat Thane, "Women and the Poor Law in Victorian and Edwardian England," *History Workshop* 6 (1978): 30.

19. Ibid., 31.

20. This provision proved extremely unpopular, and in 1844 the rules were changed so that the Poor Law guardians could sue the father for the maintenance of the child and its mother. However, throughout the century, workhouses were filled disproportionately with unwed mothers.

21. The assumption was that state charity "interfered" with the "freedom" of capital to purchase labor by supporting those who would otherwise be able to work.

22. *Blackburn Standard*, 4 May 1878, 8.

23. *Blackburn Standard*, 1 June 1878, 3.

24. *Blackburn Standard*, 25 May 1878, 6.

25. *Burnley Express*, 18 May 1878, 5.

26. Howard Marvel, "Factory Regulation: A Reinterpretation of Early English Experience," *Journal of Law and Economics* 20 (1977): 381. See also Mariana Valverde, " 'Giving the Female a Domestic Turn': The Social, Legal and Moral Regulation of Women's Work in British Cotton Mills, 1827–1850," *Journal of Social History* 21 (1988): 626.

27. Valverde, " 'Giving the Female a Domestic Turn,' " 626. See also Ava Baron, who suggests that legislators and the courts "gerrymandered" (her term) principles of laissez faire by legislating hours for women but not legislating a minimum wage: Ava Baron, "Protective Labor Legislation and the Cult of Domesticity," *Journal of Family Issues* 2 (1981): 25–38.

28. Discussions of the interests of the various proponents of the bill may be found in Raymond G. Cowherd, *The Humanitarians and the Ten Hour Movement in England* (Boston, 1958); Douglas Booth, "Karl Marx on State Regulation of the Labor Process: The English Factory Acts," *Review of Social Economy* 36 (1978). Valverde discusses the role played by operative spinners in the movement for restricting women's hours, in her " 'Giving the Female a Domestic Turn.' " Also see Catherine Hall, "The Tale of Samuel and Jemima: Gender and Working-class Culture in Nineteenth-century England," in Harvey Kaye and Keith McClelland, eds., *E. P. Thompson: Critical Perspectives* (Cambridge, England, 1990).

29. Quoted in Valverde, " 'Giving the Female a Domestic Turn,' " 627.

30. Ibid.

31. See Cowherd, *The Humanitarians and the Ten Hour Movement*. Also see L. Woodward, *The Age of Reform 1815–1870* (Oxford, 1963).

32. E. H. Hunt, *British Labour History, 1815–1914* (London, 1981), 212–13.

33. For an argument that the factory acts were a mechanism of "cartel

reinforcement," see Paul R. Lawrence, "Marx on State Regulation: A Comment," *Review of Social Economy* 38 (1980): 81–88. Howard Marvel argues that leading manufacturers intended the 1833 Factory Act to restrict output, thereby raising textile prices and disadvantaging smaller manufacturers: see "Factory Regulation."

34. Karl Marx, *Capital*, vol. 1 (New York, 1967), 270.

35. See Karl Marx and Friedrich Engels, *Collected Works*, vol. 2 (London, 1975). Also see Douglas Booth's discussions of Marx's views on the Factory Acts: "Karl Marx on State Regulation," and "Marx on State Regulation: A Rejoinder," *Review of Social Economy* 38 (1980): 89–94.

36. For a discussion of Marxian analyses of the state, see Bob Jessop, *The Capitalist State: Marxist Theories and Methods* (New York, 1982). For an extensive critique of these theories of the state, see Theda Skocpol, "Political Response to Capitalist Crisis: Neo-Marxist Theories of the State and the Case of the New Deal," *Politics and Society* 10 (1980): 156–201. For an exposition of a "state-centered" approach to public policy, see Theda Skocpol and Edwin Amenta, "States and Social Policies," *American Sociological Review* 12 (1986): 131–57. For a recent discussion from a neo-Marxian perspective, see Rhonda F. Levine, *The Class Struggle and the New Deal* (Lawrence, Kansas, 1988). Also see Jill Quadagno, *The Transformation of Old Age Security* (Chicago, 1987).

37. For a discussion of the Mines Regulation Act, see Angela V. John, *By the Sweat of Their Brow: Women Workers in Victorian Coal Mines* (London, 1984). Also see Jane Humphries, "Protective Legislation, the Capitalist State, and Working Class Men: The Case of the 1842 Mines Regulation Act," *Feminist Review* 7 (1981): 1–33; and Angela John, "Letter in Response to Jane Humphries," *Feminist Review* 7 (1981): 106–9. In analyzing the history of factory legislation, Neil Smelser has emphasized the fact that children and then women were made subject to regulation. However, rather than seeing their inclusion as due either to political expedience or to real concern with the damage long hours might inflict on working women's health and morals, he argued that these laws represented the working-out of a structural differentiation of the family: see his *Social Change in the Industrial Revolution* (Chicago, 1959), chap. 11.

38. Factory legislation reducing the hours of women's work was not an issue in the United States until the end of the nineteenth century. For a recent analysis focusing on New York state, see Susan Lehrer, *Origins of Protective Legislation for Women, 1905–1925* (Albany, N.Y., 1987). Following Poulantzas, she contends that the state is "relatively autonomous" and thus could act in a gender-biased fashion against the interests of individual capitalists, in order to protect women as the reproducers of the labor force.

39. This is one possible reading of the discussion by John, in her *By the Sweat of Their Brow*, of miners who urged passage of the 1842 Mines Regulation Act and the attempts to exclude women from the mine face in the 1880s. For the United States, see Judith Baer, *The Chains of Protection: The Judicial Response to Women's Labor Legislation* (Westport, Conn., 1978).

40. See Mary McIntosh, "The State and the Oppression of Women," in Annette Kuhn and Anne Marie Wolpe, eds., *Feminism and Materialism* (London, 1978). For the United States see Lehrer, *Origins of Protective Legislation.*

41. See Humphries, "Protective Legislation, the Capitalist State, and Working Class Men," and John, "Letter in Response to Jane Humphries." Also see the discussion by Jane Mark-Lawson and Anne Witz, "From 'Family Labour' to 'Family Wage'? The Case of Women's Labour in Nineteenth-Century Coalmining," *Social History* 13 (1988): 151–74.

42. Valverde, " 'Giving the Female a Domestic Turn,' " 629.

43. Ibid., 630.

44. Murray Edelman, *Constructing the Political Spectacle* (Chicago, 1987), 21–24.

45. Women and children were involved in tasks preparatory to spinning, which itself was generally a man's job. Women as well as men worked as weavers, and children worked at tasks auxiliary to weaving.

46. The Webbs attributed this statement to Thomas Ashton, the secretary of the Oldham Spinners and a chief protagonist for factory reform. According to the Webbs, Ashton had often made this statement. Trade union leaders such as Ashton recognized that in arguing for hours legislation, unionists had expediently focused on women and children in order to secure a legislated reduction in their own hours: see Sidney Webb and Beatrice Webb, *History of Trade Unionism,* 2d ed. (London, 1896), 297. During the Eight Hours Movement of the 1890s, the *Cotton Factory Times* on 26 May 1893 proclaimed, "now the veil must be lifted and the agitation carried on under its true colours. Women and children must no longer be made the pretext for securing a reduction of working hours for men" (quoted in Webb and Webb, *History of Trade Unionism,* 297).

47. Descriptions appear in *The Bee-Hive,* 6 January 1872, 5; *Times* (London), 3 January 1872, 5.

48. Lord Shaftesbury previously held the title Lord Ashley, and the Ten Hours Bill has often been called Ashley's Bill.

49. W. H. G. Armytage, *A. J. Mundella, 1825–1897: The Liberal Background to the Labour Movement* (London, 1951), 123. Mundella was a relatively new member of Parliament who began his political career by supporting a bill to give legal recognition to trade unions. Prior to becoming a legislator, Mundella had been instrumental in creating, in the hosiery trade, boards of conciliation and arbitration that included equal numbers of (male) workers and employers.

50. *Oldham Chronicle,* 13 January 1872, 8.

51. *Oldham Standard,* 2 December 1871, 3.

52. Webb and Webb, *History of Trade Unions,* 296.

53. Ibid.

54. Mundella wrote to his friend and political patron Robert Leader of the *Sheffield Independent,* "My Factory Bill has had no end of ill luck. Still even that gives it prominence and I shall come out all right in the end" (letter

to Robert Leader, 2 August 1873, in Mundella Papers, 6P/103/192, at the University of Sheffield).

55. While he was a member of Parliament, Disraeli apparently supported Mundella's bill.

56. *Standard* (Ashton-under-Lyne), 14 February 1872, 6.

57. *Standard* (Ashton-under-Lyne), 6 April 1872, 7.

58. Ibid.

59. The statistics on the percentages of women in the labor force and their employment are summaries based on data in Brian R. Mitchell and Phyllis Deane, *Abstract of British Historical Statistics* (Cambridge, England, 1962), 60.

60. Jane Lewis, "The Working-Class Wife and Mother and State Intervention 1870–1918," in Jane Lewis, ed., *Labour and Love: Women's Experience of Home and Family, 1850–1940* (Oxford, 1986), 99–120, esp. 100–101, 103–5. See also Jane Lewis, *The Politics of Motherhood* (London, 1980).

61. Lewis, "The Working-Class Wife," 100–103. This development may be interpreted, following Foucault, as the further development of bourgeois society in exercising control by making sex, family, and reproduction "subjects" of political discourse: see Michel Foucault, *The History of Sexuality*. Volume 1: *An Introduction* (New York, 1980), esp. part 5. Jacques Donzelot has elaborated on this idea in *The Policing of Families* (London, 1980). Recently, David Levine has situated fertility decline within this development, in "Recombinant Family Formation Strategies," *Journal of Historical Sociology* 2 (1989): 89–115.

62. Jane Lewis, *Women in England 1870–1950* (Bloomington, Ind., 1984), 47.

63. Ibid.

64. Ibid.

65. Data purporting to demonstrate the high rates of infant mortality in areas in which there were high concentrations of working women had been reported since the late 1850s. These data are discussed and accepted rather uncritically by Margaret Hewitt, in *Wives and Mothers in Victorian Industry* (London, 1958), 85–122. Hewitt maintains that high rates of infant mortality in the factory districts were caused by mothers working. She bases her statement primarily on the apparent decline in infant mortality rates during the cotton famine. That decline, however, was probably due largely to emigration. Hewitt also claims that the proportion of married women who worked rose between 1851 and 1871. However, she bases this estimate on the proportion of women aged twenty and older who were employed, but at the same time shows that age at marriage was rising, not falling, during this period. Finally, she suggests that the large proportion of married women who worked in cotton textiles were not living with their husbands or were married to men who were not in textiles; most likely they were married to men who had insufficient wages to maintain a family. It is likely that the correlation between infant mortality and married women working was spurious.

For other critiques of Hewitt's work and analyses of the connection between working mothers and infant mortality see Lewis, *The Politics of Motherhood*, 78; Carol Dyhouse, "Working Class Mothers and Infant Mortality in England, 1895–1914," *Journal of Social History* 12 (1978): 248–67. In any case, no matter what the "real facts" about infant mortality and the proportion of married women who worked, or the proportion of mothers who worked, may be, the data were used to prove that infant mortality was caused by mothers who worked in the mills and that women's hours should be further curtailed.

66. *Manchester Guardian*, 27 June 1873, 7.

67. Lewis, *Women in England*, 32. Foucault situates the eugenics movement and its racism within discourses of sexuality and the play of power in the modern world: see Foucault, *History of Sexuality*, vol. 1, 148–50.

68. Malcolm Spector and John Kitsuse, *Constructing Social Problems* (Menlo Park, 1979), speak of those who are involved in creating the perception that a social problem exists as engaged in "claim making activities." See also Joseph Gusfield, who discusses the use of scientific evidence for persuasion in what he calls "The Literary Art of Science" (*The Culture of Public Problems*, 83–110). Also see Joan W. Scott's essay on statistical representations of women's work in nineteenth-century France, "A Statistical Representation of Work," in her *Gender and the Politics of History* (New York, 1988).

69. *Times* (London), 12 June 1873, 6.

70. Ibid.

71. Ibid.

72. *Hansard*, 11 June 1873, 824.

73. *Hansard*, 9 August 1874, 1047.

74. For a provocative discussion of the position of Millicent Fawcett and other bourgeois women's rights activists on the issue of protective legislation for working-class women, see Rosemary Feurer, "The Meaning of 'Sisterhood': The British Women's Movement and Protective Labor Legislation, 1870–1900," *Victorian Studies* 31 (1988): 233–60.

75. *Hansard*, 30 July 1873, 1291.

76. *Times* (London), 5 August 1873, 8.

77. *Times* (London), 27 March 1874, 6.

78. *Hansard*, 18 May 1874, 1429.

79. These arguments suggesting that women lacked the ability to decide for themselves or negotiate with their employers focused principally on married women and mothers. Several legislators said that it would be impossible to legislate hours for married women only; others would have added special restrictions for married women and mothers. But it was common for legislators and employers to equate the term *married woman* with the terms *mother* and *widow*. This suggests that *married woman* did not signify the marital status of a woman, but, rather, equated marriage with motherhood, and motherhood with being the sole nurturer of children.

80. *Englishwoman's Review* 20 (July 1874): 200.

81. Ibid., 235–36.

82. *Third Annual Report of the Vigilance Association* (London, 1873).

83. Lewis, "Working-Class Wife," 100.
84. *Capital and Labour,* 25 March 1874, 75.
85. *Capital and Labour,* 1 April 1874, 97–98.
86. *Fourth Annual Report of the Vigilance Association* (London, 1874), 8.
87. See the statement by J. B. Baldwin at the meeting of the Leeds Factory Acts Association, *Leeds Daily News,* 9 June 1873, 3.
88. *The Bee-Hive,* 9 March 1872, 5.
89. *Leeds Evening Express,* 18 March 1872, 3. Indeed, one of Mundella's motives in pushing for an extension of state regulation of hours was to avoid labor unrest. In a letter to a constituent he said he feared that if he were not to push for an act of Parliament, the issue would be decided "through strikes and lock-outs. Leeds has already demonstrated this. And it has only been through my advice and threats of abandoning their cause that these have not become general and chronic" (letter of A. J. Mundella to Sir Swire Smith, 10 May 1872, in Mundella Papers, 6P/97/3, University of Sheffield, i).
90. *Leeds Evening Express,* 11 April 1872, 4.
91. *Leeds Evening Express,* 29 April 1872, 3.
92. *The Bee-Hive,* 27 April 1872, 5.
93. The subject of women's participation in trade unions is discussed more fully in Chapter 7.
94. Report of the Commissioners Appointed to Inquire into the Working of the Factory and Workshops Acts, *Parliamentary Papers* 30.1 (1876): 410.
95. Ibid., 255. Both Mrs. Ford and Miss Sloane testified immediately after their employers did. Their testimony was thus constrained on the one hand by the commissioners, who badgered them about the evils of married women working in factories and workshops and about the lazy husbands who forced them to work, and on the other by their employers, who opposed the extension of the Factory Acts.
96. *Women's Union Journal* 2 (1877): 45.
97. The opposition from women trade unionists, women's rights groups, and industrialists and legislators who supported "equal rights" for women was more organized and intense than it was in the debates in the early 1870s, but many of the same arguments were repeated. Henry Fawcett attempted to have women excluded from all of the regulations of the consolidated act. He was successful only in removing from regulation domestic workshops that did not employ young persons. His success was due to a coalition of interest groups who wanted to remove homework and family-run domestic industry from the legislation. Such workshops were merely excluded from the act, and the principle of women as "unfree agents" vis-à-vis work outside of family settings remained.
98. Angela John has proposed that these debates set the tone for attempts in the 1880s to prohibit women from working at the surface of coal mines (*By the Sweat of Their Brow,* 136).
99. Gusfield uses the phrase "fixing political responsibility" to refer to this aspect of public culture (*The Culture of Public Problems,* 14–15).

100. Ibid., 15, describes the cultural construction of who is to blame for a social problem as "fixing causal responsibility." Gareth Stedman Jones has described the life of casual workers in London during this period who were experiencing continuing employment instability: see his *Outcast London* (reprinted Harmondsworth, 1984).

101. Lewis, "Working-Class Wife," 103. For the United States, see Martha May, "The Historical Problem of the Family Wage: The Ford Motor Company and the Five Dollar Day," *Feminist Studies* 8 (1982): 399–424; Martha May, "Bread Before Roses: American Workingmen, Labor Unions and the Family Wage," in Ruth Milkman, ed., *Women, Work and Protest: A Century of U.S. Women's Labor History* (London, 1985), 1–21.

102. For a similar conclusion about the consequences of the U.S. Supreme Court decision in Mueller *v.* Oregon, see Ava Baron, "Protective Labor Legislation."

103. Fraser, *Unruly Practices*, chap. 8.

104. British Association for the Advancement of Science Committee on the Economic Effect of Legislation Regulating Women's Labour, Coll. 486, 1/3, British Library of Political and Economic Science, 6.

105. Recent research on the effects of factory legislation in the United States also suggests that legislation did not reduce the overall extent of women's employment: see Claudia Goldin, "Maximum Hours Legislation and Female Employment: A Reassessment," *Journal of Political Economy* 96 (1988): 189–205.

106. Baron, "Protective Labor Legislation," 37–38.

107. See, for example, testimony by Nottingham lace manufacturer William Henry Mallet, in *Parliamentary Papers* 29 (1876): 388, and by Frederick Carver, president of the Lace Merchants Association, in ibid., 391. Also see Roy A. Church, *Economic and Social Change in a Midland Town: Victorian Nottingham 1815–1900* (London, 1966), 290.

108. Marilyn Boxer has argued that in France homework proliferated as a consequence of hours legislation for women at the end of the nineteenth century: see her "Protective Legislation and Home Industry: The Marginalization of Women Workers in Late Nineteenth, Early Twentieth-Century France," *Journal of Social History* 20 (1986): 45–65.

109. Shelley Pennington and Belinda Westover, *A Hidden Workforce: Homeworkers in England, 1850–1985* (London, 1989), 37.

110. For references to debates on state formation and the development of the welfare state that take up this issue, see n. 36 above.

111. E. P. Thompson, *Whigs and Hunters* (London, 1975), 260–61.

CHAPTER 4

1. Numerous women's historians have noted the importance of wage earning among married women: see Sally Alexander, Anna Davin, and Eve Hostettler, "Labouring Women: A Reply to Eric Hobsbawm," *History Workshop* 8 (1979): 174–82. Contemporary social investigators agreed on the necessity for mar-

ried women to earn wages: see Clementina Black, ed., *Married Women's Work* (London, 1915; reprinted London, 1983). For a review of the conditions under which women engaged in waged work and those under which they remained out of the labor force, see Louise A. Tilly and Joan W. Scott, *Women, Work and Family*, 2d ed. (London, 1987; reprinted London, 1989). For the United States, see Alice Kessler-Harris, *Out to Work* (Oxford, 1982). Historians Seth Koven and Sonya Michel have written about "maternalism" as an ideology that, as they put it, "extolled the private virtues of domesticity while simultaneously legitimating women's public relationships to politics and the state, to community, workplace and marketplace." This was the ideology articulated by members of Parliament and social reformers. See Seth Koven and Sonya Michel, "Womanly Duties: Maternalist Politics and the Origins of Welfare States in France, Germany, Great Britain and the United States, 1880–1920," *American Historical Review* 95 (1990): 1079.

2. I owe this interpretation to Cynthia Rae Daniels: see "Working Mothers and the State," Ph.D. dissertation, University of Massachusetts, 1983. Also see Cynthia R. Daniels, "Between Home and Factory: Homeworkers and the State," in Eileen Boris and Cynthia R. Daniels, eds., *Homework: Historical and Contemporary Perspectives on Paid Labor at Home* (Urbana, 1989), 13–32.

3. Sheila Allen has made a similar point: see her "Locating Homework in an Analysis of the Ideological and Material Constraints on Women's Paid Work," in Boris and Daniels, eds., *Homework*, 273.

4. David Thomson, "The Decline of Social Welfare: Falling State Support for the Elderly Since Early Victorian Times," *Ageing and Society* 4 (1985): 451–82.

5. Women's Industrial Council, *Home Industries of Women in London* (London, 1897), 103.

6. Ibid., 105.

7. In the mining community of Brinsley in the same year, only 37 percent of the widows were working. Widows in Brinsley were much less likely than widows in Arnold to be household heads. Brinsley widows were found to be living in the households of relatives unless they had older children living at home who were employed. This suggests the flexibility of the family economy and that, in the absence of employment opportunities, the survival of the widowed elderly depended on alterations of household structures: see Sonya O. Rose, "The Varying Household Arrangements of the Elderly in Three English Villages, 1851–1881," *Continuity and Change* 3 (1988): 101–22.

8. Eric Hobsbawm, *Labouring Men* (London, 1964), 290.

9. Quoted in Keith McClelland, "Time to Work, Time to Live," in Patrick Joyce, ed., *The Historical Meanings of Work* (Cambridge, England, 1987), 186.

10. Ibid.

11. See Gareth Stedman Jones, *Outcast London* (Oxford, 1971; reprinted Harmondsworth, 1984), 19–158.

12. Pat Thane, *Foundations of the Welfare State* (London, 1982), 8.

13. Lynn Hollen Lees, "Getting and Spending: The Family Budgets of English Industrial Workers in 1890," in John M. Merriman, ed., *Consciousness and Class Experience in Nineteenth-Century Europe* (New York, 1979), 173 (table 2).

14. Ibid., 172.

15. See John Holley, "The Two Family Economies of Industrialism: Factory Workers in Victorian Scotland," *Journal of Family History* 6 (1981): 57–69.

16. For a recent discussion of nineteenth-century poverty, its assessment by social investigators, and attitudes toward it, see Thane, *Foundations of the Welfare State*, 8–18.

17. Charles Booth, *Life and Labour of the People in London*, 17 vols. (London, 1899–1903). Several studies conducted in the early years of the twentieth century confirm that about 30 percent of the people were living below the primary poverty line: see Lady Florence Bell, *At the Works*, 1st ed. (London, 1907); A. L. Bowley and A. R. Burnett-Hurst, *Livelihood and Poverty* (London, 1915).

18. B. Seebohm Rowntree, *Poverty: A Study of Town Life* (London, 1901), 120–21.

19. Ibid., 112.

20. Jane Lewis, *Women in England 1870–1950* (Bloomington, Ind., 1984), 48.

21. Ellen Smith, *Wage-Earning Women and Their Dependents* (London, 1915). In Yorkshire, 63 percent worked because of the inadequacy of their husbands' wages, another 6 percent were widowed, and 14 percent reported that they had been deserted by their husbands or that the husband drank: see B. L. Hutchins, "Yorkshire," in Black, ed., *Married Women's Work*, 135.

22. Maud Pember Reeves, *Round About a Pound a Week* (London, 1913; reprinted London, 1979). For the importance of the pawnshop to women in making ends meet, see Robert Roberts, *The Classic Slum* (Manchester, 1971; reprinted Harmondsworth, 1973); Ellen Ross, " 'Fierce Questions and Taunts': Married Life in Working-Class London, 1870–1914," *Feminist Studies* 8 (1982): 575–602.

23. Elizabeth Roberts, *A Woman's Place: An Oral History of Working-Class Women 1890–1940* (Oxford, 1984).

24. For a description of the range and variety of these economic strategies, see John Benson, *The Penny Capitalists* (Dublin, 1983); Ellen Ross, "Survival Networks: Women's Neighborhood Sharing in London Before World War I," *History Workshop* 15 (1983): 4–27.

25. Historian Elizabeth Roberts has compiled oral histories of women who were growing up in the Edwardian period to show that throughout the early decades of the twentieth century, the census underrepresented the number of women who were wage earners: see her *A Woman's Place*, 136.

26. Lewis, *Women in England 1870–1950*, 150. Lynn Hollen Lees, for example, shows that only among cotton and wool workers surveyed in the

Carroll D. Wright study was the proportion of households in which wives were employed as high as 11 percent. Wives of other skilled and semi-skilled workers were not listed as working: see Lees, "Getting and Spending," 173. Contemporary social investigator B. L. Hutchins estimated that at the turn of the century one-fifth of the women in the labor force were married: see Standish Meacham, *A Life Apart: The English Working Class, 1890–1914* (London, 1977), 95. Another contemporary social commentator, however, argued that women's economic contributions had been unrecognized. In her comments on the public outcry against married women's wage earning, Ada Heather Biggs said, "it is indisputable that women of the working classes always *have* been joint earners with their husbands. At no time in the world's history has the man's labour alone sufficed for the maintenance of his wife and children" (Ada Heather Biggs, "The Wife's Contribution to Family Income," *Economic Journal* 4 [1894]: 55 [emphasis in original]).

27. Sheila Allen has written, "The persistent invisibility of much of women's economic activity is not specific to homework but is institutionalized throughout the ideological separation of home and work" (Sheila Allen, "Locating Homework in an Analysis of the Ideological and Material Constraints on Women's Paid Work," in Boris and Daniels, eds., *Homework*, 273).

28. Joan W. Scott has argued that statistical accounts should be viewed as representations and analyzed in terms of the political contexts in which they were created: see her *Gender and the Politics of History* (New York, 1988), chap. 6. For a sociological argument that views statistical categories as social constructions, see Aaron V. Cicourel, *Method and Measurement in Sociology* (New York, 1964). For an important discussion of misrepresentations in censuses from nineteenth-century Britain, see Edward Higgs, "Women, Occupations and Work in the Nineteenth Century Censuses," *History Workshop* 23 (1987): 59–80.

29. For a perceptive analysis of the ideological biases in the U.S. census from 1900 to 1980, see Christine Bose, "Devaluing Women's Work: The Undercount of Women's Employment in 1900 and 1980," in Christine Bose et al., eds., *The Hidden Aspects of Women's Work* (New York, 1987), 95–115. For a similar analysis of biases in the British censuses, see Higgs, "Women, Occupations and Work."

30. See Higgs's reports of variations over time and from one enumerator's district to another in the same community, in "Women, Occupations and Work," 65–67.

31. Ibid., 70.

32. Lewis, *Women in England 1870–1950;* Higgs, "Women, Occupations and Work," 70.

33. Ibid.

34. Lewis, *Women in England 1870–1950,* 149; Clara Collet, "The Collection and Utilisation of Official Statistics Bearing on the Extent and Effects of the Industrial Employment of Women," *Journal of the Royal Statistical Society* 111 (June 1898): 229.

35. This bias probably also affected family budget studies, the major other source that historians have used in estimating women's contributions to the household economy.

36. Based on my calculations from enumerators' records in RG 11/4173, at the Public Records Office, London.

37. See Sonya O. Rose, "Proto-industry, Women's Work and the Household Economy in the Transition to Industrial Capitalism," *Journal of Family History* 13 (1988): 186. Ellen Jordan argues that although women's employment in certain industries may have been underreported, women working full-time may have been relatively faithfully represented in statistics. She proposes that the employment and unemployment of girls aged fifteen to nineteen was reported without distortion: see Ellen Jordan, "Female Unemployment in England and Wales 1851–1911: An Examination of the Census Figures for 15–19 Year Olds," *Social History* 13 (1988): 186–87.

38. James A. Schmiechen, *Sweated Industries and Sweated Labor: The London Clothing Trades, 1860–1914* (Urbana, 1984), 68; Higgs, "Women, Occupations and Work," 63.

39. Belinda Westover, "To Fill the Kids' Tummies: The Lives and Work of Colchester Tailoresses, 1880–1918," in Leonore Davidoff and Belinda Westover, eds., *Our Work, Our Lives, Our Words* (Totowa, N.J., 1986), 67.

40. Recently a good deal of research has been done on the subject of homework: see Schmiechen, *Sweated Industries;* Jenny Morris, "The Characteristics of Sweating: The Late Nineteenth-Century London and Leeds Tailoring Trade," in Angela V. John, ed., *Unequal Opportunities: Women's Employment in England 1800–1918* (Oxford, 1986), 95–124; Westover, "To Fill the Kids' Tummies," 54–75. For the United States, see Eileen Boris, "Regulating Industrial Homework: The Triumph of 'Sacred Motherhood,' " *Journal of American History* 71 (March 1985): 745–63, and her "Homework in the Past, Its Meaning for the Future," in Kathleen E. Christensen, ed., *The New Era of Home-Based Work* (Boulder, 1988), 15–29. On homework in the contemporary period, see Sheila Allen and Carol Wolkowitz, *Homeworking: Myths and Realities* (London, 1987); Lourdes Beneria and Martha Roldan, *The Crossroads of Class and Gender: Industrial Homework, Subcontracting, and Household Dynamics in Mexico City* (Chicago, 1987); Christensen, ed., *The New Era of Home-Based Work;* Eileen Boris, "Homework and Women's Rights: The Case of the Vermont Knitters, 1980–1985," *Signs* 13 (1987): 98–120. For essays on both the history and the contemporary practice of homework, see Boris and Daniels, eds., *Homework.*

41. The 1901 Census of England and Wales listed 447,480 homeworkers in England and Wales, but the actual number far exceeded that figure, for homeworkers frequently did not consider themselves to be working. Oral historians have commented that many women would not say they earned wages by working at home when the interviewer asked them if they worked after they were married. The interviewer would have to ask specifically about homework. Many women saw their industrial homework as an extension of their domestic obligations. The women who were listed in the census were

probably those who had been doing the homework for many years and considered their work as a trade.

42. For an excellent analysis of industrial homework as an employer strategy, see Allen and Wolkowitz, *Homeworking.*

43. Eileen Boris argues that flexibility was the leitmotif of the employer of homeworkers: see her "Homework in the Past," 17.

44. See Olwen Hufton, *The Poor of Eighteenth Century France* (Oxford, 1976). Not all homeworkers were casual workers. Some women worked full-time in their homes for most of their lives, sometimes doing work that had required a formal apprenticeship or a long period of training. These women, however, were a small minority of all homeworkers. For examples of skilled homeworkers who had been working at their trades all their lives, see Women's Industrial Council, *Home Industries of Women,* 109, 111.

45. Peter G. Hall, *The Industries of London Since 1861* (London, 1962), 61.

46. Westover, "To Fill the Kids' Tummies," 72.

47. V. de Vasselitsky, *The Homeworker and the Outlook* (London, 1916), 15.

48. The data are based on enumerators' books from the wards of St. Mary's and Trent. St. Mary's was adjacent to the lace market; Trent was close by and stretched into a more rural area that was still within the city limits of Nottingham. Records of all households in which someone was listed as a lace clipper were coded, along with a one-in-seven sample of non–lace-clipping households. Lace clippers were oversampled to compensate for the fact that homeworkers often do not list themselves as being employed. It is possible that these lace clippers are representative only of those who did this work on a regular basis. Because of the peculiarities of this database, combining the universe of lace clippers with a sample of non–lace-clipper households, it would make no sense to try to offer such figures as the percentage of homeworkers in the sample or in a particular age group. I have chosen to calculate percentages based on the number in various occupational categories. The data are taken from Census of Nottingham, Districts of St. Mary's (RG 11/3352) and Trent (RG 11/3348).

49. Generally it was married women who worked at home. A survey of homeworkers in Hackney in 1906 found that 66 percent were married. This calculation is based on a table from the Royal Commission on Poor Laws and the Relief of Distress, *Parliamentary Papers* 44 (1909): 598, as reprinted in Schmiechen, *Sweated Industries,* 71. According to a 1916 study of homeworkers in London, even higher percentages of boxmakers and women who worked as tailors were married. Married women made up 78.2 percent of boxmakers and 69.6 percent of female tailors: see de Vesselitsky, *The Homeworker and the Outlook,* 13. Because lace clipping was done in both warehouses and private homes, the data must be interpreted with caution. It is likely that the Nottingham sample underrepresents the proportion of homeworking lace clippers who were married, in that there are probably both some lace clippers listed who were working in warehouses and a large number of

homeworkers who were not listed. However, the general characteristics of the Nottingham sample of lace workers conform to what is known about other homeworkers in late Victorian and Edwardian England. It also conforms to the picture of homeworkers in New York in the early years of the twentieth century: see Boris, "Homework in the Past," 18–20.

50. In 1881, England was undergoing an economic depression. Workers who had regular employment were relatively well off as the cost of living declined. However, casual workers, who suffered frequent periods of unemployment even in the best of times, probably were more likely to be unemployed at this time.

51. Roberts, *The Classic Slum*, 88.

52. Stedman Jones has shown that at this time in London districts that had a heavy concentration of male casual labor, there were also heavy concentrations of casual forms of employment for women, especially homework for married women: see Stedman Jones, *Outcast London*, 85. Belinda Westover found that women tailors working at home in the city of Colchester were married to men who were building laborers. In the areas around Colchester, homeworkers often were married to agricultural laborers, sailors, or fishermen: see Westover, "To Fill the Kids' Tummies," 58, 61, 73. Also see Schmiechen, *Sweated Industries*, 70.

53. E. G. Howarth and M. Wilson, *West Ham: A Study in Social and Industrial Problems* (London, 1907), 268–69.

54. Eileen Boris reports that homeworkers in New York were overrepresented in the age group 25–44: Boris, "Homework in the Past," 48.

55. Of the married lace clippers, 22.6 percent were between thirty-five and forty-four years old, compared with 34.6 percent of lace factory hands.

56. Of the married lace clippers who were living with their husbands, 34.5 percent had at least three children under the age of fourteen. This compares with 15 percent of hosiery workers, 22.7 percent of lace menders, and 16.3 percent of lace factory hands. Nearly half of the lace clippers (47.3 percent), as opposed to only 27.6 percent of married women who did not do lace clipping, were between twenty-five and thirty-four years old.

57. Of lace clippers, 34.5 percent had three or more children under age fourteen, compared with 24 percent of married women who were not employed.

58. Oral History no. 220, Family Life and Work Archive, University of Essex, 3.

59. Index no. 58 A, B, 1, Nottingham Oral History Archive, Local Studies Library, Nottingham.

60. Index no. 58, A, B, 4, Nottingham Oral History Archive, Local Studies Library, Nottingham.

61. Oral History no. 219, Family Life and Work Archive, University of Essex, 3, 4.

62. Unfortunately, the interviewer interrupted the respondent, but we may surmise that he was about to say that his mother took in more work when his

father was out of work: see Oral History no. 219, Family Life and Work Archive, University of Essex, 4.

63. Index no. 58, A, B, 4, Nottingham Oral History Archive, Local Studies Library, Nottingham.

64. Schmiechen suggests the point that women worked in the sweated trades much as their preindustrial grandmothers had worked: see his *Sweated Industries*, 66.

65. See Rose, "Proto-industry, Women's Work and the Household Economy."

66. Belinda Westover, "Military Tailoring in Colchester 1890–1925," B.A. thesis, University of Essex, cited by Diana Gittins in *Fair Sex: Family Size and Structure* (London, 1982), 99. Present-day homeworkers in England report that their children assist them in getting the work done. A homeworker who finished sweaters for a knitwear concern in 1988 said, "My daughters (aged 13 and 14) used to come in from school, eat and start sewing. I could never have got enough money from the work if my children had not helped" (Arlen Harris, "Hardship Hides Behind Doors of Homeworkers," *Observer* [London], 5 June 1988, 7).

67. Studies of contemporary women workers have shown that women still do the bulk of the housework, but when women work full-time, less housework gets done: see Heidi Hartmann, "The Family as the Locus of Gender, Class and Political Struggle: The Example of Housework," *Signs* 6 (1981): 366–94.

68. De Vesselitsky, *The Homeworker and the Outlook*, 19–20.

69. For the importance of such societies and how they were relatively inaccessible to unskilled workers, see R. Roberts, *The Classic Slum*, 85.

70. Ibid.

71. Ibid., 84.

72. David Levine, *Reproducing Families: The Political Economy of English Population History* (Cambridge, England, 1987). See also his *Family Formation in an Age of Nascent Capitalism* (Cambridge, England, 1977). In using the term *family strategy* I am not assuming that the collective decisions or actions by family members were arrived at without debate. The "interests" of women and men in households are not necessarily identical, and power relations between husbands and wives are crucial in determining how collective family strategies are worked out. For a discussion of the concept of family strategy by scholars from several social science disciplines, see "Family Strategy: A Dialogue," *Historical Methods* 20 (1987): 113–25. The essay by Nancy Folbre is especially insightful: see "Family Strategy, Feminist Strategy," *Historical Methods* 20 (1987): 115–18.

73. Levine, *Reproducing Families*, 177. Gittins notes the high birthrates in districts of London where outwork was common. She explains the persistently high fertility rates in these districts, in comparison with those in the cotton textile areas, as due to the nature of their marriages. She suggests that because husbands worked in exclusively male industries and earned higher wages rel-

ative to their homeworking wives, "marriages were . . . likely to be characterized by segregated and unequal role-relationships, and the traditional values among local social groups were apt to deem large families and female responsibility for birth control normative" (Gittins, *Fair Sex*, 88).

74. See Levine, *Reproducing Families*, 156–57.

75. The classic essay on this subject is by Laura Oren, "The Welfare of Women in Laboring Families: England, 1860–1950," *Feminist Studies* 1 (1973): 107–21.

76. Glimpses into these private worlds are provided by Ellen Ross for London: see her " 'Fierce Questions and Taunts.' "

77. Levine, *Reproducing Families*, 157. For the experience of growing up in the Edwardian period in a time when the death of a child was a common event, see R. Roberts, *The Classic Slum*.

78. For the expense of caring for new babies, see Ellen Ross, "Labour and Love: Rediscovering London's Working-Class Mothers, 1870–1918," in Jane Lewis, ed., *Labour and Love: Women's Experience of Home and Family, 1850–1940* (Oxford, 1986), 78–79.

79. Robert Roberts writes that in the Edwardian period, working-class wives were prudish and were supposedly uninterested in sex. However, "for all their lack of interest, [they] felt bound in duty to a fiction they thought existed, legally and morally, called 'conjugal rights'. These, they believed, entitled a husband to the liberty of copulation at almost any time, whatever his or his wife's state or condition" (*The Classic Slum*, 56). His descriptions of the local working-class male culture suggest that an ideology of virility may have contributed to the perception that a husband had sexual rights to his wife regardless of her wishes. Although birth-control devices that women could use were known among members of the working class, what evidence exists suggests that abstinence and withdrawal were the most frequently used methods: see E. Roberts, *A Woman's Place*, 95. These, however, required the cooperation of the husband. Abortion was the most frequently practiced method of family limitation: see Barbara Brooks, "Women and Reproduction c. 1860–1919," in Lewis, ed., *Labour and Love*, 149–74. For a recent essay on the beginnings of fertility decline, see Wally Seccombe, "Starting to Stop: Working Class Fertility Decline in Britain," *Past and Present* 126 (1990): 151–88.

80. See Ross, "Rediscovering London's Working-class Mothers," 76–79; E. Roberts, *A Woman's Place*, 83–104.

81. This may have been exacerbated by the practice of giving the most food to the male head of household: see Oren, "The Welfare of Women in Laboring Families," 107–25; R. Roberts, *The Classic Slum*, 111, 117; Carol Dyhouse, *Girls Growing Up in Late Victorian and Edwardian England* (London, 1981), 8–9.

82. See Angus McLaren, *Reproductive Rituals* (London, 1984), 64–70. In preindustrial societies, childbirths were widely spaced because mothers nursed their babies for as much as two or three years. Second and subsequent children were born when earlier-born children became able to make some contribution to the household economy or at least to provide child care while the mother

was working. Working-class women in the Edwardian period may have known about the connection between breast-feeding and fecundity: see E. Roberts, *A Woman's Place*, 99.

83. See Ross, "Labour and Love," 78–79.

84. Johanna Brenner and Maria Ramas, "Rethinking Women's Oppression," *New Left Review* 144 (1984): 33–71.

85. The contrast between the lack of state involvement in infant and child care and the relatively early state support for education is noteworthy.

86. Jane Lewis, *The Politics of Motherhood* (London, 1980); Dyhouse, *Girls Growing Up*. For a contemporary's assessment, see Anna Martin, *The Married Working Woman* (London, 1911; reprinted London, 1980).

87. In addition, as Cynthia Rae Daniels has proposed, the ideological opposition between motherhood and employment, home and factory was embedded in the structure of the labor market. The labor market was designed to accommodate single persons without childcare responsibilities. Policy makers and others based the logic of this structure in nature: see Daniels, "Working Mothers and the State," 134.

88. For a helpful discussion about conceptualizing social reproduction, see Johanna Brenner and Barbara Laslett, "Social Reproduction and the Family," in Ulf Himmelstrand, ed., *Sociology from Crisis to Science?* Vol. 2: *The Social Reproduction of Organization and Culture* (London, 1986), 116–31.

89. Lewis, *The Politics of Motherhood*.

90. See Oren, "The Welfare of Women in Laboring Families." For the financial costs and hardships of bearing many children in London, see Ross, "Labour and Love."

91. Margaret Llewelyn Davies, ed., *Life as We Have Known It: By Co-operative Working Women* (London, 1931; reprinted New York, 1975), 35.

92. Hewitt, *Wives and Mothers*.

93. Quoted from Hewitt, *Wives and Mothers*, 180. France passed a measure in 1913 that provided for a possible prenatal and compulsory postnatal leave. A daily allowance was available for eight weeks before and after childbirth, to compensate for wages lost: see Jane Jenson, "Gender and Reproduction: Or, Babies and the State," *Studies in Political Economy* 20 (1986): 16–17.

94. George Newman, *Infant Mortality* (New York, 1907), 124.

95. *Annual Report of Chief Inspector of Factories* (1904), 275, cited in Newman, *Infant Mortality*, 126. See also Black, *Married Women's Work*, 160.

96. Westover, "To Fill the Kids' Tummies," 71.

97. *Woman Worker*, 7 April 1909, 319.

98. See R. Roberts, *The Classic Slum*, 112; E. Roberts, *A Woman's Place*, 165–66; Hewitt, *Wives and Mothers*, 137.

99. Peter Laslett, *The World We Have Lost* (London, 1965); Peter Laslett, "Size and Structure of the Household in England over Three Centuries," *Population Studies* 23 (1969): 199–223; Peter Laslett, "Mean Household Size in England Since the Sixteenth Century," in Peter Laslett and Richard Wall, eds.,

Household and Family in Past Time (Cambridge, England, 1972); Richard Wall, "The Household: Demographic and Economic Change in England, 1650–1970," in Richard Wall, Jean Robin, and Peter Laslett, eds., *Family Forms in Historic Europe* (Cambridge, England, 1983).

100. Richard M. Smith argues that English household formation was a culturally distinctive pattern involving economic and residential independence for the newly married: see "Fertility, Economy and Household Formation in England over Three Centuries," *Population and Development Review* 7 (1981): 615.

101. Michael Anderson, "The Impact on the Family Relationships of the Elderly Since Victorian Times in Governmental Income-Maintenance Provision," in Ethel Shanas and Marvin Sussman, eds., *Family, Bureaucracy and the Elderly* (Durham, 1977); Laslett, *The World We Have Lost;* Rose, "The Varying Household Arrangements." Preston in 1851 was an exception. Michael Anderson has reported that in this city in which cotton manufacture dominated, widowed mothers were found living with their factory-working married daughters: see Michael Anderson, *Family Structure in Nineteenth Century Lancashire* (Cambridge, England, 1971), 139–47.

102. Hewitt does not indicate whether the percentage is based on all households, households in which a married woman was working, or households in which mothers were working: see Hewitt, *Wives and Mothers,* 129. Generally, elderly parents did not live with their married children, and when they did so, according to Robert Roberts, their loss of independence, signified by giving up their own homes, was a mark of shame: see R. Roberts, *The Classic Slum.* See also Rose, "The Varying Household Arrangements."

103. Calculated from the 1881 census enumerators' listings of households in Low Moor, RG 11/4035, and Ashton-under-Lyne, RG 11/4173, at the Public Record Office, London.

104. Calculated from the 1881 census enumerators' listings of households in Nottingham districts, RG 11/3352 and RG 11/3348.

105. Jill Liddington and Jill Norris, *One Hand Tied Behind Us* (London, 1978), 59.

106. Ibid.

107. Ross, "Labour and Love," 85. See also Joy Parr, *Labouring Children: British Immigrant Apprentices to Canada, 1869–1924* (London, 1980).

108. Letter 7, "The Condition of Factory Women and Their Families," in P. E. Razzell and R. W. Wainwright, eds., *The Victorian Working Class: Selections from Letters to the Morning Chronicle* (London, 1973), 295.

109. Davies, ed., *Life as We Have Known It,* 4.

110. Dyhouse, *Girls Growing Up,* 102. Dyhouse reports that some parliamentary commissioners in 1904 even proposed that this system of keeping girls out to help at home be formalized by allowing parents to apply for permission to keep daughters at home on washing or baking days, to help out with younger children.

111. E. Roberts, *A Woman's Place,* 138.

112. Oral History no. 241, Family Life and Work Archive, University of Essex, 5.

113. Select Commission on Homework, *Parliamentary Papers* 8 (1908): Q. 1721.

114. Ibid., Q. 2722.

115. Ibid., Q. 2728.

116. Elizabeth Roberts reports that a woman minding only a few children in Preston could earn as much as a full-time weaver. There were apparently no fixed rates, but the amounts given by her respondents ranged from 3 shillings to 10 shillings per week: see her *A Woman's Place*, 141.

117. See, for example, the discussion of contemporary women homeworkers in a rural area of the United States in Betty A. Beach, "The Family Context of Home Shoe Work," in Boris and Daniels, eds., *Homework*. For Edwardian England, see Meacham, *A Life Apart*, 99.

118. E. Roberts, *A Woman's Place*, 142.

119. Judy Lown, *Women and Industrialization* (Cambridge, England, 1990), 146–47.

120. Hewitt, *Wives and Mothers*, 164.

121. Ibid.

122. Ibid., 163.

123. Ibid., 158.

124. Ibid., 158–59.

125. Newman, *Infant Mortality*, 271.

126. Hewitt, *Wives and Mothers*, 161.

127. Newman, *Infant Mortality*, 273.

128. Ibid., 261.

129. Hewitt, *Wives and Mothers*, 163.

130. This was also true in the United States, according to Sonya Michel's research: see her *The History of Daycare in America* (forthcoming).

131. This is discussed more fully in Chapter 2, above.

132. Oral History no. 220, Family Life and Work Archive, University of Essex, 3.

133. As Eileen Boris has suggested about depression-era homeworkers in the United States, since married women experienced discrimination in gaining employment outside their households, most women chose to do industrial homework: see Boris, "Homework in the Past," 19.

134. Ibid., 18. For variations in the rates of homework by black and white women in the contemporary period in the United States, see Robert E. Kraut, "Homework: What Is It and Who Does It?" in Christensen, ed., *The New Era of Home-Based Work*, 30–48.

135. Most of those who did work at home worked as washerwomen. For an excellent discussion of how racism affected black women's work and their ability to care for their families, see Jacqueline Jones, *Labor of Love, Labor of Sorrow: Black Women, Work and the Family, from Slavery to the Present* (New York, 1985).

136. In the United States certain ethnic groups were more likely to be homeworkers than others. The variations have been explained as resulting from ideological differences: see Boris, "Homework in the Past," 18–19.

137. Boris shows how the discourses both of those who opposed homework and of those who wanted to preserve it during the Depression in the United States emphasized the primacy of motherhood: see Boris, "Regulating Industrial Homework."

138. Quoted in Gertrude M. Tuckwell, *The Life of the Rt. Honorable Sir Charles W. Dilke*, vol. 2 (London, 1917), 360.

139. Christine Stansell notes that sweated labor in home and workshop in New York City in the nineteenth century either was based on traditional family patterns and relationships or replicated them: see her *City of Women: Sex and Class in New York 1789–1860* (New York, 1982; reprinted Urbana, 1987), chap. 6.

140. Stedman Jones shows how casual workers, especially women, were immobilized by being dependent on particular and erratic forms of work: see his *Outcast London*, 60, 81–88, 92, 97, 155, 183.

CHAPTER 5

1. The use made of such symbolic representations is similar to William Sewell's understanding of the "language of labor" as constructing people's experiences of industrial transformation: see his *Work and Revolution in France: The Language of Labor from the Old Regime to 1848* (Cambridge, England, 1980).

2. Hosiery industry: Sonya O. Rose, "Gender Segregation in the Transition to the Factory: The English Hosiery Industry, 1850–1910," *Feminist Studies* 13 (1987): 163–84. Tailoring: Barbara Taylor, *Eve and the New Jerusalem: Socialism and Feminism in the Nineteenth Century* (New York, 1983), 94–116. Metalworking: Sonya O. Rose, "Gender Antagonism and Class Conflict: Exclusionary Strategies of Male Trade Unionists in Nineteenth Century Britain," *Social History* 13 (1988): 199. Printing: Cynthia Cockburn, *Brothers: Male Dominance and Technical Change* (London, 1983), 151–59.

3. A great deal of research on the issue of "deskilling" and the struggle for control over the capitalist labor process was stimulated by the publication of Harry Braverman's *Labor and Monopoly Capital* (New York, 1974). Much of the recent debate over the labor process concerns whether or not deskilling is the inevitable consequence of technology and how worker resistance has continued to shape managerial strategies. For reviews of this literature, see Paul Thompson, *The Nature of Work: An Introduction to Debates on the Labor Process* (London, 1989); Andrew Friedman, *Industry and Labour: Class Struggle at Work and Monopoly Capitalism* (London, 1977); Richard Edwards, *Contested Terrain: The Transformation of the Workplace in the Twentieth Century* (New York, 1979); Stephen Wood, ed., *The Transformation of Work? Skill, Flexibility and the Labour Process* (London, 1989). For

analyses of gender and the labor process, see David Knight and Hugh Willmott, eds., *Gender and the Labour Process* (Aldershot, 1986).

4. Webb Trade Union Papers, sec. A, vol. 47, 94, at the British Library of Political and Economic Science.

5. *Kidderminster Shuttle*, 8 September 1894, 4.

6. See *Leeds Evening Express*, 5 April 1872, 2; 10 April 1872, 3; 29 April 1872, 3. See the discussion of the strike in chapter 3, above.

7. Letter to Sidney Webb dated July 1891, Webb Trade Union Papers, sec. A, vol. 47, 59–60v.

8. Taylor, *Eve and the New Jerusalem*, 107.

9. Webb Trade Union Papers, sec. A, vol. 34, 105–6.

10. Webb Trade Union Papers, sec. A, vol. 40, 49.

11. Cockburn, *Brothers*, 151–59.

12. Webb Trade Union Papers, sec. A, vol. 19, 56.

13. Ibid., 32.

14. British Association for the Advancement of Science Committee on the Economic Effect of Legislation Regulating Women's Labour, Coll. 486, 2/6, 45, at the British Library of Political and Economic Science. (Hereafter British Association for the Advancement of Science Papers.)

15. Ibid., 47.

16. Webb Trade Union Papers, sec. A, vol. 47, 59.

17. Edna Bonacich's theory of the split labor market is an important effort to explain ethnic antagonism among workers and strategies of exclusion: see "A Theory of Ethnic Antagonism: The Split Labor Market," *American Sociological Review* 37 (1972): 547–59. As I have argued elsewhere, her theory claims that this antagonism is caused by the wage differential between workers inherent in the split or dual labor market and ignores the influence of race and gender: see Rose, "Gender Antagonism and Class Conflict," 191–208.

18. J. M. Barlett, "The Mechanization of the Kidderminster Carpet Industry," *Business History* 9 (1967): 49–69.

19. Ibid., 52.

20. Alex Murie, *The Carpet Weavers of Kidderminster* (Kidderminster, 1966), 14.

21. Ibid., 15.

22. Bright and the Crossleys hired men as well as women to work "the women's machines" at the "women's rate of pay." The unionists determined that the loom Bright had caused to be designed enabled women and men to earn the same wages: see *Halifax Courier*, 31 October 1874, 4. A letter Francis Crossley wrote to his manager, Mr. Musgrave, confirms this: "I object," he said, "to this proposed plan of paying men one price and women another; let everything be done for a man that would be done for a woman—let him have neither more nor less price. This is the plan that Bright adopts and in my opinion it is the only sound course" (letter dated 17 March 1870, Francis Crossley's letters from Suffolk to Musgrave, Crossley archives, C300/B8/1, at the West Yorkshire Archive Service, Wakefield, Yorkshire). On 18 November 1870 Crossley wrote to Musgrave requesting information about the firm's

average cost for weaving tapestries: "What I mean is some are woven by men at 1 1/2d per yard; some by men at 1 1/5d per yd, some by men at 1d per yard and some by girls at 1d per yard and I want to know what is the average price for the whole we make."

23. Although Brussels weaving remained a male occupation in Kidderminster, at a carpet mill in Halifax male Brussels weavers were threatened with a piece-rate reduction on looms of a particular type. When the men insisted that their wages not be lowered, the employer fired them and hired women and boys to take their places (Report by May E. Abraham on the Conditions of Work in the Textile Industries of Yorkshire, in Royal Commission on Labour: The Employment of Women, *Parliamentary Papers* 37 [1893–1894]: 648).

24. *Kidderminster Shuttle*, 24 October 1874, 5.

25. Moxon Loom Arbitration Proceedings, (1879), E III (3), Kid. 677, Carpet Trade Pamphlets 25, at the Local Studies Library, Kidderminster.

26. *Rochdale Observer*, 30 November 1861, 5.

27. The machines Brinton had purchased were principally used in Rochdale by John Bright's firm. It is possible that Brinton was entering the trade to compete against Bright, who was the major and long-term rival of Brinton's son-in-law, Francis Crossley. In the early 1870s Crossley's firm introduced a new type of loom and hired women to work the new looms; although they had some men working tapestry looms, by 1874 most of those hired for this work were women.

28. Minutes of the Power Loom Carpet Weavers' Association, 14 October 1874, Coll. 705, Box 1, 875, at the Worcester and Hereford County Record Office. Women earned 1d. per yard on the women's tapestry machines in Halifax and Rochdale, and men earned 1½d. per yard, plus 20 percent of their total piece-rate earnings, on the tapestry looms running in Kidderminster.

29. *Kidderminster Shuttle*, 24 October 1874, 7.

30. Ibid. See Chapter 2, above, for a more general discussion of employers' assumptions about women and technological competence.

31. *Kidderminster Shuttle*, 17 October 1874, 8.

32. *Halifax Courier*, 17 October 1874, 4.

33. *Kidderminster Shuttle*, 24 October 1874, 8.

34. Ibid.

35. See letter to the editor from a Brinton weaver, *Kidderminster Shuttle*, 31 October 1874, 5. See also the minutes of the Power Loom Carpet Weavers' Association meeting of 22 October 1874, at which the members gave a vote of thanks to Mayor Dixon and Messrs. Hughes and Hamilton. On 24 October 1874, the minutes recorded that the membership gave a vote of thanks to Mr. W. Green "re the action taken in the matter." Dixon and Green both were tapestry manufacturers, and it is possible that Hughes and Hamilton were as well.

36. Minutes of the Power Loom Carpet Weavers' Association, 13 February 1879.

37. Ibid.

38. It is an interesting comment on labor relations in this period that a few months after the arbitration award had been decided, a celebration was held at Brinton's to honor the inauguration of a new and very large steam engine called the Hercules. Apparently, it was Mrs. Brinton's idea that the firm give a feast to the employees. All fifteen hundred of them were invited to dinner. The workpeople presented John Brinton with an illuminated address and gave Mrs. Brinton a bracelet. The *Kidderminster Shuttle,* 27 September 1879, commented: "It is not for us to analyse the feeling with which Mr. Brinton is sometimes regarded by a section of the manufacturers and of the workpeople. His position as the head of the Brinton carpet trade is sufficient to account for the occasional jealousy of his brother-manufacturers, while the prominent part he and his partner are compelled to take, by their position, in all questions between Capital and Labour exposes them from time to time to temporary unpopularity." The illuminated address read: "As those who have to gain their daily bread by manly toil, we are not unmindful of the value and dignity of labour; and we hope to be found faithful both in the discharge of its duties and in maintaining its just rights. But we do not forget how much Labour stands in need of Capital and how largely dependent it is upon the energy and capacity of those who direct the operations of Industry and who open up the markets of the world to its products." The illuminated address still hangs on the walls in Brinton's offices at their factory in Kidderminster. The article from the *Kidderminster Shuttle* was found in the Brinton's Ltd. Diary Extracts, 1677 to 1888, K1–K399, in the Brinton company archives (called the Muniments Room).

39. Bernard Elbaum et al., "Symposium: The Labour Process, Market Structure and Marxist Theory," *Cambridge Journal of Economics* 3 (1979): 228.

40. Richard Price, "The Labour Process and Labour History," *Social History* 8 (1983): 62.

41. See Minutes of the Power Loom Carpet Weavers' Association, 28 March 1881 through 9 June 1881, 875.

42. *Kidderminster Shuttle,* 8 December 1883, 5.

43. Minutes of the Power Loom Carpet Weavers' Association, 6 December 1883.

44. About fourteen hundred members participated in business meetings during the period; at one meeting, the union official had tickets handed out, to keep out nonunionists and reporters, some of whom had been writing about the feud in a manner unsympathetic to the union: see Minutes of the Power Loom Carpet Weavers' Association for the period from 29 February 1884 to 10 April 1884.

45. *Kidderminster Shuttle,* 8 March 1874, 7.

46. *Kidderminster Shuttle,* 15 March 1884, 6.

47. *Kidderminster Shuttle,* 29 March 1884, 5.

48. *Kidderminster Shuttle,* 12 April 1884, 8.

49. Ibid.

50. *Kidderminster Shuttle,* 12 April 1884, 8.

51. Minutes of the Power Loom Carpet Weavers' Association, 9 April 1884.

52. *Kidderminster Shuttle,* 1 March 1884, 7.

53. *Kidderminster Shuttle,* 2 February 1884, 6. There had never before been a strike at Dixon's; according to one of Dixon's weavers, all previous disputes had been settled in an amicable way.

54. *Kidderminster Shuttle,* 16 February 1884, 5.

55. *Kidderminster Shuttle,* 8 March 1884, 7.

56. *Kidderminster Shuttle,* 1 March 1884, 7.

57. Ibid.

58. *Kidderminster Shuttle,* 15 March 1884, 6.

59. *Kidderminster Shuttle,* 12 April 1884, 2.

60. See Minutes of the Power Loom Carpet Weavers' Association, 5 April 1884; *Kidderminster Shuttle,* 12 April 1884, 2.

61. *Kidderminster Shuttle,* 19 April 1884, 5.

62. Minutes of the Power Loom Carpet Weavers' Association, 30 May 1884.

63. See *Kidderminster Shuttle,* 16 February 1895, 6, and 2 March 1894, 6.

64. Ken Tomkinson and George Hall, *Kidderminster Since 1800* (Kidderminster, 1985), 89.

65. See report of the annual meeting of the carpet weavers' association in *Kidderminster Shuttle,* 2 February 1884, 6.

66. *Kidderminster Shuttle,* 9 March 1895, 8.

67. The only looms women worked were rug looms, a job men refused to consider, presumably because it was hard work for very low wages. Rug weaving was not considered to fall within the purview of the union.

68. See letter from Thomas Edwards to *Kidderminster Shuttle,* 25 August 1894, 8.

69. See Minutes of Power Loom Carpet Weavers' Association, 22 April 1891 and 17 June 1891.

70. Minutes of the Power Loom Carpet Weavers' Association, 17 June 1891.

71. See Minutes of the Power Loom Carpet Weavers' Association, 2 July 1891, 13 July 1891, 19 October 1892, 11 January 1892.

72. See Minutes of the Power Loom Carpet Weavers' Association, 14 April 1894, 6 May 1894.

73. *Kidderminster Shuttle,* 9 February 1895, 5.

74. Ibid.

75. See *Kidderminster Shuttle,* 22 September 1894, 5; 22 December 1894, 5; 29 December 1894, 5.

76. *Kidderminster Shuttle,* 9 February 1895, 5.

77. *Kidderminster Shuttle,* 9 March 1895, 8.

78. Ibid.

79. The employers told the unionists that women's wages did not exceed

15 shillings to 1 pound per week. One of the employers said that the women working for him averaged 16*s*. per week, which was more than girls earned for the same work in America: see *Kidderminster Shuttle*, 9 March 1895, 8.

80. Webb Trade Union Papers, sec. A, vol. 37, 271.

81. *Kidderminster Shuttle*, 9 March 1985, 8.

82. *Kidderminster Shuttle*, 17 October 1874, 5.

83. *Kidderminster Shuttle*, 31 October 1874, 5.

84. Quoted in Arthur Smith, "Carpet Weaving and Trade Union Activity, Kidderminster and District," N.D., Kid. 677, no. 4359, at the Kidderminster Local Studies Library.

85. *Kidderminster Shuttle*, 24 October 1874, 5.

86. Carole Pateman has shown how the ideas behind such thinking were deeply gendered. In fact, she suggests that they were based on an implicit sexual contract that guaranteed that men would have sexual access to women: see Carole Pateman, *The Sexual Contract* (Stanford, 1988).

87. See *Englishwoman's Review* 21 (January 1875): 38; *Kidderminster Shuttle*, 1 March 1884, 7.

88. Reprinted in *Kidderminster Shuttle*, 17 October 1874, 5.

89. *Kidderminster Shuttle*, 10 October 1874, 6.

90. *Kidderminster Shuttle*, 31 October 1874, 4.

CHAPTER 6

1. Reprinted, from *The Furniture Gazette*, in *Kidderminster Shuttle*, 10 October 1874, 6.

2. *Oldham Evening Express*, 14 April 1871, 2–3.

3. In the United States, racism and ethnic antagonisms did divide male workers from one another. Relations between Irish and native-born Englishmen were not as divisive, although unskilled Irish and English working men battled for jobs in the 1830s and 1840s: see E. P. Thompson, *The Making of the English Working Class* (Harmondsworth, 1968; reprinted Harmondsworth, 1980), 479–85.

4. *Hosiery and Lace Trades Review* (June 1890): 813.

5. *Kidderminster Shuttle*, 31 October 1874, 7.

6. Arthur Smith, "Carpet Weaving and Trade Union Activity, Kidderminster and District," N.D., Kid. 677, no. 4359, 65, at the Kidderminster Local Studies Library.

7. Friedrich Engels, *The Condition of the Working Class in England* (Oxford, 1958; reissued Stanford, 1968), 162–63.

8. Ibid., 164. Engels, however, recognized that all asymmetrical constructions of gender relations are arbitrary: "If the rule of the wife over her husband—a natural consequence of the factory system—is unnatural, then the former rule of the husband over the wife must also have been unnatural" (ibid.).

9. *Kidderminster Shuttle*, 25 August 1894, 8.

10. *Kidderminster Shuttle*, 1 March 1884, 7.

11. Ibid.

12. *Kidderminster Shuttle*, 8 March 1884, 8.

13. *Kidderminster Shuttle*, 15 March 1884, 6.

14. *Kidderminster Shuttle*, 9 March 1895, 8.

15. *Kidderminster Shuttle*, 15 March 1884, 6.

16. Keith McClelland, "Time to Work, Time to Live," in Patrick Joyce, ed., *The Historical Meanings of Work* (Cambridge, England, 1987), 192.

17. Ava Baron, "An Other Side of Gender Antagonism: Men, Boys and the Remasculinization of Work in the Printing Trade, 1830–1920," in Ava Baron, ed., *Work Engendered: Towards a New Understanding of Men, Women and Work* (Ithaca, 1991).

18. Ava Baron, "Questions of Gender: De-skilling and De-masculinization in the U.S. Printing Industry 1830–1915," *Gender and History* 1 (1989): 179.

19. Cynthia Cockburn, *Brothers: Male Dominance and Technological Change* (London, 1983), 139. Also see her *Machinery of Dominance: Women, Men and Technical Know-How* (London, 1985), for analyses of a range of occupations in which masculinity and technology are conflated in the construction of male identity.

20. Ava Baron, "Contested Terrain Revisited: Technology and Gender Definitions of Work in the Printing Industry, 1850–1920," in Barbara Wright et al., eds., *Women, Work, and Technology: Transformations* (Ann Arbor, 1987).

21. Paul Willis, *Learning to Labor* (Farnsborough, 1977); Paul Willis, "Shop Floor Culture, Masculinity and the Wage Form," in John Clarke et al., eds., *Working Class Culture* (London, 1979).

22. David Halle, *America's Working Man* (Chicago, 1984).

23. Hilary Land, "The Family Wage," *Feminist Review* 6 (1980): 55–76; Michele Barrett and Mary McIntosh, "The 'Family Wage': Some Problems for Socialists and Feminists," *Capital and Class*, 1980, no. 11: 51–72. For the United States, see Alice Kessler-Harris's discussion of the gendering of wages in *A Woman's Wage* (Lexington, Ky., 1990).

24. Eric Hobsbawm, *Labouring Men* (London, 1964), 278–84. Although most economic historians have agreed that real wages were rising in the second half of the nineteenth century, economic insecurity was still the lot of most workers. For an overview, see Neville Kirk, *The Growth of Working Class Reformism in Mid-Victorian England* (Urbana, 1985), 91–109.

25. Heidi Hartmann, "Capitalism, Patriarchy and Job Segregation by Sex," *Signs* 1 (1976): 137–69; Jane Humphries, "Class Struggle and the Persistence of the Working-Class Family," *Cambridge Journal of Economics* 1 (1977): 241–58.

26. Martha May, "Bread Before Roses: American Workingmen, Labor Unions and the Family Wage," in Ruth Milkman, ed., *Women, Work and Protest: A Century of U.S. Women's Labor History* (London, 1985). See also Martha May, "The Historical Problem of the Family Wage: The Ford Motor Company and the Five Dollar Day," *Feminist Studies* 8 (1982): 399–424.

Mary Blewett suggests that at times both class and gender models of the family wage could be argued in labor conflicts: see her *Men, Women and Work: Class, Gender, and Protest in the New England Shoe Industry 1780–1910* (Urbana, 1988), 139–40.

27. In a vivid analysis of a strike involving male and female shoeworkers, Blewett has argued that both Hartmann's and Humphries's versions of the family wage were in play. In other words, she proposed that the family wage rhetoric had different meanings for different workers: see *Men, Women, and Work* chap. 5, esp. 138–41.

28. See the critique by Barrett and McIntosh, "The 'Family Wage.' " In a private communication, Mariana Valverde has suggested that another problem with these conceptions of the "family wage" is the assumption that wages determined power relations within households. Clearly, wages do affect gender relations in households, but these relations are not solely determined by wages. I am arguing that for men, wage levels signified manliness by linking their status as household heads with their status at work. However, wages did not determine men's family status as heads of households. Also, I am not talking about whose interests were at stake in the ideology of the family wage. For example, I am not here trying to assess whether the family wage ideology was in men's interests, family interests, or women's interests. Rather, I am discussing how men's interests were constituted. In the next chapter I will discuss some consequences of how interests were constituted for working-class solidarity.

29. Report of a Meeting of Brass and Metal Workers, 19 October 1909, in "Brass and Metal Workers Crusade Against Sweating," George Howell Collection, Q 2(4), at the Bishopsgate Institute, London. See also David Montgomery's description of manliness as part of the moral code of the American craftsman, in *Workers' Control in America* (Cambridge, England, 1979), 13–14.

30. *Report of the Fifth Crusade Meeting of the National Society of Amalgamated Brassworkers and Metal Workers' Crusade Against Sweating*, 9 November 1909, 3–4, George Howell Collection, Q 2(4), at the Bishopsgate Institute, London.

31. Employers also used national and imperial language to communicate their class position: see, for example, employers' statements quoted in Chapter 2, above.

32. *Kidderminster Shuttle*, 1 March 1884, 5.

33. Ibid., 7.

34. *Kidderminster Shuttle*, 8 March 1884, 8.

35. *Kidderminster Shuttle*, 15 March 1884, 6.

36. *Kidderminster Shuttle*, 9 March 1884, 8.

37. Reprinted in *Kidderminster Shuttle*, 24 October 1874, 5.

38. *Kidderminster Shuttle*, 1 March 1884, 5.

39. Ibid.

40. *Kidderminster Shuttle*, 22 March 1884, 2.

41. *Kidderminster Shuttle*, 31 October 1874, 5.

42. *Kidderminster Shuttle,* 24 October 1874, 5.

43. *Kidderminster Shuttle,* 9 February 1895, 5.

44. *Kidderminster Shuttle,* 23 February 1895, 8.

45. Mariana Valverde, "The Love of Finery: Fashion and the Fallen Woman in Nineteenth-Century Social Discourse," *Victorian Studies* 32 (1989): 169.

46. Ibid.

47. In a private communication, Jane Hunter suggested this interpretation.

48. *Kidderminster Shuttle,* 2 March 1895, 2.

49. Barbara Drake, *Women in the Engineering Trades* (London, 1917), 7.

50. *Kidderminster Shuttle,* 22 March 1884, 2.

51. Ivy Pinchbeck, *Women Workers and the Industrial Revolution, 1750–1850,* 3d ed. (London, 1981).

52. K. D. M. Snell, *Annals of the Labouring Poor* (Cambridge, England, 1987), 305.

53. Sonya O. Rose, "Proto-industry, Women's Work and the Household Economy in the Transition to Industrial Capitalism," *Journal of Family History* 13 (1988): 181–93.

54. David Vincent, *Bread, Knowledge and Freedom* (New York, 1981), 68.

55. *Poor Man's Guardian,* 7 September 1833, 292, as quoted in I. J. Prothero, *Artisans and Politics in Early Nineteenth Century London* (London, 1981), 334.

56. Barbara Taylor, *Eve and the New Jerusalem* (New York, 1983), 102.

57. William Felkin, *The History of the Machine-Wrought Hosiery and Lace Manufacture* (London, 1867; reprinted Newton Abbott, 1967), 380.

58. Vincent, *Bread, Knowledge and Freedom,* 53.

59. Sonya O. Rose, "Gender Segregation in the Transition to the Factory: The English Hosiery Industry, 1850–1910," *Feminist Studies* 13 (1987): 163–84.

60. Vincent, *Bread, Knowledge and Freedom,* 80.

61. "Select Committee on the Stoppage of Wages in Hosiery Manufacture," *Parliamentary Papers* 14 (1854): 289.

62. Sally Alexander, "Women, Class and Sexual Difference," *History Workshop* 17 (1984): 125–49.

63. Eric Hobsbawm, *Worlds of Labour* (London, 1984), 182.

64. See Alexander, "Women, Class and Sexual Difference"; Vincent, *Bread, Knowledge and Freedom,* esp. chap. 4. Neil Smelser argues that the breakdown in this "inheritance pattern" was a source of dissent and protest for fathers because they lost control over their children: see his *Social Change in the Industrial Revolution* (Chicago, 1959), 198–200.

65. Vincent, *Bread, Knowledge and Freedom,* 74.

66. Ibid.

67. Ibid., 85–86. Vincent recognizes the interconnectedness of men's economic and familial roles and the ways that the former were important to the latter. Neil Smelser's interpretation is on the structural level, not on the level

of either personal experience or human agency. See also Smelser, *Social Change in the Industrial Revolution*.

68. See John Rule, "The Property of Skill in the Period of Manufacture," in Patrick Joyce, ed., *The Historical Meanings of Work* (Cambridge, England, 1987), 107–8.

69. Wally Seccombe argues that the norm of male breadwinning emerged from the ranks of skilled artisans: see his insightful "Patriarchy Stabilized: The Construction of the Male Breadwinner Wage Norm in Nineteenth-century Britain," *Social History* 11 (1986): 53–76.

70. Thompson, *The Making of the English Working Class;* William Reddy, *The Rise of Market Culture* (Cambridge, England, 1984), 116; Rule, "The Property of Skill"; Catherine Hall, "The Tale of Samuel and Jemima: Gender and Working-class Culture in Nineteenth-century England," in Harvey Kaye and Keith McClelland, eds., *E. P. Thompson, Critical Perspectives* (Cambridge, England, 1990), 82.

71. Maxine Berg, *The Age of Manufactures, 1700–1820* (London, 1985), 159.

72. Harold Benenson, "Victorian Sexual Ideology and Marx's Theory of the Working Class," *International Labor and Working Class History* 25 (1984): 1–23.

73. Berg, *The Age of Manufactures*, 160.

74. Snell, *Annals of the Labouring Poor*, 307–8.

75. Dorothy Thompson, *The Chartists: Popular Politics in the Industrial Revolution* (New York, 1984), 130.

76. As John Rule has put it, "Indeed in many instances skilled workers reacting to pressures upon their customary expectations and ways, explicitly looked back to a past when their rights had been respected" ("The Property of Skill," 114).

77. Alexander, "Women, Class and Sexual Difference," 136.

78. Rule, "The Property of Skill."

79. William Lazonick, "Industrial Relations and Technical Change: The Case of the Self-acting Mule," *Cambridge Journal of Economics* 3 (1979): 231–62.

80. Seccombe, "Patriarchy Stabilized," 65.

81. Smelser, *Social Change and the Industrial Revolution*, 232.

82. Ibid.

83. Ibid., 236.

84. Taylor, *Eve and the New Jerusalem*, 94.

85. Ibid., 106.

86. Ibid., 107.

87. Ibid., 114–16.

88. Mariana Valverde, " 'Giving the Female a Domestic Turn': The Social, Legal and Moral Regulation of Women's Work in British Cotton Mills, 1820–1850," *Journal of Social History* 21 (1988): 619–34.

89. Taylor, *Eve and the New Jerusalem*, 83–117.

90. Ibid., 115.

91. Joan Scott has made a similar point about the significance of Taylor's work: see her *Gender and the Politics of History* (New York, 1988), 84–85.

92. See, for example, Alexander, "Women, Class and Sexual Difference"; Taylor, *Eve and the New Jerusalem;* Valverde, "Giving the Female a Domestic Turn"; Benenson, "Victorian Sexual Ideology."

93. *The Ten Hours' Question: A Report Addressed to the Short-Time Committees of the West Riding of Yorkshire* (London, 1842), 4–5, cited in Valverde, " 'Giving the Female a Domestic Turn,' " 628.

94. Ibid.

95. Quoted by Smelser, *Social Change and the Industrial Revolution,* 301.

96. *Hansard,* 15 March 1844, 1088–1100.

97. Ashley was particularly fond of making this point. See his speech to Parliament introducing the Mines and Collieries Act in 1842, in *Hansard,* 7 June 1842, 1327, and his speech on the Factory Act of 1844, in *Hansard,* 15 March 1844, 1097. Carole Pateman discusses the belief in women's essential subversiveness which is fundamental to Western political thought: see Carole Pateman, *The Disorder of Women: Democracy, Feminism and Political Theory* (Stanford, 1989).

98. Thompson, *The Chartists.* Also see Gareth Stedman Jones, "The Chartist Experience," in *Languages of Class: Studies in English Working-Class History, 1832–1982* (Cambridge, England, 1983). Also see Scott's critique, *Gender and the Politics of History,* chap. 3.

99. Thompson, *The Chartists.* Also see Hall, "Samuel and Jemima," 85.

100. Taylor, *Eve and the New Jerusalem,* 268.

101. Quoted in Janet Murray, ed., *Strong Minded Women* (New York, 1982), 341–42.

102. Taylor, *Eve and the New Jerusalem,* 268.

103. Thompson, *The Chartists,* 337. See also Joan W. Scott, "On Language, Gender, and Working-Class History," *International Labor and Working Class History* 31 (1987): 1–13.

104. This theory is suggested by Taylor, *Eve and the New Jerusalem,* 268–69. The idea that Chartism articulated a vision of the working class as male, based as it was on producers who argued for their political rights because they held property in labor, has been suggested by Joan W. Scott: see *Gender and the Politics of History,* 62–65.

105. Quoted in Taylor, *Eve and the New Jerusalem,* 269.

106. Quoted in ibid.

107. See Gareth Stedman Jones, "Working-class Culture and Working-class Politics in London, 1870–1900: Notes on the Remaking of a Working Class," in *Languages of Class,* 179–238.

108. Vincent, *Bread, Knowledge and Freedom,* 55.

109. Prothero, *Artisans and Politics in Early Nineteenth Century London,* 328.

110. Seccombe, "Patriarchy Stabilized," 55.

111. Elizabeth Roberts, *A Woman's Place: An Oral History of Working-Class Women 1890–1940* (Oxford, 1984), 137.

112. Pierre Bourdieu, *Distinctions: A Social Critique of the Judgement of Taste* (Cambridge, Mass., 1988).

113. The middle class's preoccupation with categorization and classification has been noted by Catherine Hall: see "Gender Divisions and Class Formation in the Birmingham Middle Class, 1780–1850," in R. Samuel, ed., *People's History and Socialist Theory* (London, 1981); also see Catherine Hall, "The Early Formation of Victorian Domestic Ideology," in Sandra Burman, ed., *Fit Work for Women* (London, 1979).

114. See Geoffrey Crossick, *An Artisan Elite in Victorian Society* (London, 1978); Robert Roberts, *The Classic Slum* (Manchester, 1971; reprinted Harmondsworth, 1973); Ellen Ross, " 'Not the Sort That Would Sit on the Doorstep': Respectability in Pre–World War I London Neighborhoods," *International Labor and Working Class History* 27 (1985): 39–59; Robert Gray, *The Aristocracy of Labour in Nineteenth-Century Britain* (London, 1981); David Levine, *Reproducing Families: The Political Economy of English Population History* (Cambridge, England, 1987); Kirk, *The Growth of Working Class Reformism.*

115. Levine, *Reproducing Families,* 175.

116. Peter Bailey, "Will the Real Bill Banks Please Stand Up?" *Journal of Social History* 7 (1979): 336–53.

117. See especially Ross, " 'Not the Sort,' " and Stedman Jones, "Working-class Culture."

118. The significance of avoiding a pauper's funeral as symbolic of working-class independence has been noted by numerous social historians. For an autobiographical account, see Roberts, *The Classic Slum.*

119. F. M. L. Thompson, *The Rise of Respectable Society: A Social History of Victorian Britain, 1830–1900* (London, 1988), 193.

120. Ibid., 194.

121. Ibid.

122. Stedman Jones, "Working-class Culture," 217; Kirk, *The Growth of Working Class Reformism.*

123. Stedman Jones, "Working-class Culture," 217–18.

124. As David Rubenstein has shown, school attendance by children of the very poor was not regular, as they frequently had to earn wages to help their families make ends meet: see David Rubenstein, *School Attendance in London, 1870–1904* (New York, 1969), 44, 56, 89. For resistance to the demands of regular school attendance on the part of children of stockingers, see Rose, "Proto-industry, Women's Work and the Household Economy," 188.

125. *The Reporter* (Ashton-under-Lyne), 15 December 1877, 5.

126. *The Bee-Hive,* 4 March 1876, 5.

127. *Women's Union Journal* 2 (1877): 72.

128. Taylor, *Eve and the New Jerusalem,* 111.

129. *Women's Union Journal* 4 (1879): 83.

130. Wally Seccombe also makes this argument: see his "Patriarchy Stabilized," 73.

131. Robert Gray makes a similar argument: see *The Labour Aristocracy in Victorian Edinburgh* (Oxford, 1976).

CHAPTER 7

1. William Shakespeare, *Othello*, 3: 3, lines 155–56. This was not an exact quote. The lines are: "Good name in man and woman, dear my lord, is the immediate jewel of their souls."

2. There are two recent and notable exceptions. The work of Jill Liddington and Jill Norris on late-nineteenth-century Lancashire women active in the suffrage movement is an especially rich resource for learning about women's lives and jobs in the cotton mills: see their *One Hand Tied Behind Us* (London, 1978). Patrick Joyce, in a carefully researched analysis of paternalism and deference in textile communities, suggests that gender difference and the replication of familial patterns of authority in the family and community were more important in working-class formation in Lancashire than were the commonalities in the relations of production for women and men: see his *Work, Society and Politics* (Brighton, Sussex, 1980), chap. 3. For discussions of the labor process in spinning, see William Lazonick, "Industrial Relations and Technical Change: The Case of the Self-acting Mule," *Cambridge Journal of Economics* 3 (1979): 231–62; Mary Freifeld, "Technological Change and the 'Self-acting' Mule: A Study of Skill and the Sexual Division of Labour," *Social History* 11 (1986): 319–43; Isaac Cohen, "Workers' Control in the Cotton Industry: A Comparative Study of British and American Mule Spinning," *Labor History* 26 (1985): 53–85. On the ideology of domesticity and female exclusion from mule spinning, see Mariana Valverde, " 'Giving the Female a Domestic Turn': The Social, Legal and Moral Regulation of Women's Work in British Cotton Mills, 1820–1850," *Journal of Social History* 21 (1988): 619–34.

3. Webb Trade Union Papers, sec. A, vol. 37, 76–77, at the British Library of Political and Economic Science.

4. Sidney J. Chapman suggests that the decline of the handloom industry was occasioned by a glut of workers. Some workers entered handloom weaving to supplement agricultural work, and wives of weavers who had been spinners turned to weaving. Trade societies were weakened, and handloom weavers' unions were less able than other trade societies to maintain apprenticeship and other restrictions. Handloom weaving absorbed the unemployed and the displaced, including discharged soldiers after 1815: see *The Lancashire Cotton Industry* (Manchester, 1904; reprinted Clifton, N.J., 1973), 46.

5. Ibid. The major work on the decline of work for the handloom weavers and their responses remains that of E. P. Thompson, *The Making of the English Working Class* (Harmondsworth, 1968; reprinted Harmondsworth, 1980).

6. See Ivy Pinchbeck's analysis of the relationship between declining piece

rates, early age at marriage, and the household economy of handloom weavers: *Women Workers and the Industrial Revolution,* 3d ed. (London, 1981), 179.

7. Stanley D. Chapman, *The Cotton Industry in the Industrial Revolution* (London, 1977), 33–34.

8. Pinchbeck, *Women Workers and the Industrial Revolution,* 180.

9. Chapman, *The Cotton Industry,* 48.

10. Pinchbeck, *Women Workers and the Industrial Revolution,* 188.

11. Ibid.

12. Powerloom weaving began as an addition to yarn manufacture. It was probably adopted by employers who had already experienced the muscle of the mule spinners, and it is possible that their difficulties with the spinners' union influenced their hiring practices in powerloom weaving.

13. Chapman, *The Lancashire Cotton Industry,* 48.

14. Notes on interview with D. J. Shackleton, 11 November 1913, Webb Trade Union Papers, sec. A, vol. 37, 218.

15. Liddington and Norris note that by the 1880s more than three-fifths of the looms were worked in the northern area and three-quarters of the spindles were in operation in the southern region: see *One Hand Tied Behind Us,* 57.

16. Statement of T. Christopher Brooks, 1892, Webb Trade Union Papers, sec. A, vol. 37, 103.

17. Overlookers tuned the weaving machines and were responsible for securing the quantity of output from the weavers that was demanded by management.

18. Owen Ashmore, "Low Moor, Clitheroe: a Nineteenth-Century Factory Community," *Transactions of the Lancashire and Cheshire Antiquarian Society* 73–74 (1963–1964): 142.

19. Social mobility was practically nonexistent in the weaving towns. The Blackburn journalist W. A. Abram reported in 1868: "Should our typical workman close his career as the manager of a loom-shed, he may set himself down as a favourite of the gods. For one who reaches that elevation fifty super-annuated weavers are relegated to the duties of oddmen, messengers, casual labourers, and the like, until death rescues them from the buffeting and contumely of circumstances" ("The Social Condition and Political Prospects of Lancashire Workmen," *Fortnightly Review* [October 1868]: 432).

20. Webb Trade Union Papers, sec. A, vol. 47, 270.

21. C. Evans, a woman weaver from Chorley, wrote to B. L. Hutchins that young weavers had only two or three looms, but older weavers worked on four looms; she did not mention differences between women's and men's work (Webb Trade Union Papers, sec. A, vol. 47, 273). The secretary of the Burnley Weavers' Association told the Royal Commission on Labour that in Burnley women worked under similar conditions to men, ran the same number of looms, and were paid the same rates and earned as much money as the men (Royal Commission on Labour, *Parliamentary Papers* 35 [1892]: Q. 761).

22. O'Neill's diary simply stated, "Jane and me has joined the Power Loom

Weavers' Union" (William O'Neill, *Journals of a Lancashire Weaver,* ed. Mary Briggs [Manchester, 1982], entry dated 7 February 1859).

23. D. Holmes, president of the Darwen Weavers' Association, told the Webbs that women and men (who worked separately) tended to have unequal rates of pay in weaving. He said that if only women worked at a shed, employers would lower their wages because the women did not "take the trouble to ascertain whether they are being paid the list price" (Webb Trade Union Papers, sec. A, vol. 37, 185). Another weavers' association official told B. L. Hutchins in 1913 that male weavers earned a few shillings a week more than female weavers (Webb Trade Union Papers, sec. A, vol. 47, 219).

24. Sidney Webb and Beatrice Webb, *Industrial Democracy* (London and New York, 1902), 501. Also see the discrepancy between male and female weavers in Liddington and Norris, *One Hand Tied Behind Us,* 95–96.

25. In a strike at the mill in the fall of 1877, the employer, aided by the overlookers, attempted to play the narrow-loom weavers off against the broadloom weavers. Although the weavers lost the dispute, the turmoil had the consequence of bringing the narrow-loom weavers together with the broadloom weavers to form a trade union: see *The Reporter* (Ashton-under-Lyne), 6 October 1877, 3; 13 October 1877, 3; 20 October 1877, 5; 17 November 1877, 5.

26. Webb Trade Union Papers, sec. A, vol. 47, 49. She believed that there was a general tendency on the part of men to keep women out of the unions and to discourage them from taking leadership positions. B. L. Hutchins commented in her notes on the interview that Mrs. Dickinson "showed no bitterness about this attitude on the part of the men, and seemed to regard it as a law of nature."

27. "The 1906 Earnings and Hours Inquiry," *Parliamentary Papers* 80 (1909), shows slight differences in wages earned by women and men weavers.

28. Liddington and Norris, *One Hand Tied Behind Us,* 95; Joyce, *Work, Society and Politics,* 113; F. M. L. Thompson, *The Rise of Respectable Society: A Social History of Victorian Britain, 1830–1900* (London, 1988), 216; Barbara Drake, *Women in Trade Unions* (London, 1920; reprinted London, 1984), 121.

29. See Drake, *Women in Trade Unions,* 216. To what extent hours legislation was actually enforced, even as late as the last quarter of the nineteenth century, is open to question. One of the complaints of Preston weavers just before the great strike and lockout of 1878 was that not only were their wages threatened with a 10 percent reduction, but that mill managers were working the mills over the hours permitted by the Factory Bill of 1874. According to one speaker at a weavers' strike rally, some mills in Preston were running eleven hours and ten minutes: see *Preston Chronicle and Lancashire Advertiser,* 13 April 1878, 1. A main point of contention between the weavers and their employers was the cause and cure for the lower profits that manufacturers claimed they were receiving. The workers claimed the cause was overproduction and argued that short time would solve the problem. The employers

claimed that it was competition from America and India that was the problem, for which a reduction in wages was the solution.

30. "Report of Inquiry by the Board of Trade into Working-Class Rents," *Parliamentary Papers* 107 (1908): 380.

31. Drake, *Women in Trade Unions*, 121. On the one hand, women lost time by having to wait for a "fixer" to tune their looms, but, on the other, men contributed more labor to the manufacturing process than women and yet were paid the same wages. This situation was similar to that of the Canadian hosiery industry, where women and men worked the same machines, earning the same piece rates, but women worked during the day and men worked at night; men but not women tuned their own looms. As Joy Parr points out, the employer "took the material gain and encouraged gender pride based on mechanical proficiency among their knitter-fixers": see Joy Parr, *The Gender of Breadwinners: Women, Men, and Change in Two Industrial Towns* (Toronto, 1990), 75. As she notes, in the English hosiery industry, women worked machines during the day which men worked at night, but there, if they were unionized, the men earned higher wages. I discuss this, as well, in my article "Gender Segregation in the Transition to the Factory: The English Hosiery Industry, 1850–1910," *Feminist Studies* 13 (1987): 177.

32. Drake, *Women in Trade Unions*, 121.

33. Webb Trade Union Papers, sec. A, vol. 37, 185.

34. William H. Lockwood, a Yorkshire union official, reported that the women complained that they had to "leave off at 5:30 while the men go on until 8 o'clock" (Webb Trade Union Papers, sec. A, vol. 38, 183). He added that the women considered themselves to be unjustly treated and were placed at a disadvantage relative to the men "and are loud in their attacks on the Factory Acts in consequence."

35. For a discussion of the significance of overlookers in the overlapping worlds of factory and community in Lancashire, see Joyce, *Work, Society and Politics*, 100–103.

36. *Standard* (Oldham), 11 May 1878, 2.

37. Joyce, *Work, Society and Politics*, 100.

38. Evidence of Thomas Birtwhistle, Royal Commission on Labour, *Parliamentary Papers* 35 (1892): 777.

39. Statement by T. Christopher Brooks in 1892, Webb Trade Union Papers, sec. A, vol. 34, 105. Brooks remarked to the Webbs, "This may be one reason why a vicious and licentious overlooker prefers to have women only" (ibid., 106). It is likely that the incidence of such harassment was much lower where male and female family members were employed in the same mills and, in the case of weaving, at the same jobs. Most likely, working women in towns like Wigan (also known to have a relatively weak weavers' union), where men were employed in the mines, and in towns in South Lancashire and Cheshire, where women's and men's jobs were segregated, were particularly subject to such victimization.

40. Webb Trade Union Papers, sec. A, vol. 40, 22.

41. The clergymen also said that such actions were not uncommon: see Amy Bulley and Margaret Whitley, *Women's Work* (London, 1894), 99–100.

42. See the reference made by a strike leader in 1888 to employers who "go tickling the winders": *Standard* (Ashton-under-Lyne), 22 September 1888, 8.

43. See Ashmore, "Low Moor, Clitheroe," 143. Ashmore comments on these data, "It certainly looks as if, when it was necessary to reduce the hands, women were the first to go." It is likely that women's jobs in weaving were reduced more substantially than men's jobs in weaving during the cotton famine.

44. See, for example, *The Herald* (Preston), 1 May 1878, 3.

45. Edwin Hopwood, *A History of the Lancashire Cotton Industry and the Amalgamated Weavers' Association* (Manchester, 1969), 38–44. On women's special vulnerability, see Webb Trade Union Papers, sec. A, vol. 47, 217.

46. Statistical descriptions of workers in Low Moor were based on an analysis of census data on all residents aged ten and older as indicated in RG 11/4173.

47. O'Neill, *Journals of a Lancashire Weaver*, ed. M. Briggs, entry dated 31 December 1856.

48. Overall, the number of girls who were half-time school attendees exceeded the number of boys who were half-timers.

49. Liddington and Norris, *With One Hand Tied Behind Us*, 35.

50. See Robert Roberts, *A Ragged Schooling* (Manchester, 1976), 5; Liddington and Norris, *With One Hand Tied Behind Us*, 35; June Purvis, *Hard Lessons: The Lives and Education of Working-class Women in Nineteenth-Century England* (Minneapolis, 1989), chap. 4.

51. Liddington and Norris, *With One Hand Tied Behind Us*, 35.

52. Elizabeth Roberts, *A Woman's Place: An Oral History of Working-Class Women 1890–1940* (Oxford, 1984), 23.

53. The Education Code of 1876 mandated that every girl was required to study domestic economy: see Lords Committee of the Privy Council of Education, *New Code of Regulations for Education* 59 (1876), Cd. 1458, 1 (reference from E. Roberts, *A Woman's Place*, 30–31).

54. Oral history of Mr. Gaskell in E. Roberts, *A Woman's Place*, 118.

55. Edward Cadbury, M. Cecile Matheson, and George Shann found in Birmingham that "Where women and men both work during the day, the woman accepts it as right that she should do all the housework at night while the man amuses himself in any way he thinks fit. And often where a working man assists his wife in household duties, he does not like his mates to know": see Edward Cadbury, M. Cecile Matheson, and George Shann, *Women's Work and Wages* (London, 1906), 137.

56. Harry Pollitt, *Serving My Time* (London, 1940), 18, as quoted in Liddington and Norris, *With One Hand Tied Behind Us*, 47.

57. Walter Greenwood, *There Was a Time*, 67, as quoted in Liddington and Norris, *With One Hand Tied Behind Us*, 94.

58. *Preston Chronicle and Lancashire Advertiser,* 20 April 1878, 3.

59. For a similar pattern in the Leicester hosiery industry, see Nancy Grey Osterud, "Gender Divisions and the Organization of Work in the Leicester Hosiery Industry," in Angela V. John, ed., *Unequal Opportunities: Women's Employment in England 1800–1918* (Oxford, 1986), but compare Louise A. Tilly and Joan W. Scott, who suggest that most women in Britain and in France withdrew from factory work when they married or when they had children: see their *Women, Work and Family,* 2d ed. (London, 1987; reprinted London, 1989), 126–27.

60. Union leaders of Lancashire weavers were generally concerned about respectable behavior of the membership. The Preston Powerloom Weavers Committee, for example, fined union members for swearing in the meeting hall: see Preston Powerloom Weavers Minutes, 25 May 1878, DDX 1089/1/3, at the Lancashire County Record Office.

61. H. I. Dutton and J. E. King, *Ten Percent and No Surrender: The Preston Strike of 1853–1854* (Cambridge, England, 1981), 51.

62. See *Preston Chronicle,* 12 November 1852, 6. The newspaper reported that Mrs. Margaret Fletcher of Preston and various other delegates spoke at a meeting at the Wheat Sheaf Inn in Clitheroe. Either Ann or Margaret spoke at Glossop: a Mrs. Fletcher called the employers "grinding capitalists, men who had risen from the dunghill" (Dutton and King, *Ten Percent and No Surrender,* 51).

63. See Chapter 6, above, for a discussion of the exclusion of women from working-class politics and its connection with the development of the ideal of domesticity for working-class women.

64. *Blackburn Standard,* 30 March 1878, 2.

65. Ibid.

66. *Blackburn Standard,* 20 April 1878, 2.

67. *Blackburn Standard,* 13 April 1878, 3.

68. See *Blackburn Standard,* 1 June 1878, 2, 3; 15 June 1878, 3; 22 June 1878, 3.

69. *Burnley Express,* 20 April 1878, 6. In the Ashton weavers' strike during the preceding summer, women were especially persuasive in having strike relief distributed to those who were most needy rather than to everyone on strike. For example, at one meeting a middle-aged woman in the body of the room rose and said: "Let those having families and little ones be relieved, and let those with no families 'frab for thersell.' " She continued, "I paid the last farthing that I had last Saturday, but I will manage another fortnight before I'll be licked." She then made a formal motion (which was unusual for a woman to do) which passed handily, that those who were in need should have the relief (*Standard* [Ashton-under-Lyne], 4 August 1877, 6).

70. *Blackburn Standard,* 18 June 1878, 3.

71. Reported in *Industrial Review* (formerly *The Bee-Hive*), 18 May 1878, 1.

72. *Preston Chronicle and Lancashire Advertiser,* 18 May 1878, 4.

73. *The Standard* (Oldham), 4 May 1878, 6. Note here the workers' use

of the imperial or colonialist metaphor of "slaves," from the song "Rule Britannia," to articulate class conflict.

74. See *Preston Chronicle and Lancashire Advertiser*, 11 May 1878, 6.

75. *Burnley Express*, 25 May 1878, 6.

76. Although the rioting did not start in Blackburn, the consequences in Blackburn were perhaps more serious than elsewhere. Strike leaders condemned the attacks, but the employers used the riots as a way of condemning the unionists.

77. *Blackburn Standard*, 18 May 1878, 2. Blackburn residents, including Colonel Jackson, the press, and trade union leaders, made a concerted effort to preserve the "good name" of Blackburn in the face of the destruction of property and reports of terror experienced by mill owners' wives, children, and servants. This context gives additional point to the press's focus on Irish women, as opposed to native men.

78. *Blackburn Standard*, 18 May 1878, 4.

79. *Blackburn Standard*, 15 June 1878, 3.

80. For example, the chair of a meeting of the Amalgamated Weavers in Preston said to the assembly, "if everyone had been in the union, or more united, they would never have been on strike": see *Standard* (Oldham), 4 May 1878, 6.

81. *Standard* (Oldham), 11 May 1878, 2.

82. *Burnley Express*, 6 April 1878, 6.

83. Placards calling for all weavers, "especially females to attend in the hundreds," announced a meeting at Burnley in the early days of the dispute that drew a crowd of three thousand people, including an unspecified number of women: see *Blackburn Standard*, 6 April 1878, 2.

84. *Burnley Express*, 6 April 1878, 6.

85. *Blackburn Standard*, 6 April 1878, 2.

86. See report of Bamber Bridge meeting, *Preston Chronicle and Lancashire Advertiser*, 13 April 1878, 6; meeting in Preston Corn Exchange, *Preston Chronicle and Lancashire Advertiser*, 20 April 1878, 3; meeting at Padiham, *Burnley Express*, 20 April 1878, 6; meeting at Darwen, *Burnley Express*, 20 April 1878, 6; placard posted by the combined strike committees at Padiham, *Burnley Express*, 25 May 1878, 5. Meeting at Burnley reported in *Blackburn Standard*, 6 April 1878, 2.

87. Elizabeth Faue, "Gender and Solidarity in the American Labor Movement," *Gender and History* 1 (1989): 147.

88. *Blackburn Standard*, 30 March 1878, 2.

89. *Burnley Express*, 25 May 1878, 5.

90. *Blackburn Standard*, 18 May 1878, 3.

91. *Blackburn Standard*, 25 May 1878, 5.

92. *Burnley Express*, 25 May 1878, 5.

93. *Blackburn Standard*, 6 April 1878, 2.

94. Memorial dated 30 March 1878, *Preston Chronicle and Lancashire Advertiser*, 6 April 1878, 5.

95. *The Herald* (Preston), 24 April 1878, 5.

96. *Blackburn Standard,* 15 June 1878, 3. The operatives voted to reject the call to end the strike, and the strike committee members' speeches were received with opposition and anger. People in the crowd, including women, yelled that they were being sold. By the eighth week of the strike, the Blackburn leaders were trying to find a way of ending the strike without the mandate of the membership. Word of their efforts was leaked, and resistance began to crumble. After the membership voted down the proposal to end the strike, the leadership supported an unofficial movement, in which overlookers were heavily involved, to end the strike. Eventually, at shop-floor meetings at which the overlookers had a great deal of influence, workers voted to end the strike. The strike was over before the last week of June. It had cost the operatives £200,000 in lost wages and had cost the Blackburn association £3,500. The Amalgamated spent more than £5,000, cutting its reserves in half. The defeat led many unions to withdraw from the Amalgamated, and it was reorganized: see Andrew Bullen, *The Lancashire Weavers' Union: A Commemorative History* (Manchester, 1984).

97. *Preston Chronicle and Lancashire Advertiser,* 13 April 1878, 6. See also the speech by an operative in Preston at a meeting of six thousand to seven thousand people, reported by *Preston Chronicle and Lancashire Advertiser,* 20 April 1878, 3.

98. *Standard* (Oldham), 11 May 1878, 2.

99. Ibid. It is clear from other comments that both women and men were present in the audience. Banks urged every "working man and woman in Ashton to try . . . to stop production, save money and go for a holiday." Another speaker applauded the women and contrasted their attitude about the strike levy on their wages with the attitudes of the men, saying that the men "would rather spend it in beer than give their assistance to the distressed operatives." He railed against drink as a curse and then ended his speech by encouraging "factory girls" to wear more print dresses and fewer clothes made of imported material: see *Standard* (Oldham), 11 May 1878, 2.

100. In fact, they resented such assistance because it meant the perpetuation of the dual-paycheck family.

101. I owe this insight to the work of Joanna Bornat on gender, work, and unionism among woolen and worsted weavers in Yorkshire. She has argued that in Yorkshire, where the wages of women and men differed for the same work, women were construed to be marginal workers: see her "Home and Work: A New Context for Trade Union History," *Oral History* 5 (1977); her "Lost Leaders: Women, Trade Unionism and the Case of the General Union of Textile Workers, 1875–1914," in John, ed., *Unequal Opportunities;* and her " 'What about That Lass of Yours Being in the Union?': Textile Workers and Their Union in Yorkshire, 1888–1922," in Leonore Davidoff and Belinda Westover, eds., *Our Work, Our Lives, Our Words* (Totowa, N.J., 1986).

102. The relationship between what is constructed as primary and secondary, or center and periphery, has been conceptualized by Jacques Derrida as being in a relationship of supplementarity. According to Derrida, the supplement appears to be exterior, or an inessential addition, but it is needed to

replace what is lacking in the whole. See, for example, Jacques Derrida, *Of Grammatology* (Baltimore, 1974), 141–64, and his *Writing and Difference* (Chicago, 1978), 289–93.

103. Unfortunately, the enumerator in Low Moor combined piecers and spinners, recording both as spinners. To arrive at the percentage of spinners with wives in the labor force or at home, I looked only at married spinners who were at least twenty-five years old. In one enumerator's district that I studied in Ashton-under-Lyne, where the enumerator made very detailed lists of people's occupations, all of the piecers were twenty-two or younger.

104. See speech by Margaret Fletcher in Clitheroe, *Preston Chronicle,* 12 November 1853, 3. In her speech she said, "To the young women present, I would say whenever a young man pays his address to you and wishes to make you his wife, ask if he is able to maintain you. If he says he is not, tell him to go about his business, for you never intend when married to go out to work." At the same meeting Ann Fletcher said, "The day is come when we are determined to do nothing until every man is employed; and then if there is anything left for the women, we'll do a little, but we'll not do much." See also Margaret Fletcher's fervent oratory at Bolton, where she talked of employers as "grinding capitalists, the majority of whom thirty or forty years ago, were nothing but scavengers, sweeping under the spinning jenny, but who also now claimed the right of ruling them, and if they asked for anything, would turn her majesty's subjects into the streets, to die, to starve, steal, beg or to do what they would." She finished her speech by calling upon "all married women to stop at home, to nurse their children and keep their husbands comfortable": see *Bolton Chronicle and South Lancashire Advertiser,* 10 December 1853, 8.

105. Dorothy Thompson, *The Chartists: Popular Politics in the Industrial Revolution* (New York, 1984).

106. The weavers not only did not recover the 10 percent they had lost in 1878, but they suffered 5 percent reductions in March 1879 and December 1883, the latter of which was the cause of the districtwide strike in the winter of 1884. Employers gave advances of 5 percent in January 1881 and July 1884, but the 10 percent reduction in piece rates that the weavers were forced to accept in June 1878 was to remain throughout the century. See report by Joshua Rawlinson, secretary of the Blackburn Cotton Spinners and Manufacturers Association, N.D., Webb Trade Union Papers, sec. A, vol. 37, 74.

107. *Blackburn Standard,* 5 January 1884, 8.

108. Bornat, " 'What about That Lass of Yours?' "

109. George Howell, *The Conflicts of Capital and Labour,* 2d ed. (London, 1890), 341.

110. "Report of the 10th Annual Trades Union Congress in Leicester," *Women's Union Journal* 2 (1877): 72.

111. "Report on 11th Trades Union Congress at Bristol," *Women's Union Journal* 3 (1878): 70.

112. *The Bee-Hive,* 25 January 1873, 13.

113. *Cotton Factory Times,* 14 August 1891, quoted in Liddington and Norris, *With One Hand Tied Behind Us,* 53.

114. Lady Dilke, "Benefit Societies and Trades Unions for Women," in *Tracts Relating to Marriage, Women, Etc.,* reprinted from the *Fortnightly Review* (June 1889): 5, at the British Library.

115. *Women's Union Journal* 1 (1876): 14. John Ruskin's letter may be found in *Women's Union Journal* 1 (1876): 1–2.

116. *Women's Union Journal* 4 (1879): 83.

117. *Women's Union Journal* 4 (1879): 9.

118. A woman weaver said in a letter to B. L. Hutchins: "I strongly suspect they have not time. I think the amount of work most mill workers are expected to do, chiefly in the evenings is perfectly appalling" (letter dated 20 December 1913, Webb Trade Union Papers, sec. A, vol. 37, 275).

119. Webb Trade Union Papers, sec. A, vol. 37, report by secretary of Preston and District Power Loom Weavers, 263, and report by Bolton and District Power Loom Weavers, Winders and Warpers, 248. Whereas the male secretary of the Nelson weavers insisted that women had opportunities for leadership but would not take them, a woman weaver from Nelson said she would like to be a collector, but she could get no support from the other women members (interview notes dated 30/1/14, Webb Trade Union Papers, sec. A, vol. 37, 234–37).

120. Webb Trade Union Papers, sec. A, vol. 47, 148.

121. Letter dated 20 December 1913, Webb Trade Union Papers, sec. A, vol. 37, 275.

122. In an interview done on the same day, the secretary of the Nelson Weavers Association attributed women's lack of interest to "the way they've been brought up" or "perhaps modesty," and said that the indifference of women is an argument against giving them the vote (interview notes dated 30/1/14, Webb Trade Union Papers, sec. A, vol. 37, 234–36). The woman weaver, "Miss S.," was described by the interviewer (possibly B. L. Hutchins) in her notes as "very thin, hard driven and tense, flat-chested, plain and slightly deaf but very eager and interested with a good deal of power of expression" (236).

123. Webb Trade Union Papers, sec. A, vol. 37, 246.

124. The implication in his comments was that the union had not invited any women to speak, because, as he also commented, "we've never felt the need of asking them": see Webb Trade Union Papers, sec. A, vol. 37, 252.

125. Webb Trade Union Papers, sec. A, vol. 47, 49 (N.D., probably 1914).

126. Webb Trade Union Papers, sec. A, vol. 47, 226.

127. Webb Trade Union Papers, sec. A, vol. 37, 255. The Webbs' respondent commented that all of the membership voted and some women are "real good trade unionists."

128. Webb Trade Union Papers, sec. A, vol. 37, 226.

129. Bornat, " 'What about That Lass of Yours?' " 222.

130. *Blackburn Standard,* 30 March 1878, 2. Note that the paper printed that declarative sentence with a question mark as punctuation.

131. *Women's Union Journal* 3 (1878): 53.

132. Drake, *Women in Trade Unions,* 15; Bornat, "Lost Leaders," 213.
133. Drake, *Women in Trade Unions,* 11.
134. Liddington and Norris, *With One Hand Tied Behind Us,* chap. 9.
135. Ibid., 145.
136. Historian Joan W. Scott has written, "It was not lack of imagination or male chauvinism that prevented serious defense of the position of women workers, but a construction of class that equated productivity and masculinity" (Joan W. Scott, *Gender and the Politics of History* [New York, 1988], 64).

137. It could be argued that union leaders addressed their appeals to adult men, which excluded both young, single men and all women. For an elaboration of the idea of a generational aspect of gender, see Ava Baron, "Questions of Gender: De-skilling and De-masculinization in the U.S. Printing Industry 1830–1915," *Gender and History* 1 (1989): 178–99. For an analysis of how females have been portrayed as disorderly in Western thought, see Carole Pateman, *The Disorder of Women: Democracy, Feminism and Political Theory* (Stanford, 1989), esp. chap. 1. For the development of the insight that discourses that are meant to control particular subjects create the possibility of resistance, see Michel Foucault, *The History of Sexuality.* Vol. 1: *An Introduction* (New York, 1980), 101. Foucault writes, "discourse can be both an instrument and an effect of power, but also a hindrance, a stumbling-block, a point of resistance and a starting point for an opposing strategy."

CHAPTER 8

1. Cynthia Cockburn, "The Gendering of Jobs: Workplace Relations and the Reproduction of Sex Segregation," in Sylvia Walby, ed., *Gender Segregation at Work* (Milton Keynes, 1988), 32.
2. Jane Lewis, "The Debate on Sex and Class," *New Left Review* 167 (1985): 115.
3. Veronica Beechey, "Conceptualizing Part-time Work," in Veronica Beechey, ed., *Unequal Work* (London, 1987), 156, 157. Also see Sheila Kishler Bennett and Leslie B. Alexander, who suggest that women who do part-time employment must choose between unemployment and a job that is minimally compatible with child care—a requirement which marks its similarity to homework: see their "The Mythology of Part-time Work: Empirical Evidence from a Study of Working Mothers," in Lourdes Beneria and Catharine R. Stimpson, eds., *Women, Households and the Economy* (New Brunswick, N.J., 1987), 225–42.
4. Joan W. Scott, *Gender and the Politics of History* (New York, 1988), 42.
5. Cynthia Cockburn, "The Gendering of Jobs," 40. See R. W. Connell's discussion of gender difference and unequal power relations between women and men as crucial aspects of the social construction of heterosexual attraction: *Gender and Power* (Stanford, 1987), 113.
6. Lewis, "The Debate on Sex and Class"; Mary Ann Clawson, *Construct-*

ing Brotherhood (Princeton, 1989), 246. This was the point of Michèle Barrett's *Women's Oppression Today* (London, 1980) and is made clear in the introduction to the second edition (London, 1988), xii. Also see Joy Parr, *The Gender of Breadwinners: Women, Men, and Change in Two Industrial Towns* (Toronto, 1990), 229–46.

7. Parr, *The Gender of Breadwinners*, 245.

8. Raymond Williams, *Towards 2000* (London, 1983), 266–67. Also see his critique of the concept of production in *Marxism and Literature* (Oxford, 1977), 90–94. R. E. Pahl has argued that focusing on household work strategies is more fruitful than focusing on paid employment for understanding changes in work practices: see R. E. Pahl, *Divisions of Labor* (Oxford, 1984), 17–20.

9. For a discussion of strategies see Pierre Bourdieu, *Outline of a Theory of Practice* (Cambridge, England, 1977). Also see Ann Swidler, "Culture in Action: Symbols and Strategies," *American Sociological Review* 51 (1986): 273–86. For a critique of Bourdieu's ideas about habitus-forming strategies, see Michel de Certeau, *Everyday Practices* (Berkeley and Los Angeles, 1988), 50–60. The idea of family or household strategy has been important both to family and demographic historians and to feminist historians. Feminists have argued that the "interests" of women and men in households are never identical and that therefore strategies should not be seen as the uncontested practices that family and demographic historians have described them as being: see "Family Strategy: A Dialogue," *Historical Methods* 20 (1987): 113–25.

10. John Benson, *The Penny Capitalists* (Dublin, 1983).

11. Ellen Ross, " 'Fierce Questions and Taunts': Married Life in Working-Class London, 1870–1914," *Feminist Studies* 8 (Fall 1982): 575–602; Ellen Ross, "Survival Networks: Women's Neighborhood Sharing in London Before World War I," *History Workshop* 15 (1983): 4–27; Elizabeth Roberts, *A Woman's Place: An Oral History of Working-Class Women 1890–1940* (Oxford, 1984).

12. See Anna Clark, *Women's Silence, Men's Violence: Sexual Assault in England 1770–1840* (London, 1987); Nancy Tomes, "A 'Torrent of Abuse': Crimes of Violence Between Working Class Men and Women in London, 1840–1875," *Journal of Social History* 11 (1978): 328–45; Laura Oren, "The Welfare of Women in Laboring Families: England, 1860–1950," *Feminist Studies* 1 (1973): 107–21.

13. Keith McClelland, "Time to Work, Time to Live," in Patrick Joyce, ed., *The Historical Meanings of Work* (Cambridge, England, 1987), 185–86.

14. Roslyn L. Feldberg and Evelyn Nakano Glenn, "Male and Female: Job Versus Gender Models in the Sociology of Work," in Rachel Kahn-Hut and Arlene Kaplan Daniels, eds., *Women and Work* (New York, 1982).

15. Leonore Davidoff and Catherine Hall, *Family Fortunes: Men and Women of the English Middle Class, 1780–1850* (London, 1987).

16. Joan Kelly, "The Doubled Vision of Feminist Theory," *Feminist Studies* 5 (1979): 216–27.

17. Pahl, *Divisions of Labour* (Oxford, 1984).

18. See, for example, Parr, *The Gender of Breadwinners,* 243–46, and numerous empirical examples throughout her book; and Judy Lown, *Women and Industrialization* (Cambridge, England, 1990), 210–12.

Select Bibliography

ARCHIVAL SOURCES

Annual Reports of the Vigilance Association. Second: 1872; *Third:* 1873; *Fourth:* 1874; *Fifth:* 1875; *Seventh:* 1877; *Eighth:* 1878. George Howell Collection at the Bishopsgate Institute, London.

Blackburn Manufacturers' Association Minute Books, 1877–1896. DDX 1115/1/1, at the Lancashire County Record Office, Preston.

"Brass and Metal Workers Crusade Against Sweating." 1909. George Howell Collection, Q 2(4), at the Bishopsgate Institute, London.

British Association for the Advancement of Science Committee on the Effect of Legislation Regulating Women's Labour. Coll. 486. At the British Library of Political and Economic Science.

Crossley Business Archives. At the West Yorkshire Archive Service, Wakefield, Yorkshire.

Family Life and Work Archive. At the University of Essex.

Illuminated Address dated 4 October 1879. Muniments Room, Brinton's Inc., Kidderminster.

Master Cotton Spinners Association Archives. Letter Books 1870, 1871, at the John Rylands University Library, Manchester.

Minutes of the Power Loom Carpet Weavers' Association, 1874–1895. Coll. 705, at the Worcester and Hereford County Record Office.

Minutes of the Thomas Mason and Sons Oxford Mills Workpeople and Tenants Committee. At the Tameside Local Studies Library, Staleybridge.

Moxon Loom Arbitration Proceedings, 1879. E III (3), Kid. 677, Carpet Trade Pamphlets 25, at the Local Studies Library, Kidderminster.

Mundella Papers. At the University of Sheffield.

Nottingham Oral History Archive. At the Local Studies Library, Nottingham.

Preston Powerloom Weavers Minutes, 1872–1878. DDX 1089/1/3, at the Lancashire County Record Office, Preston.

Secretary's Notes of Proceedings of the Fourth Annual Trade Union Congress, 1872. George Howell Collection, at the Bishopsgate Institute Library, London.

Smith, Arthur. "Carpet Weaving and Trade Union Activity, Kidderminster and District." N.D. Kid. 677, no. 4359, at the Kidderminster Local Studies Library.

Webb Trade Union Papers. At the British Library of Political and Economic Science.

GOVERNMENT DOCUMENTS

CENSUS

1881 enumerators' listings of households in Low Moor, RG 11/4035 and Ashton-under-Lyne, RG 11/4173, at the Public Records Office, London.

1881 enumerators' listing of households in Nottingham. Districts of St. Mary's, RG 11/3352 and Trent, RG 11/3348, at the Public Records Office, London.

PARLIAMENTARY PAPERS [LISTED IN DATE ORDER]

Royal Commission on Children's Employment, 20 (1833).

Royal Commission on Children's Employment, 13, 14, 15 (1843).

Report of the Commission to Inquire into the Condition of the Framework Knitters, 15 (1845).

Select Committee on the Stoppage of Wages in Hosiery Manufacture, 14 (1854–1855).

Report to Home Secretary upon the Expediency of Subjecting Lace Manufacture to the Factory Acts, 22 (1861).

First Report of the Children's Employment Commission with Minutes of Evidence, 17 (1863).

Report of the Commission on Trade Unions, 39 (1867).

Reports of the Commissioners on the Truck Acts, 36 (1871).

Hansard, 11 June 1873, 216, 824; 30 July 1873, 217, 1291; 18 May 1874, 219, 1429; 9 August 1874, 220, 1047.

Report of the Commissioners Appointed to Inquire into the Working of the Factory and Workshops Acts, with Minutes of Evidence, 30 (1876).

Report of the Royal Commission on Depression of Trade and Industry, 21 (1886).

Returns of Rates of Wages in Principal Textiles, 70 (1889).

Returns of Rates of Wages in Minor Textile Trades, 68 (1890).

Royal Commission on Labour, 36 (1892).

Royal Commission on Labour: The Employment of Women, 37 (1893–1894).

Report on Earnings and Hours of Labour in Textile Trades, 34 (1906).

Report of Select Committee on Homework, 6 (1907).

Report of Select Committee on Homework, 8 (1908).

Report of Inquiry by the Board of Trade into Working-Class Rents, etc., 107 (1908).

NEWSPAPERS

Standard (Ashton-under-Lyne); *The Bee-hive*; *Birmingham Mail*; *Blackburn Standard*; *Bolton Chronicle and South Lancashire Advertiser*; *Burnley Express*; *Capital and Labour*; *Cotton Factory Times*; *Englishwoman's Review*;

Furniture Gazette; *Halifax Courier*; *Hosiery and Lace Trades Review*; *Industrial Review*; *Kidderminster Shuttle*; *Leeds Daily News*; *Leeds Evening Express*; *Leicester Journal*; *Manchester Guardian*; *Nottingham Daily Guardian*; *Observer* (London); *Oldham Chronicle*; *Oldham Evening Express*; *Oldham Standard*; *Poor Man's Guardian*; *Preston Chronicle*; *Preston Chronicle and Lancashire Advertiser*; *The Herald* (Preston); *Rochdale Observer*; *Woman Worker*; *Women's Union Journal*

BOOKS AND ARTICLES

Abbott, Edith. *Women in Industry: A Study in American Economic History.* New York, 1910; reprinted New York, 1969.

Abram, W. A. "The Social Condition and Political Prospects of Lancashire Workmen." *Fortnightly Review* (October 1868).

Abrams, Philip. *Historical Sociology.* Ithaca, 1982.

Acker, Joan. "The Problem with Patriarchy." *Sociology* 23 (1989).

———— "What Happened to the Paradigm Shift? Making Gender Visible." In Phyllis A. Wallace, ed., *Sociological Theory and Feminism.* Beverly Hills, 1989.

Alexander, Sally. "Women, Class and Sexual Difference." *History Workshop* 17 (1984).

———— "Women's Work in Nineteenth-Century London: A Study of the Years 1820–1850." In Juliet Mitchell and Ann Oakley, eds., *The Rights and Wrongs of Women.* Harmondsworth, 1976.

Alexander, Sally, Anna Davin, and Eve Hostettler. "Labouring Women: A Reply to Eric Hobsbawm." *History Workshop* 8 (1979).

Allen, Sheila, and Carol Wolkowitz. *Homeworking: Myths and Realities.* London, 1987.

Althusser, Louis. *For Marx.* London, 1969.

———— "Ideology and Ideological State Apparatuses (Notes Towards an Investigation)." In Louis Althusser, *Lenin and Philosophy.* New York, 1971.

Anderson, Michael. *Family Structure in Nineteenth Century Lancashire.* Cambridge, England, 1971.

———— "The Impact on the Family Relationships of the Elderly Since Victorian Times in Governmental Income-Maintenance Provision." In Ethel Shanas and Marvin Sussman, eds., *Family, Bureaucracy and the Elderly.* Durham, 1977.

———— "Sociological History and the Working-Class Family: Smelser Revisited." *Social History* 6 (1976).

Armytage, W. H. G. *A. J. Mundella, 1825–1897: The Liberal Background to the Labour Movement.* London, 1951.

Arnold, Erik, and Wendy Faulkner. "Smothered by Invention: The Masculinity of Technology." In Wendy Faulkner and Erik Arnold, eds., *Smothered by Invention: Technology in Women's Lives.* London, 1985.

Ashmore, Owen. "Low Moor, Clitheroe: A Nineteenth-Century Factory

Community." *Transactions of the Lancashire and Cheshire Antiquarian Society* 73–74 (1963–1964).

Baer, Judith. *The Chains of Protection: The Judicial Response to Women's Labor Legislation.* Westport, Conn., 1978.

Bailey, Peter. "Will the Real Bill Banks Please Stand Up?" *Journal of Social History* 7 (1979).

Barker, Diana L. "Regulation of Marriage." In Gary Littlejohn et al., eds., *Power and the State.* London, 1978.

Barlett, J. M. "The Mechanization of the Kidderminster Carpet Industry." *Business History* 9 (1967).

Baron, Ava. "Acquiring Manly Competence: The Demise of Apprenticeship and the Remasculinization of Printers' Work, 1830–1915." In Clyde Griffen and Mark C. Carnes, eds., *Meanings for Manhood: Constructions of Masculinity in Victorian America.* Chicago, 1991.

——— "An Other Side of Gender Antagonism: Men, Boys and the Remasculinization of Work in the Printing Trade, 1830–1920." In Ava Baron, ed., *Work Engendered: Towards a New Understanding of Men, Women and Work.* Ithaca, 1991.

——— "Contested Terrain Revisited: Technology and Gender Definitions of Work in the Printing Industry, 1850–1920." In Barbara Wright et al., eds., *Women, Work and Technology: Transformations.* Ann Arbor, 1987.

——— "Gender and Labor History: Learning from the Past, Looking to the Future." In Ava Baron, ed., *Work Engendered: Towards a New Understanding of Men, Women and Work.* Ithaca, 1991.

——— "Questions of Gender: De-skilling and De-masculinization in the U.S. Printing Industry 1830–1915." *Gender and History* 1 (1989).

Baron, Ava, ed. *Work Engendered: Towards a New Understanding of Men, Women and Work.* Ithaca, 1991.

Barrett, Michèle. *Women's Oppression Today.* Revised ed. London, 1988.

Barrett, Michèle, and Mary McIntosh. "The 'Family Wage': Some Problems for Socialists and Feminists." *Capital and Class,* 1980, no. 11.

Beale, H. L. "The New Poor Law." *History* 15 (1931).

Beechey, Veronica. *Unequal Work.* London, 1987.

Bell, Lady Florence. *At the Works.* London, 1907.

Bendix, Reinhardt. *Work and Authority in Industry.* New York, 1956.

Benenson, Harold. "Victorian Sexual Ideology and Marx's Theory of the Working Class." *International Labor and Working Class History* 25 (1984).

Beneria, Lourdes, and Martha Roldan. *The Crossroads of Class and Gender: Industrial Homework, Subcontracting, and Household Dynamics in Mexico City.* Chicago, 1987.

Beneria, Lourdes, and Catherine R. Stimpson, eds. *Women, Households and the Economy.* New Brunswick, N.J., 1987.

Bennett, Sheila Kishler, and Leslie B. Alexander. "The Mythology of Part-time Work: Empirical Evidence from a Study of Working Mothers." In Lourdes Beneria and Catherine R. Stimpson, *Women, Households and the Economy.* New Brunswick, N.J., 1987.

Benson, John. *The Penny Capitalists*. Dublin, 1983.

Berg, Maxine. *The Age of Manufactures, 1700–1820*. London, 1985.

Biggs, Ada Heather. "The Wife's Contribution to Family Income." *Economic Journal* 4 (1894).

Black, Clementina, ed. *Married Women's Work*. London, 1915; reprinted London, 1983.

Blewett, Mary. *Men, Women, and Work: Class, Gender, and Protest in the New England Shoe Industry 1780–1910*. Urbana, 1988.

Block, Fred. *Postindustrial Possibilities: A Critique of Economic Discourse*. Berkeley and Los Angeles, 1990.

Block, Fred, and Margaret R. Somers. "Beyond the Economistic Fallacy: The Holistic Social Science of Karl Polanyi." In Theda Skocpol, ed., *Vision and Method in Historical Sociology*. Cambridge, England, 1984.

Blumer, Herbert. *Symbolic Interaction: Perspective and Method*. Englewood Cliffs, 1969.

Bock, Gisela. "Women's History and Gender History: Aspects of an International Debate." *Gender and History* 1 (1989).

Bonacich, Edna. "A Theory of Ethnic Antagonism: The Split Labor Market." *American Sociological Review* 37 (1972).

Booth, Charles. *Life and Labour of the People in London*. 17 vols. London, 1899–1903.

Booth, Douglas. "Karl Marx on State Regulation of the Labor Process: The English Factory Acts." *Review of Social Economy* 36 (1978).

———— "Marx on State Regulation: A Rejoinder." *Review of Social Economy* 38 (1980).

Boris, Eileen. "Homework in the Past, Its Meaning for the Future." In Kathleen E. Christensen, ed., *The New Era of Home-Based Work*. Boulder, 1988.

———— "Regulating Industrial Homework: The Triumph of 'Sacred Motherhood.' " *Journal of American History* 71 (March 1985).

Boris, Eileen, and Cynthia R. Daniels, eds. *Homework: Historical and Contemporary Perspectives on Paid Labor at Home*. Urbana, 1989.

Bose, Christine. "Devaluing Women's Work: The Undercount of Women's Employment in 1900 and 1980." In Christine Bose, Roslyn Feldberg, and Natalie Sokoloff, eds., *The Hidden Aspects of Women's Work*. New York, 1987.

Bose, Christine, Roslyn Feldberg, and Natalie Sokoloff, eds. *The Hidden Aspects of Women's Work*. New York, 1987.

Bourdieu, Pierre. *Distinctions: A Social Critique of the Judgement of Taste*. Cambridge, Mass., 1984.

———— *Outline of a Theory of Practice*. Cambridge, England, 1977.

———— "Social Space and Symbolic Power." *Sociological Theory* 7 (1989).

Bowley, A. L., and A. R. Burnett-Hurst. *Livelihood and Poverty*. London, 1915.

Boxer, Marilyn. "Protective Legislation and Home Industry: The Marginalization of Women Workers in Late Nineteenth, Early Twentieth-Century France." *Journal of Social History* 20 (1986).

Bradley, Harriet. *Men's Work, Women's Work: A Sociological History of the Sexual Division of Labour in Employment.* Cambridge, England, 1989.

Braverman, Harry. *Labor and Monopoly Capital.* New York, 1974.

Brenner, Johanna, and Barbara Laslett. "Social Reproduction and the Family." In Ulf Himmelstrand, ed., *Sociology from Crisis to Science?* Vol. 2: *The Social Reproduction of Organization and Culture.* London, 1986.

Brenner, Johanna, and Maria Ramas. "Rethinking Women's Oppression." *New Left Review* 144 (1984).

Breugel, Irene. "Women as a Reserve Army of Labour: A Note on Recent British Experience." *Feminist Review* 3 (1979).

Brooks, Barbara. "Women and Reproduction c. 1860–1919." In Jane Lewis, ed., *Labour and Love: Women's Experience of Home and Family 1850–1940.* London, 1986.

Bullen, Andrew. *The Lancashire Weavers' Union: A Commemorative History.* Manchester, 1984.

Bulley, Amy, and Margaret Whitley. *Women's Work.* London, 1894.

Burawoy, Michael. *Manufacturing Consent.* Chicago, 1979.

——— *The Politics of Production.* London, 1985.

Burke, Kenneth. *On Symbols and Society.* Chicago, 1989.

Burman, Sandra, ed. *Fit Work for Women.* London, 1979.

Bythell, Duncan. *The Handloom Weavers.* Cambridge, England, 1969.

Cadbury, Edward. *Experiments in Industrial Organization.* London, 1912.

Cadbury, Edward, M. Cecile Matheson, and George Shann. *Women's Work and Wages.* London, 1906.

Calhoun, Craig. *The Question of Class Struggle.* Chicago, 1982.

Caplan, Jane. "The Point Is to Change It." *The Nation,* 13 August 1990.

Chapman, Sidney J. *The Lancashire Cotton Industry.* Manchester, 1904; reprinted Clifton, N.J., 1973.

Chapman, Stanley D. *The Cotton Industry in the Industrial Revolution.* London, 1977.

Charles, Lindsey, and Lorna Duffin, eds. *Women and Work in Pre-Industrial England.* London, 1985.

Christensen, Kathleen E., ed. *The New Era of Home-Based Work.* Boulder, 1988.

Church, Roy A. *Economic and Social Change in a Midland Town: Victorian Nottingham 1815–1900.* London, 1966.

Cicourel, Aaron V. *Method and Measurement in Sociology.* New York, 1964.

Clapham, Sir John. *An Economic History of Modern Britain.* Vol. 1. London, 1939.

Clark, Alice. *Working Life of Women in the Seventeenth Century.* London, 1919; reprinted London, 1982.

Clark, Anna. *Women's Silence, Men's Violence: Sexual Assault in England 1770–1840.* London, 1987.

Clarke, John, C. Critcher, and Richard Johnson, eds. *Working Class Culture.* London, 1979.

Clawson, Mary Ann. *Constructing Brotherhood.* Princeton, 1989.

Cockburn, Cynthia. *Brothers: Male Dominance and Technological Change.* London, 1983.

———— "The Gendering of Jobs: Workplace Relations and the Reproduction of Sex Segregation." In Sylvia Walby, ed., *Gender Segregation at Work.* Milton Keynes, 1988.

———— *Machinery of Dominance: Women, Men and Technical Know-How.* London, 1985.

———— "The Relations of Technology: What Implications for Theories of Sex and Class?" In Rosemary Crompton and Michael Mann, eds., *Gender and Stratification.* Cambridge, England, 1986.

Cocks, Joan. *The Oppositional Imagination.* London, 1990.

Cohn, Samuel. *The Process of Occupational Sex-Typing.* Philadelphia, 1985.

Collet, Clara. "The Collection and Utilisation of Official Statistics Bearing on the Extent and Effects of the Industrial Employment of Women." *Journal of the Royal Statistical Society* 111 (June 1898).

Connell, R. W. *Gender and Power.* Stanford, 1987.

Corr, Helen, and Lynn Jamieson, eds. *The Politics of Everyday Life: Continuity and Change in Work, Labour and the Family.* London, 1990.

Corrigan, Philip, and Derek Sayer. "How the Law Rules: Variation on Some Themes in Karl Marx." In Bob Fryer et al., eds., *Law, State and Society.* London, 1981.

———— *The Great Arch: English State Formation as Cultural Revolution.* Oxford, 1985.

Cowherd, Raymond G. *The Humanitarians and the Ten Hour Movement in England.* Boston, 1958.

Crompton, Rosemary, and Michael Mann, eds. *Gender and Stratification.* Cambridge, England, 1986.

Crossick, Geoffrey. *An Artisan Elite in Victorian Society.* London, 1978.

Daniels, Cynthia Rae. "Between Home and Factory: Homeworkers and the State." In Eileen Boris and Cynthia Rae Daniels, *Homework: Historical and Contemporary Perspectives on Paid Labor at Home.* Urbana, 1989.

———— "Working Mothers and the State." Ph.D. dissertation, University of Massachusetts, 1983.

Davidoff, Leonore. " 'Adam Spoke First and Named the Orders of the World': Masculine and Feminine Domains in History and Sociology." In Helen Corr and Lynn Jamieson, eds., *The Politics of Everyday Life: Continuity and Change in Work, Labour and the Family.* London, 1990.

Davidoff, Leonore, and Catherine Hall. *Family Fortunes: Men and Women of the English Middle Class, 1780–1850.* London, 1987.

Davidoff, Leonore, and Belinda Westover, eds. *Our Work, Our Lives, Our Words.* Totowa, N.J., 1986.

Davies, Margaret Llewelyn, ed. *Life as We Have Known It: By Co-operative Working Women.* London, 1931; reprinted New York, 1975.

de Certeau, Michel. *Everyday Practices.* Berkeley and Los Angeles, 1988.

Deem, Rosemary, and Graham Salaman, eds. *Work, Culture and Society.* Milton Keynes, 1985.

De Lauretis, Teresa. *Alice Doesn't: Feminism, Semiotics, Cinema.* Blooming-
ton, Ind., 1984.
——— *Technologies of Gender.* Bloomington, Ind., 1987.
Derrida, Jacques. *Of Grammatology.* Baltimore, 1974.
——— *Writing and Difference.* Chicago, 1978.
de Vasselitsky, V. *The Homeworker and the Outlook.* London, 1916.
Dilke, Lady Emilia. "Benefit Societies and Trades Unions for Women." In
Tracts Relating to Marriage, Women, Etc. Reprinted from the *Fortnightly
Review* (June 1889). At the British Library, London.
Drake, Barbara. *Women in the Engineering Trades.* London, 1917.
——— *Women in Trade Unions.* London, 1920; reprinted London, 1984.
Dutton, H. I., and J. E. King. "The Limits of Paternalism: The Cotton Tyrants
of North Lancashire, 1836–54." *Social History* 7 (1982).
——— *Ten Percent and No Surrender: The Preston Strike of 1853–1854.*
Cambridge, England, 1981.
Dyhouse, Carol. *Girls Growing Up in Late Victorian and Edwardian En-
gland.* London, 1981.
——— "Working Class Mothers and Infant Mortality in England, 1895–1914."
Journal of Social History 12 (1978).
Edelman, Murray. *Constructing the Political Spectacle.* Chicago, 1987.
——— *The Symbolic Uses of Politics.* Urbana, 1984.
Edwards, Richard. *Contested Terrain: The Transformation of the Workplace
in the Twentieth Century.* New York, 1979.
Eisenstein, Zillah. *The Female Body and the Law.* Berkeley and Los Angeles,
1988.
Elbaum, Bernard, et al. "Symposium: The Labour Process, Market Structure
and Marxist Theory." *Cambridge Journal of Economics* 3 (1979).
Eley, Geoff. "Edward Thompson, Social History and Political Culture: The
Making of a Working-class Public, 1780–1850." In Harvey Kaye and Keith
McClelland, eds., *E. P. Thompson: Critical Perspectives.*
Elson, Diane, and Ruth Pearson. " 'Nimble Fingers Make Cheap Workers':
An Analysis of Women's Employment in Third World Export Manufac-
turing." *Feminist Review* 7 (1981).
Engels, Friedrich. *The Condition of the Working Class in England.* Oxford,
1958; reissued Stanford, 1968.
Epstein, Cynthia Fuchs. *Deceptive Distinctions: Sex, Gender and the Social
Order.* New Haven, 1988.
Erikson, Charlotte. *British Industrialists: Steel and Hosiery, 1850–1950.*
Cambridge, England, 1959.
——— "Family Strategy: A Dialogue." *Historical Methods* 20 (1987).
Faue, Elizabeth. "Gender and Solidarity in the American Labor Movement."
Gender and History 1 (1989).
Faulkner, Wendy, and Erik Arnold, eds. *Smothered by Invention: Technology
in Women's Lives.* London, 1985.
Feldberg, Roslyn L., and Evelyn Nakano Glenn. "Male and Female: Job Ver-

sus Gender Models in the Sociology of Work." In Rachel Kahn-Hut and Arlene Kaplan Daniels, eds., *Women and Work*. New York, 1982.

Felkin, William. *The History of the Machine-Wrought Hosiery and Lace Manufacture*. London, 1867; reprinted Newton Abbott, 1967.

Feurer, Rosemary. "The Meaning of 'Sisterhood': The British Women's Movement and Protective Labor Legislation, 1870–1900." *Victorian Studies* 31 (1988).

Foster, John. *Class Struggle and the Industrial Revolution*. London, 1974.

Foucault, Michel. *Discipline and Punish*. New York, 1979.

————— *The History of Sexuality*. Vol. 1: *An Introduction*. New York, 1980.

————— *The Order of Things: An Archaeology of the Human Sciences*. New York, 1973.

Fraser, Derek. *The Evolution of the British Welfare State*. London, 1973; 2d ed. London, 1984.

Fraser, Nancy. *Unruly Practices: Power, Discourse and Gender in Contemporary Social Theory*. Minneapolis, 1989.

Freifeld, Mary. "Technological Change and the 'Self-acting' Mule: A Study of Skill and the Sexual Division of Labour." *Social History* 11 (1986).

Friedman, Andrew. *Industry and Labour: Class Struggle at Work and Monopoly Capitalism*. London, 1977.

Gallagher, Catherine. *The Industrial Reformation of English Fiction, 1832–1867*. Chicago, 1985.

Game, Ann, and Rosemary Pringle. *Gender at Work*. Sydney, 1983.

Garnsey, Elizabeth, Jill Rubery, and Frank Wilkinson. "Labour Market Structure and Workforce Divisions." In Rosemary Deem and Graham Salaman, eds., *Work, Culture and Society*. Milton Keynes, 1985.

Gaskell, Elizabeth. *North and South*. London, 1855; reprinted London, 1970.

Giddens, Anthony. *Central Problems in Social Theory: Action, Structure and Contradiction in Social Analysis*. Berkeley and Los Angeles, 1979.

————— *The Constitution of Society*. Berkeley and Los Angeles, 1984.

————— *Social Theory and Modern Sociology*. Stanford, 1987.

————— "Structuralism, Post-structuralism and the Production of Culture." In Anthony Giddens and Jonathan Turner, eds., *Social Theory Today*. Stanford, 1987.

Gittins, Diana. *Fair Sex: Family Size and Structure*. London, 1982.

Godelier, Maurice. "The Ideal in the Real." In Raphael Samuel and Gareth Stedman Jones, eds., *Culture, Ideology and Politics*. London, 1982.

Goldin, Claudia. "Maximum Hours Legislation and Female Employment: A Reassessment." *Journal of Political Economy* 96 (1988).

Gramsci, Antonio. *Selections from the Prison Notebooks*. New York, 1971.

Gray, Robert. *The Aristocracy of Labour in Nineteenth-Century Britain*. London, 1981.

————— *The Labour Aristocracy in Victorian Edinburgh*. Oxford, 1976.

Griffen, Clyde, and Mark C. Carnes, eds. *Meanings for Manhood: Constructions of Masculinity in Victorian America*. Chicago, 1991.

Gurevitch, Michael, et al., eds. *Culture, Society and the Media*. London, 1982.

Gusfield, Joseph. *The Culture of Public Problems: Drinking, Driving and the Symbolic Order*. Chicago, 1981.

Hall, Catherine. "The Early Formation of Victorian Domestic Ideology." In Sandra Burman, ed., *Fit Work for Women*. London, 1979.

—— "Gender Divisions and Class Formation in the Birmingham Middle Class, 1780–1850." In Raphael Samuel, ed., *People's History and Socialist Theory*. London, 1981.

—— "The Tale of Samuel and Jemima: Gender and Working-class Culture in Nineteenth-century England." In Harvey Kaye and Keith McClelland, eds., *E. P. Thompson: Critical Perspectives*. Cambridge, England, 1990.

Hall, Peter G. *The Industries of London Since 1861*. London, 1962.

Hall, Stuart. "The Rediscovery of 'Ideology': Return of the Repressed In Media Studies." In Michael Gurevitch et al., eds., *Culture, Society and the Media*. London, 1982.

—— "The Toad in the Garden: Thatcherism among the Theorists." In Cary Nelson and Lawrence Grossberg, eds., *Marxism and the Interpretation of Culture*. Urbana, 1988.

Halle, David. *America's Working Man*. Chicago, 1984.

Hamilton, Roberta, and Michèle Barrett, eds. *The Politics of Diversity*. London, 1986.

Hammond, John L., and Barbara Hammond. *The Skilled Laborer, 1760–1832*. London, 1919.

Hanawalt, Barbara. "Peasant Women's Contribution to the Home Economy in Late Medieval England." In Barbara Hanawalt, ed., *Women and Work in Preindustrial Europe*. Bloomington, Ind., 1986.

—— *The Ties That Bind*. Bloomington, Ind., 1986.

Hanawalt, Barbara, ed. *Women and Work in Preindustrial Europe*. Bloomington, Ind., 1986.

Harding, Sandra. *The Science Question in Feminism*. Ithaca, 1986.

—— "What Is the Real Material Base of Patriarchy and Capital?" In Lydia Sargent, ed., *Women and Revolution*. Boston, 1981.

Harley, C. R. "British Industrialization Before 1841: Evidence of Slower Growth During the Industrial Revolution." *Journal of Economic History* 42 (1982).

Harrison, Royden. *Before the Socialists*. London, 1965.

Hartmann, Heidi. "Capitalism, Patriarchy and Job Segregation by Sex." *Signs* 1 (1976).

—— "The Family as the Locus of Gender, Class and Political Struggle: The Example of Housework." *Signs* 6 (1981).

—— "The Unhappy Marriage of Marxism and Feminism: Towards a More Progressive Union." In Lydia Sargent, ed., *Women and Revolution*. Boston, 1981.

Herbert, George. *Mind, Self and Society*. Chicago, 1934.

Hewitt, Margaret. *Wives and Mothers in Victorian Industry*. London, 1958.

Higgs, Edward. "Women, Occupations and Work in the Nineteenth Century Censuses." *History Workshop* 23 (1987).

Hill, Christopher. *The Collected Essays of Christopher Hill*. Amherst, Mass., 1985.

—— "Pottage for Freeborn Englishmen: Attitudes to Wage Labour in the 16th and 17th Centuries." In *The Collected Essays of Christopher Hill*. Amherst, 1985.

Hilton, R. H. *The English Peasantry in the Later Middle Ages*. Oxford, 1975.

Hobsbawm, Eric J. *Industry and Empire*. Harmondsworth, 1969.

—— *Labouring Men*. London, 1964.

—— *Worlds of Labour*. London, 1984.

Holley, John. "The Two Family Economies of Industrialism: Factory Workers in Victorian Scotland." *Journal of Family History* 6 (1981).

Honeyman, Katrina. *Origins of Enterprise*. Manchester, 1982.

Hopwood, Edwin. *A History of the Lancashire Cotton Industry and the Amalgamated Weavers' Association*. Manchester, 1969.

Howarth, Edward G., and Mona Wilson. *West Ham: A Study in Social and Industrial Problems*. London, 1907.

Howe, Anthony. *The Cotton Masters 1830–1860*. Oxford, 1984.

Howell, George. *The Conflicts of Capital and Labour*. 2d ed. London, 1890.

Hufton, Olwen. *The Poor of Eighteenth Century France*. Oxford, 1976.

Humphries, Jane. "Class Struggle and the Persistence of the Working Class Family." *Cambridge Journal of Economics* 1 (1977).

—— "Protective Legislation, the Capitalist State, and Working Class Men: The Case of the 1842 Mines Regulation Act." *Feminist Review* 7 (1981).

Hunt, E. H. *British Labour History, 1815–1914*. London, 1981.

Hunt, Lynn. Introduction to Lynn Hunt, ed., *The New Cultural History*. Berkeley and Los Angeles, 1989.

—— *Politics, Culture and Class*. Berkeley and Los Angeles, 1985.

Hutchins, B. L. *Women in Modern Industry*. New York, 1915.

—— "Yorkshire." In Clementina Black, ed., *Married Women's Work* (London, 1915; reprinted London, 1983).

Hutton, Diane. "Women in Fourteenth Century Shrewsbury." In Lindsey Charles and Lorna Duffin, eds., *Women and Work in Pre-Industrial England*. London, 1985.

Jenson, Jane. "Gender and Reproduction: Or, Babies and the State." *Studies in Political Economy* 20 (1986).

—— "Paradigms and Political Discourse: Protective Legislation in France and the United States Before 1914." *Canadian Journal of Political Science* 22 (1989).

Jessop, Bob. *The Capitalist State*. New York, 1982.

John, Angela V. *By the Sweat of Their Brow: Women Workers in Victorian Coal Mines*. London, 1984.

—— "Letter in Response to Jane Humphries." *Feminist Review* 7 (1981).

John, Angela V., ed. *Unequal Opportunities: Women's Employment in England 1800–1918*. Oxford, 1986.

Jones, Gareth Stedman. *Languages of Class: Studies in English Working-Class History, 1832–1982*. Cambridge, England, 1983.

Jordan, Ellen. "Female Unemployment in England and Wales 1851–1911: An Examination of the Census Figures for 15–19 Year Olds." *Social History* 13 (1988).

Jordanova, Ludmilla. *Sexual Visions: Images of Gender in Science and Medicine Between the Eighteenth and Twentieth Centuries.* Hemel Hempstead, Hertfordshire, 1989.

Joyce, Patrick. *Work, Society and Politics.* Brighton, Sussex, 1983.

Joyce, Patrick, ed. *The Historical Meanings of Work.* Cambridge, England, 1987.

Kahn-Hut, Rachel, and Arlene Kaplan Daniels, eds. *Women and Work.* New York, 1982.

Katznelson, Ira. "Constructing Cases and Comparisons." In Ira Katznelson and Aristide R. Zolberg, eds., *Working-class Formation: Nineteenth-Century Patterns in Western Europe and the United States.* Princeton, 1986.

Katznelson, Ira, and Aristide R. Zolberg, eds. *Working-class Formation: Nineteenth-Century Patterns in Western Europe and the United States.* Princeton, 1986.

Kaye, Harvey, and Keith McClelland, eds. *E. P. Thompson: Critical Perspectives.* Cambridge, England, 1990.

Kelly, Joan. "The Doubled Vision of Feminist Theory." *Feminist Studies* 5 (1979).

Kent, Susan. *Sex and Suffrage in Britain 1860–1914.* Princeton, 1987.

Kertzer, David I. *Ritual, Politics and Power.* New Haven, 1988.

Kessler-Harris, Alice. "Gender Ideology in Historical Reconstruction: A Case Study from the 1930s." *Gender and History* 1 (1989).

——— *Out to Work: A History of Wage-Earning Women in the United States.* New York, 1982.

——— *A Woman's Wage.* Lexington, Ky., 1990.

Kirk, Neville. *The Growth of Working Class Reformism in Mid-Victorian England.* Urbana, 1985.

Knight, David, and Hugh Willmott, eds. *Gender and the Labour Process.* Aldershot, 1986.

Koven, Seth, and Sonya Michel. "Womanly Duties: Maternalist Politics and the Origins of Welfare States in France, Germany, Great Britain and the United States, 1880–1920." *American Historical Review* 95 (1990).

Kraut, Robert E. "Homework: What Is It and Who Does It?" In Kathleen E. Christensen, ed., *The New Era of Home-Based Work.* Boulder, 1988.

Kriedte, Peter, Hans Medick, and Jurgen Schlumbohm, eds. *Industrialization Before Industrialization.* Cambridge, England, 1981.

Kuhn, Annette, and Anne Marie Wolpe, eds. *Feminism and Materialism.* London, 1978.

Kussmaul, Ann. *Servants in Husbandry in Early Modern England.* Cambridge, England, 1981.

Laclau, Ernesto, and Chantal Mouffe. "Post-Marxism Without Apologies." *New Left Review* 166 (1987).

Land, Hilary. "The Family Wage." *Feminist Review* 6 (1980).

Laslett, Peter. "Mean Household Size in England Since the Sixteenth Century." In Peter Laslett and Richard Wall, eds., *Household and Family in Past Time*. Cambridge, England, 1972.

———— "Size and Structure of the Household in England over Three Centuries." *Population Studies* 23 (1969).

———— *The World We Have Lost*. London, 1965.

Laslett, Peter, and Richard Wall, eds. *Household and Family in Past Time*. Cambridge, England, 1972.

Lawrence, Paul R. "Marx on State Regulation: A Comment." *Review of Social Economy* 38 (1980).

Lazonick, William. "Industrial Relations and Technical Change: The Case of the Self-acting Mule." *Cambridge Journal of Economics* 3 (1979).

———— "Production Relations, Labor Productivity and Choice of Technique: British and U.S. Cotton Spinning." *Journal of Economic History* 41 (1981).

Lees, Lynn Hollen. "Getting and Spending: The Family Budgets of English Industrial Workers in 1890." In John M. Merriman, ed., *Consciousness and Class Experience in 19th Century Europe*. New York, 1979.

Lehrer, Susan. *Origins of Protective Legislation for Women, 1905–1925*. Albany, N.Y., 1987.

Levine, David. *Family Formation in an Age of Nascent Capitalism*. Cambridge, England, 1977.

———— "Recombinant Family Formation Strategies." *Journal of Historical Sociology* 2 (1989).

———— *Reproducing Families: The Political Economy of English Population History*. Cambridge, England, 1987.

Levine, Rhonda F. *The Class Struggle and the New Deal*. Lawrence, Ks., 1988.

Lewis, Jane. "The Debate on Sex and Class." *New Left Review* 146 (1985).

———— *The Politics of Motherhood*. London, 1980.

———— *Women in England 1870–1950*. Bloomington, Ind., 1984.

———— "The Working-Class Wife and Mother and State Intervention 1870–1918." In Jane Lewis, ed., *Labour and Love: Women's Experience of Home and Family 1850–1940*. Oxford, 1986.

Lewis, Jane, ed. *Labour and Love: Women's Experience of Home and Family 1850–1940*. Oxford, 1986.

Liddington, Jill, and Jill Norris. *One Hand Tied Behind Us*. London, 1978.

Littlejohn, Gary, et al., eds. *Power and the State*. London, 1978.

Lowe, David, and Jack Richards. *The City of Lace*. Nottingham, 1983.

Lown, Judy. *Women and Industrialization*. Cambridge, England, 1990.

McClelland, Keith. "Some Thoughts on Masculinity and the 'Representative Artisan' in Britain, 1850–1880." *Gender and History* 1 (1989).

———— "Time to Work, Time to Live." In Patrick Joyce, ed., *The Historical Meanings of Work*. Cambridge, England, 1987.

McIntosh, Mary. "The State and the Oppression of Women." In Annette Kuhn and Anne Marie Wolpe, eds., *Feminism and Materialism*. London, 1978.

McLaren, Angus. *Reproductive Rituals*. London, 1984.

MacLennan, Gregor. "The Labour Aristocracy and Incorporation: Notes on Terms in the Social History of the Working Class." *Social History* 6 (1981).

Mark-Lawson, Jane, and Anne Witz. "From 'Family Labour' to 'Family Wage'? The Case of Women's Labour in Nineteenth-Century Coalmining." *Social History* 13 (1988).

Martin, Anna. *The Married Working Woman*. London, 1911; reprinted London, 1980.

Marvel, Howard. "Factory Regulation: A Reinterpretation of Early English Experience." *Journal of Law and Economics* 20 (1977).

Marx, Karl. *Capital*, vol. 1. New York, 1967.

Marx, Karl, and Friedrich Engels. *The German Ideology*. London, 1965.

Mathias, Peter, and M. M. Postan, eds. *The Cambridge Economic History of Europe*. Vol. 7, Part 1: *The Industrial Economies: Capital, Labour and Enterprise*. Cambridge, England, 1978.

May, Martha. "Bread Before Roses: American Workingmen, Labor Unions and the Family Wage." In Ruth Milkman, ed., *Women, Work and Protest: A Century of U.S. Women's Labor History*. London, 1985.

——— "The Historical Problem of the Family Wage: The Ford Motor Company and the Five Dollar Day." *Feminist Studies* 8 (1982).

Meacham, Standish. *A Life Apart: The English Working Class, 1890–1914*. London, 1977.

Medick, Hans. "The Proto-Industrial Family Economy." In Peter Kriedte, Hans Medick, and Jurgen Schlumbohm, eds., *Industrialization before Industrialization*. Cambridge, England, 1981.

Merriman, John M., ed. *Consciousness and Class Experience in Nineteenth-Century Europe*. New York, 1979.

Michel, Sonya. *The History of Daycare in America*. Forthcoming.

Middleton, Chris. "The Familiar Fate of the 'Famulae': Gender as a Principle of Stratification in the Historical Organisation of Labour." In R. E. Pahl, ed., *On Work*. Oxford, 1988.

——— "Peasants, Patriarchy and the Feudal Mode of Production in England: A Marxist Appraisal." *Sociological Review* 29 (1981).

——— "The Sexual Division of Labour in Feudal England." *New Left Review* 113–14 (1979).

——— "Women's Work and the Transition to Pre-industrial Capitalism." In Lindsey Charles and Lorna Duffin, eds., *Women and Work in Pre-Industrial England*. London, 1985.

Milkman, Ruth. *Gender at Work: The Dynamics of Job Segregation by Sex During World War II*. Urbana, 1987.

Milkman, Ruth, ed. *Women, Work and Protest: A Century of U.S. Women's Labor History*. London, 1985.

Minow, Martha. *Making All the Difference: Inclusion, Exclusion, and American Law*. Ithaca, 1990.

Mitchell, Brian R., and Phyllis Deane. *Abstract of British Historical Statistics*. Cambridge, England, 1962.

Mitchell, Juliet, and Ann Oakley, eds. *The Rights and Wrongs of Women.* Harmondsworth, 1976.

Molyneux, Maxine. "Beyond the Domestic Labour Debate." *New Left Review* 116 (1979).

Montgomery, David. *Workers' Control in America.* Cambridge, England, 1979.

Moorhouse, H. F. "The Marxist Theory of the Labour Aristocracy." *Social History* 3 (1978).

———— "The Significance of the Labour Aristocracy." *Social History* 6 (1981).

Morris, Jenny. "The Characteristics of Sweating: The Late Nineteenth-Century London and Leeds Tailoring Trade." In Angela V. John, ed., *Unequal Opportunities: Women's Employment in England 1800–1918.* Oxford, 1986.

Murie, Alex. *The Carpet Weavers of Kidderminster.* Kidderminster, 1966.

Murray, Janet, ed. *Strong Minded Women.* New York, 1982.

Musson, A. E. "Class Struggle and the Labour Aristocracy, 1830–1860." *Social History* 1 (1976).

———— *The Growth of British Industry.* London, 1978.

Nelson, Cary, and Lawrence Grossberg, eds. *Marxism and the Interpretation of Culture.* Urbana, 1988.

Newman, George. *Infant Mortality.* New York, 1907.

O'Neill, William. *Journals of a Lancashire Weaver.* Edited by Mary Briggs. Manchester, 1982.

Oren, Laura. "The Welfare of Women in Laboring Families: England, 1860–1950." *Feminist Studies* 1 (1973).

Osterud, Nancy Grey. "Gender Divisions and the Organization of Work in the Leicester Hosiery Industry." In Angela V. John, ed., *Unequal Opportunities: Women's Employment in England 1800–1918.* Oxford, 1986.

Pahl, R. E. *Divisions of Labor.* Oxford, 1984.

Pahl, R. E., ed. *On Work.* Oxford, 1988.

Palmer, Bryan. *Descent into Discourse.* Oxford, 1990.

Parr, Joy. "Disaggregating the Sexual Division of Labour: A Transatlantic Case Study." *Comparative Studies in Society and History* 30 (1988).

———— *The Gender of Breadwinners: Women, Men, and Change in Two Industrial Towns.* Toronto, 1990.

———— *Labouring Children: British Immigrant Apprentices to Canada, 1869–1924.* London, 1980.

Pateman, Carole. *The Disorder of Women: Democracy, Feminism and Political Theory.* Stanford, 1989.

———— *The Sexual Contract.* Stanford, 1988.

Pennington, Shelley, and Belinda Westover. *A Hidden Workforce: Homeworkers in England, 1850–1985.* London, 1989.

Perkin, Frank. *The Origins of Modern English Society, 1780–1880.* London, 1969.

Phillips, Anne, and Barbara Taylor. "Sex and Skill: Notes Towards a Feminist Economics." *Feminist Review* 6 (1980).

Pike, E. Royston. *Human Documents of the Industrial Revolution*. London, 1966.

Pinchbeck, Ivy. *Women Workers and the Industrial Revolution, 1750–1850*. 3d ed. London, 1981.

Polanyi, Karl. *The Great Transformation*. Boston, 1957.

Pollard, Sidney. "Labour in Great Britain." In Peter Mathias and M. M. Postan, eds., *The Cambridge Economic History of Europe*. Vol. 7, Part 1: *The Industrial Economies: Capital, Labour and Enterprise*. Cambridge, England, 1978.

Poovey, Mary. *Uneven Developments: The Ideological Work of Gender in Mid-Victorian England*. Chicago, 1988.

Price, Richard. "Conflict and Cooperation: A Reply to Patrick Joyce." *Social History* 9 (1984).

——— *Labour in British Society*. London, 1986; reprinted London, 1990.

——— "The Labour Process and Labour History." *Social History* 8 (1983).

——— "The Other Face of Respectability: Violence in the Manchester Brickmaking Trade 1859–1970." *History Workshop Journal* 23 (1987).

——— "Structures of Subordination in Nineteenth-Century British Industry." In Pat Thane, Geoffrey Crossick, and Roderick Floud, eds., *The Power of the Past: Essays for Eric Hobsbawm*. Cambridge, England, 1984.

Prothero, I. J. *Artisans and Politics in Early Nineteenth Century London*. London, 1981.

Quadagno, Jill. *The Transformation of Old Age Security*. Chicago, 1987.

Rapp, Rayna, Ellen Ross, and Renate Bridenthal. "Examining Family History." *Feminist Studies* 5 (1979).

Razzell, P. E., and R. W. Wainwright, eds. *The Victorian Working Class: Selections from Letters to the Morning Chronicle*. London, 1973.

Reddy, William. *The Rise of Market Culture*. Cambridge, England, 1984.

Reeves, Maud Pember. *Round About a Pound a Week*. London, 1913; reprinted London, 1979.

Riley, Denise. *"Am I That Name?" Feminism and the Category of "Women" in History*. Minneapolis, 1988.

Roberts, David. *Paternalism in Early Victorian England*. London, 1979.

Roberts, Elizabeth. *A Woman's Place: An Oral History of Working-Class Women 1890–1940*. Oxford, 1984.

Roberts, Michael. "Sickles and Scythes: Women's Work and Men's Work at Harvest Time." *History Workshop* 7 (1979).

——— " 'Words They Are Women, and Deeds They Are Men': Images of Work and Gender in Early Modern England." In Lindsey Charles and Lorna Duffin, eds., *Women and Work in Pre-Industrial England*. London, 1985.

Roberts, Robert. *The Classic Slum*. Manchester, 1971; reprinted Harmondsworth, 1973.

——— *A Ragged Schooling*. Manchester, 1976.

Rogers, Thorold. *Wages of Agricultural Labourers*. Vol. 2. London, 1866.

Rose, Michael E. *The Relief of Poverty 1834–1914*. London, 1972; 2d ed. London, 1986.

Rose, Sonya O. "Gender Antagonism and Class Conflict: Exclusionary Strategies of Male Trade Unionists in Nineteenth-Century Britain." *Social History* 13 (1988).

———— " 'Gender at Work': Sex, Class and Industrial Capitalism." *History Workshop* 21 (1986).

———— "Gender Segregation in the Transition to the Factory: The English Hosiery Industry, 1850–1910." *Feminist Studies* 13 (1987).

———— "Proto-industry, Women's Work and the Household Economy in the Transition to Industrial Capitalism." *Journal of Family History* 13 (1988).

———— "The Varying Household Relations of the Elderly in Three English Villages, 1851–1881." *Continuity and Change* 3 (1988).

Ross, Ellen. " 'Fierce Questions and Taunts': Married Life in Working-Class London, 1870–1914." *Feminist Studies* 8 (Fall 1982).

———— "Labour and Love: Rediscovering London's Working-Class Mothers, 1870–1918." In Jane Lewis, ed., *Labour and Love: Women's Experience of Home and Family, 1850–1940*. Oxford, 1986.

———— " 'Not the Sort That Would Sit on the Doorstep': Respectability in Pre–World War I London Neighborhoods." *International Labor and Working Class History* 27 (1985).

———— "Survival Networks: Women's Neighborhood Sharing in London Before World War I." *History Workshop* 15 (1983).

Rowntree, B. Seebohm. *Poverty: A Study of Town Life*. London, 1901.

Rubenstein, David. *School Attendance in London, 1870–1904*. New York, 1969.

Rubery, Jill. "Structured Labour Markets, Worker Organization and Low Pay." In Alice Amsden, ed., *The Economics of Women and Work*. Harmondsworth, 1980.

Rule, John. "The Property of Skill in the Period of Manufacture." In Patrick Joyce, ed., *The Historical Meanings of Work*. Cambridge, England, 1987.

Ryan, Mary. *Cradle of the Middle Class: The Family in Oneida County, New York, 1790–1865*. Cambridge, England, 1983.

Sahlins, Marshall. *Culture and Practical Reason*. Chicago, 1976.

Said, Edward. *Orientalism*. New York, 1979.

Samuel, Raphael. "Workshop of the World: Steam Power and Hand Technology in Mid-Victorian Britain." *History Workshop Journal* 3 (1977).

Samuel, Raphael, ed. *People's History and Socialist Theory*. London, 1981.

Sargent, Lydia, ed. *Women and Revolution*. Boston, 1981.

Sayer, Derek. *The Violence of Abstraction: The Analytic Foundations of Historical Materialism*. Oxford, 1987.

Schmiechen, James A. *Sweated Industries and Sweated Labor: The London Clothing Trades, 1860–1914*. Urbana, 1984.

Scott, Alison. "Industrialization, Gender Segregation and Stratification Theory." In Rosemary Crompton and Michael Mann, eds., *Gender and Stratification*. Oxford, 1986.

Scott, Joan W. *Gender and the Politics of History*. New York, 1988.

———— "On Language, Gender, and Working-Class History." *International Labor and Working-Class History* 31 (1987).

Seccombe, Wally. "Patriarchy Stabilized: The Construction of the Male Breadwinner Wage Norm in Nineteenth-Century Britain." *Social History* 11 (1986).

———— "Starting to Stop: Working-Class Fertility Decline in Britain." *Past and Present* 126 (1990).

Seed, John. "Unitarianism, Political Economy and the Antinomies of Liberal Culture in Manchester, 1830–50." *Social History* 7 (1982).

Sewell, William H. "How Classes Are Made: Critical Reflections on E. P. Thompson's Theory of Working-class Formation." In Harvey Kaye and Keith McClelland, eds., *E. P. Thompson: Critical Perspectives.* Cambridge, England, 1990.

———— *Work and Revolution in France: The Language of Labor from the Old Regime to 1848.* Cambridge, England, 1980.

Shanas, Ethel, and Marvin Sussman, eds. *Family, Bureaucracy and the Elderly.* Durham, 1977.

Shephard, Michael. "The Origins and Incidence of the Term Labour Aristocracy." *Bulletin of the Society for the Study of Labour History* 37 (1978).

Skocpol, Theda. "Political Response to Capitalist Crisis: Neo-Marxist Theories of the State and the Case of the New Deal." *Politics and Society* 10 (1980).

Skocpol, Theda, ed. *Vision and Method in Historical Sociology.* Cambridge, England, 1984.

Skocpol, Theda, and Edwin Amenta. "States and Social Policies." *American Sociological Review* 12 (1986).

Smart, Carol. *Feminism and the Power of the Law.* London, 1989.

Smelser, Neil. *Social Change in the Industrial Revolution.* Chicago, 1959.

Smith, Ellen. *Wage-Earning Women and Their Dependents.* London, 1915.

Smith, Paul. *Discerning the Subject.* Minneapolis, 1988.

Smith, Richard M. "Fertility, Economy and Household Formation in England over Three Centuries." *Population and Development Review* 7 (1981).

Snell, K. D. M. *Annals of the Labouring Poor.* Cambridge, England, 1987.

Spector, Malcolm, and John Kitsuse. *Constructing Social Problems.* Menlo Park, 1979.

Spruill, Julia Cherry. *Women's Life and Work in the Southern Colonies.* Chapel Hill, 1938.

Stacey, Judith, and Barrie Thorne. "The Missing Feminist Revolution in Sociology." *Social Problems* 32 (1985).

Stansell, Christine. *City of Women: Sex and Class in New York 1789–1860* (New York, 1982; reprinted Urbana, 1987).

———— "A Response to Joan Scott." *International Labor and Working-Class History* 31 (1987).

Stark, David. "Class Struggle and the Transformation of the Labor Process." *Theory and Society* 9 (1980).

Swidler, Ann. "Culture in Action: Symbols and Strategies." *American Sociological Review* 51 (1986).

Taylor, Acton. *History of the Carpet Trade*. Heckmondwike, 1874.

Taylor, Barbara. *Eve and the New Jerusalem*. New York, 1983.

Thane, Pat. *Foundations of the Welfare State*. London, 1982.

——— "Women and the Poor Law in Victorian and Edwardian England." *History Workshop* 6 (1978).

Thane, Pat, Geoffrey Crossick, and Roderick Floud, eds. *The Power of the Past: Essays for Eric Hobsbawm*. Cambridge, England, 1984.

Tholfson, Trygve R. *Working Class Radicalism in Mid-Victorian England*. London, 1976.

Thompson, Dorothy. *The Chartists: Popular Politics in the Industrial Revolution*. New York, 1984.

Thompson, E. P. *The Making of the English Working Class*. Harmondsworth, 1968; reprinted Harmondsworth, 1980.

——— *Whigs and Hunters*. London, 1975.

Thompson, F. M. L. *The Rise of Respectable Society: A Social History of Victorian Britain, 1830–1900*. London, 1988.

Thompson, Paul. *The Nature of Work: An Introduction to Debates on the Labor Process*. London, 1989.

Thomson, David. "The Decline of Social Welfare: Falling State Support for the Elderly Since Early Victorian Times." *Ageing and Society* 4 (1985).

Tilly, Louise A., and Joan W. Scott. *Women, Work and Family*. 2d ed. London, 1987; reprinted London, 1989.

Tomes, Nancy. "A 'Torrent of Abuse': Crimes of Violence Between Working Class Men and Women in London, 1840–1875." *Journal of Social History* 11 (1978).

Tomkinson, Ken. "Lottie Mary Cooper." In Ken Tomkinson, *Characters of Kidderminster*. Kidderminster, 1977.

Tomkinson, Ken, and George Hall. *Kidderminster Since 1800*. Kidderminster, 1985.

Tuckwell, Gertrude M. *The Life of the Rt. Honorable Sir Charles W. Dilke*, vol. 2. London, 1917.

Turberville, A. S. *John Bright—His Character and Career*. Swindon, 1945.

United Kingdom. Parliament. *Women in Industry*. Cmd. 3508. 1930.

Valverde, Mariana. " 'Giving the Female a Domestic Turn': The Social, Legal and Moral Regulation of Women's Work in British Cotton Mills, 1820–1850." *Journal of Social History* 21 (1988).

——— "The Love of Finery: Fashion and the Fallen Woman in Nineteenth-Century Social Discourse." *Victorian Studies* 32 (1989).

——— "The Making of a Gendered Working Class." *Labour/Le Travail* 22 (1988).

Vincent, David. *Bread, Knowledge and Freedom*. New York, 1981.

Von Plener, Ernst Edler. *The English Factory Legislation*. Translated from the German edition, with an introduction by A. J. Mundella. London, 1873.

Walby, Sylvia. *Patriarchy at Work.* Minneapolis, 1986.

Walby, Sylvia, ed. *Gender Segregation at Work.* Milton Keynes, 1988.

Wall, Richard. "The Household: Demographic and Economic Change in England, 1650–1970." In Richard Wall, Jean Robin, and Peter Laslett, eds., *Family Forms in Historic Europe.* Cambridge, England, 1983.

Wall, Richard, Jean Robin, and Peter Laslett, eds. *Family Forms in Historic Europe.* Cambridge, England, 1983.

Wallace, Phyllis A., ed. *Sociological Theory and Feminism.* Beverly Hills, 1989.

Waugh, Edwin. *Home-Life of the Lancashire Factory Folk During the Cotton Famine.* London, 1867.

Webb, Sidney, and Beatrice Webb. *English Poor Law History.* Part 2: *The Last Hundred Years.* London, 1929.

—— *History of Trade Unionism.* 2d ed. London, 1896.

Wells, F. A. *Nottingham Industries: A Hundred Years of Progress, 1851–1951.* Nottingham, 1951.

Westover, Belinda. "Military Tailoring in Colchester 1890–1925." B.A. thesis, University of Essex. Cited in Diana Gittins, *Fair Sex: Family Size and Structure.* London, 1982.

—— "To Fill the Kids' Tummies: The Lives and Work of Colchester Tailoresses, 1880–1918." In Leonore Davidoff and Belinda Westover, eds., *Our Work, Our Lives, Our Words.* Totowa, N.J., 1986.

Whipp, Richard. "The Art of Good Management: Managerial Control of Work in the British Pottery Industry, 1900–25." *International Review of Social History* 29 (1984).

Wilentz, Sean. *Chants Democratic.* New Haven, 1984.

Wilkinson, Frank, ed. *The Dynamics of Labor Market Segmentation.* London, 1981.

Williams, Raymond. *Culture and Society.* London, 1958.

—— *Marxism and Literature.* Oxford, 1977.

—— *Politics and Letters.* London, 1979.

—— *Towards 2000.* London, 1983.

Willis, Paul. *Learning to Labor.* Farnsborough, 1977.

—— "Shop Floor Culture, Masculinity and the Wage Form." In John Clarke, C. Critcher, and Richard Johnson, eds., *Working Class Culture.* London, 1979.

Women's Industrial Council. *Home Industries of Women in London.* London, 1897.

Wood, Stephen, ed. *The Transformation of Work? Skill, Flexibility and the Labour Process.* London, 1989.

Wright, Barbara, et al., eds. *Women, Work and Technology: Transformations.* Ann Arbor, 1987.

Zukin, Sharon, and DiMaggio, Paul. Introduction to Sharon Zukin and Paul DiMaggio, eds., *Structures of Capital: The Social Organization of the Economy.* Cambridge, England, 1990.

Index

Compositor: Maple-Vail Book Mfg. Group
Text: 10/13 Sabon
Display: Sabon
Printer: Maple-Vail Book Mfg. Group
Binder: Maple-Vail Book Mfg. Group